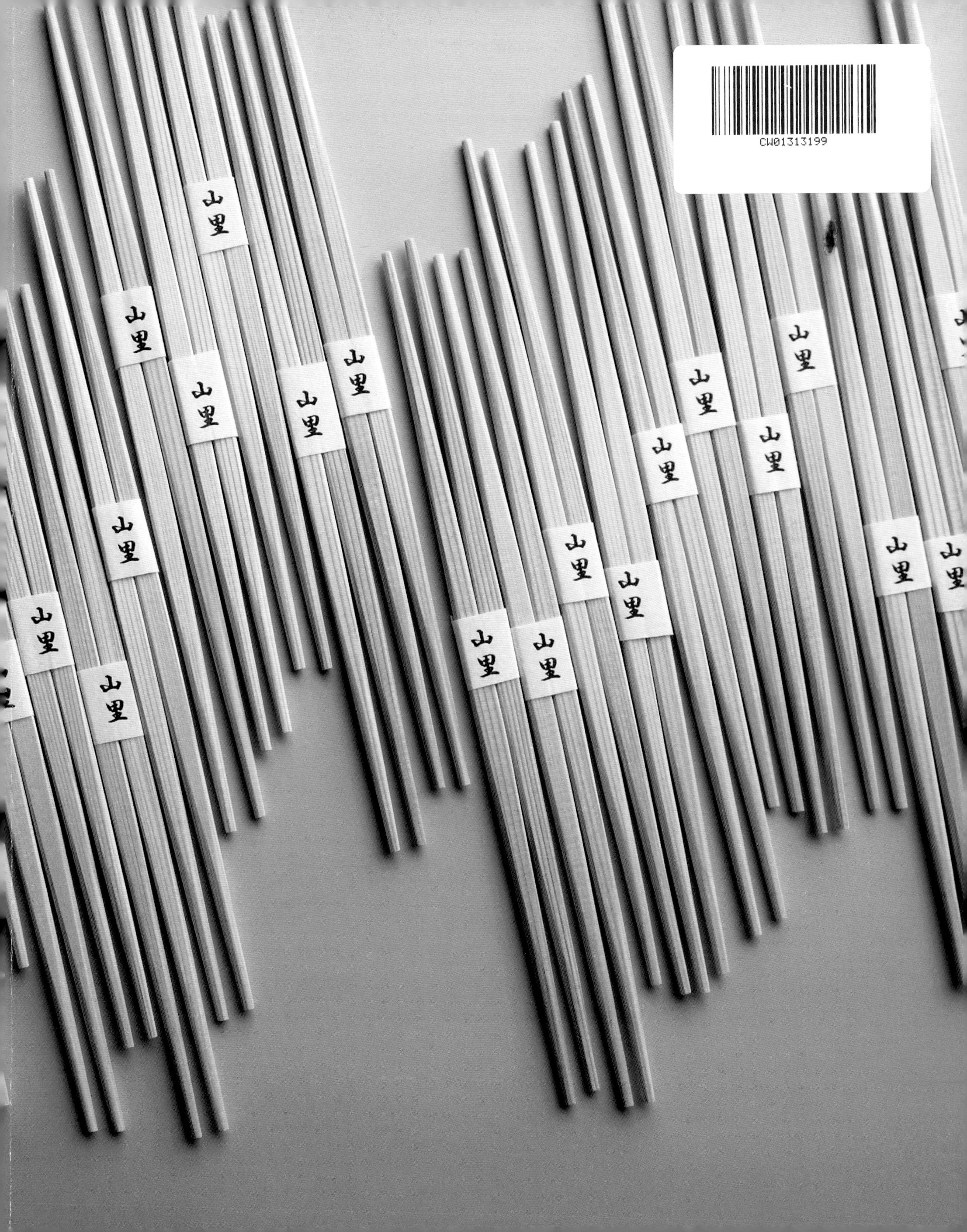
山里

山里

*Yamazato*
Kaiseki cuisine
Hotel Okura Amsterdam

Akira Oshima
Patrick Faas
Katarzyna Cwiertka

Photography: Bart Van Leuven

stichting kunstboek

Dear reader,

In recent years Japanese cuisine has gained popularity, and not only sushi but more traditional dishes as well. In this book Akira Oshima introduces the Japanese culinary culture, kaiseki cuisine in its many different nuances. Oshima is the first Japanese chef ever to receive a Guide Michelin star, for his Japanese kitchen at the Yamazato restaurant of Hotel Okura Amsterdam.

No other cuisine in the world pays as much attention to the various seasons and their respective colors and festivals as the Japanese, seeking balance in every aspect.

The growing interest in the Japanese cuisine by both hobby cooks and professional chefs led us to the initiative to create 'Taste of Okura': a culinary center in which interested professionals as well as consumers can learn about the cooking methods of Akira Oshima and his team.

We owe a lot of gratitude to author Patrick Faas and co-author Dr. Katarzyna Cwiertka for helping to make this book unique in its kind. Photographer Bart van Leuven made the splendid photographs of the creations of Akira Oshima, his Chef de Cuisine Masanori Tomikawa and their team of Japanese chefs.

I wish you a wonderful time exploring this book and Japanese cuisine at its very best.

— Marcel P. Van Aelst —
President and General Manager
Hotel Okura Amsterdam

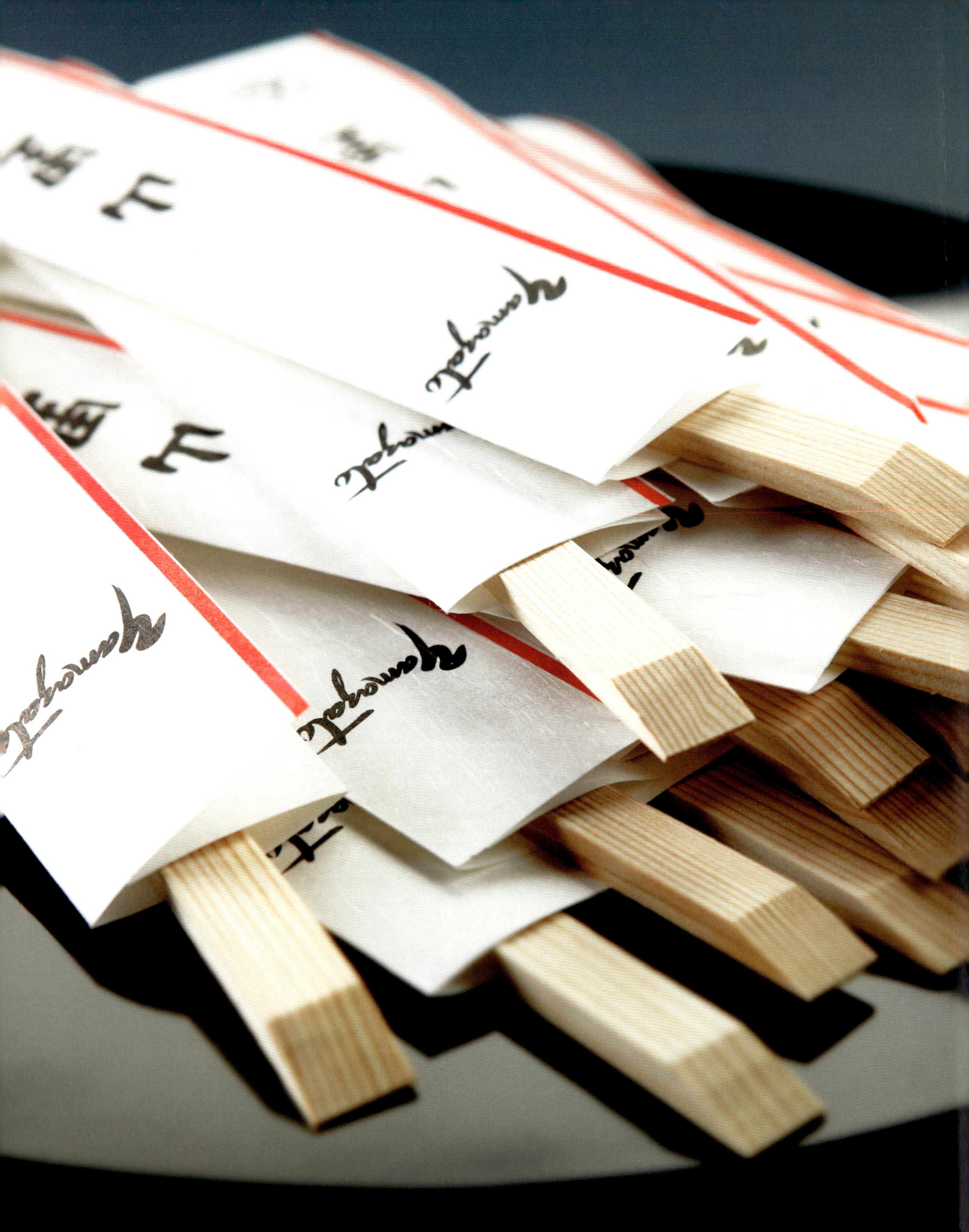

3	Preface Van Aelst
6	Oshima and the Yamazato restaurant
14	Change of climate
16	Origins of kaiseki
24	Courses of enkaiseki ryōri
56	Kaiseki art
70	Japanese festivals
72	New Year
90	Winter
100	Spring
110	Vegetarian
120	Early Summer
132	Summer
142	Autumn
154	Sushi
158	Teppanyaki
164	Unagi
170	Condiments
174	Index

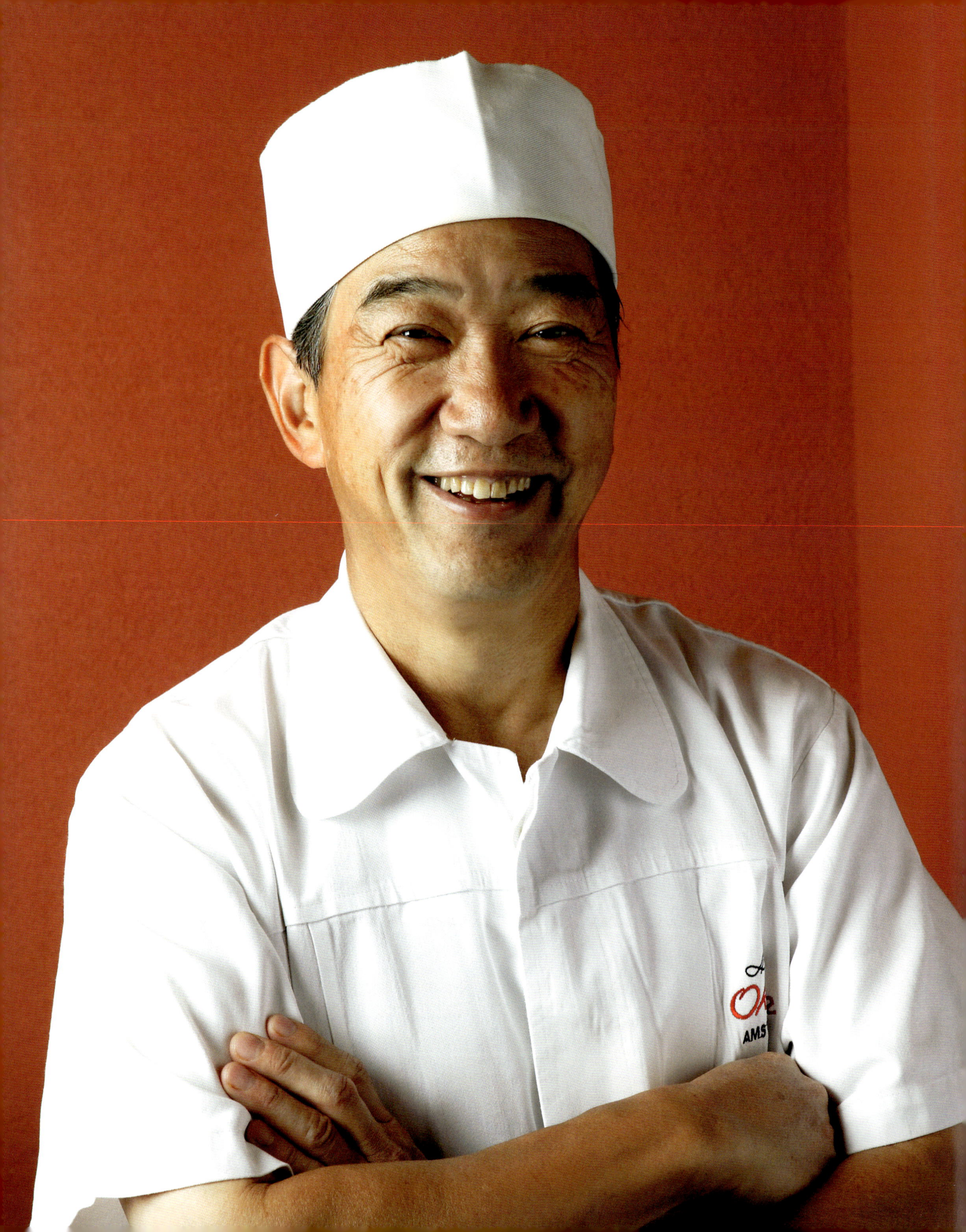

Oshima and the Yamazato restaurant

Executive chef Akira Oshima[1] was born in Tokyo in 1943. His father was a musician who had not continued the family trade, which had been the kimono trade, and so likewise, he left his own son free in his choice of career. Akira Oshima decided to cook. In 1962 Oshima started as a trainee in the Japanese kitchens of the newly opened Hotel Okura Tokyo.

To further his education Oshima had originally wanted to study French cuisine, but so did most of his peers. Cleverly he opted for Japanese cuisine and was given the chance to study *kaiseki* cuisine *(kaiseki ryōri)* at the famous Traditional Japanese Restaurant Tsuruya in Osaka.

The training at Tsuruya was tough. The students always humbly obeyed their master, slept twenty to a room and worked all waking hours. When they made mistakes they were punished, but they learned to clean, cut, chop, slice, grind, measure, season, cure, dry, simmer, steam, roast, fry and bake to perfection all of the products of Japan's seas, mountains and fields. They were instilled with the traditions and teachings of *kaiseki* philosophy, and learned to concentrate and to display food gracefully.

When Oshima had learned what he could in the Traditional Japanese Restaurant Tsuruya, he left Osaka and went back to Tokyo, where he worked for Mr Kamata in the equally famous restaurant Shinkiraku. Now Oshima was ready for a challenge. He considered specializing in the preparation of *fugu* (known under the names of puffer, blowfish or globefish), a fish which contains a poison (a form of tetrodotoxin) in the liver and ovaries, but is much appreciated by daring gourmets. If prepared incorrectly the fish can be lethal, which is why *fugu* chefs have to pass an exam every year. Oshima was advised against it, however. He was warned that he would never cook *fugu* for important people, since they weren't allowed the risky dish. Oshima still prepares *fugu* dishes, but substitutes slices of sea bass or brill, which have the same structure and transparency.

Oshima's big challenge arrived. He was well on his way of making a name for himself, when Mr Noda arrived on the steps of restaurant Shinkiraku and asked if he would go to Holland with Mr Shiraki, chef in the Hotel Okura Tokyo, to introduce *kaiseki* cuisine to foreign shores. Oshima took up the challenge.

The first years, in which not Oshima but Shiraki was the executive chef, were very hard. When the Japanese chefs arrived on the Dutch shores they found a food culture that was rather different to what they had been accustomed to. The character of Dutch food production has since been heavily debated and was consequently improved, but was still unchallenged in the early 1970s.

In the beginning, many products – including rice, vegetables and fish – were flown in from Japan. Because of the cost involved, this was not a sustainable solution in the long run. For this reason, and also because *kaiseki ryōri* tends to pay homage to local products, Oshima did his best to find European products that sufficed. Where necessary, Oshima helped food producers to upgrade the quality of their produce.

Fish was a big issue, especially tuna, which the Japanese eat raw *(sashimi)*. Tuna, a favourite *sashimi* dish, was in Holland sold only in cans or frozen, and was of inferior quality; totally unsuitable for *sashimi*. Oshima used to drive to Paris every week to buy fresh tuna. There he looked for blue-fin tuna *(kuromaguro)*, yellow-fin tuna *(kihada maguro)* and big-eye tuna *(mebachi maguro)*, and drove the catch back to Amsterdam himself.

Refrigeration was still a problem. Because of all the fat and blood it contains, tuna can go rancid. Freezing seemed to totally ruin the structure of the meat, but Oshima did not quite understand why this should have to be; if human organs can be refrigerated in hospitals and implanted in living people, why can't tuna be kept fresh? He found out about shock freezing and bought medical freezers, which cool tissues to -86 °C in a matter of moments. It worked perfectly for tuna.

Nowadays tuna no longer has to come all the way from Paris. Oshima explains that tunas are nice and fat when they enter the Mediterranean to lay eggs. As tunas swim clockwise through the Mediterranean their condition is checked by Japanese agents in Spain, Italy, Greece and Turkey. They reserve the best for the Okura. Oshima wants fat fish. Fish fat is very healthy. 'Remember cod liver oil?' asks Wim van As, director of Jan van As fishmongers in Amsterdam. 'It is why the Japanese live so long.' Moreover, the fatty parts of the tuna *(toro)* are most sought after for sashimi.

Two types of tuna meat are taken from the 'back' of the fish, close to the spine:
>Ordinary 'red meat' tuna *(akami)*
>Half-fatty tuna, coming from between the skin of the fish and 'red meat' *(chiaigishi)*

Three types are taken from the belly:
>Low-fatty *(chūtoro)*
>Medium-fatty *(toro)*
>Fatty *(ōtoro)*

'We have learned a lot from Oshima-san[2],' says Wim van As. 'The first time we imported a tuna for him, he wept because we were handling the fish so roughly and were bruising the meat.' Now the tunas are wrapped in bandages and wheeled in like sacred mummies. Van As also learned the value of many other fish. 'We used to throw sepia, cuttlefish and squid overboard, until we realised the Okura would pay good money for them', he says. Some fish, like flying fish and fresh *awabi* (a costly shellfish much liked for its texture) are flown in especially for Oshima.

In Japan herring roe is appreciated quite as much as caviar. It is especially popular salted and dried, as *kazunoko*. Oshima has taught Dutch fishermongers how to prepare it. Herring roe should be readily available in a country that consumes so much herring, but the roe was treated as waste. Oshima changed that and gave it some local value. Also the precious liver of monkfish used to be thrown out, until Oshima came along.

Van As Fishmongers learned to be more careful with fish: 'Oshima taught us the Japanese use all parts – head, tail and guts – so we treat them with the utmost care.' The firm is currently abandoning chipped ice as a way of cooling the fish, since it damages them too much. They are changing to 'liquid ice'.

One might have hoped that Oshima would think of Holland as Eel Paradise, but somehow Dutch eels are not fatty enough. 'They don't get enough food,' says Oshima. It pays to listen to the master. 'He can be very demanding,' says Van As, 'but because of his approval we are now able to export large quantities of mackerel and horse mackerel to Japan.'

Rice doesn't have to come from Japan anymore either. For a while rice from California was used but representatives of the Okura Trading Company asked rice farmers in the delta of the Ebro river in Spain to grow a Japanese brand of rice called *akita komachi*. The seed of this rice, now indeed grown in Spain, is registered under the name 'Okura.'

Naturally this is the rice served in the Yamazato restaurant. Vegetables could be acquired closer to home. Oshima spoke with a number of Dutch farmers and stimulated them to grow *daikon* radish, Chinese cabbage and certain spring onions. At first there was some reluctance, but in the course of the 1970s and 1980s the vegetables became very fashionable, eventually being generally accepted as normal. Takii, the company that provided the seeds for the Japanese vegetables, still sells to Dutch farmers. Oshima seems somewhat surprised by the success. 'You can buy *daikon* in so many places now, but old Dutch vegetables like the ramanas are forgotten', he says.

Japanese cuisine has indeed conquered the Netherlands. Japanese soy sauce, *sake*, *miso* and *nori* seaweed can be found in many Dutch shops. The Netherlands' colonial past meant that the Dutch had been familiar with the phenomenon of Chinese chopsticks for centuries, but they did not learn to eat with them until Japanese cuisine became popular. *Sushi*, *sashimi* and *tempura* are now widely appreciated, and recently Japanese noodles were added to the list. Japanese herbs like *shiso* and chrysanthemum leaves are grown in Holland, as well as mushrooms like the *shiitake*.

This is a far cry from the situation in the first decade of the Yamazato restaurant. Japanese cuisine was unknown and unloved. The whole style of *kaiseki* dining seemed very formal and severely minimalist to diners used to the abundance of European and Chinese cuisine. In 1977, when many changes were made to the Okura, Oshima was made executive chef. He decided to turn the space previously occupied by the failing Chinese restaurant into a *teppanyaki* restaurant, the Sazanka. There had been a few *teppanyaki* tables in Yamazato, which were now removed. *Teppanyaki* is more meat oriented than *kaiseki*, and had proved to be much appreciated by westerners.

The *kaiseki* cuisine of Yamazato, however, remained the focus of Oshima's attention and with pure *kaiseki ryōri* he became the first Japanese chef in the Netherlands to earn a Michelin star.

1 — The name is really 'Ōshima,' which means 'big island' but for convenient use in the West he dropped the elongation of the first letter to 'Oshima'.
2 — 'Oshima-san' is the Japanese way of saying 'Mr Oshima'.

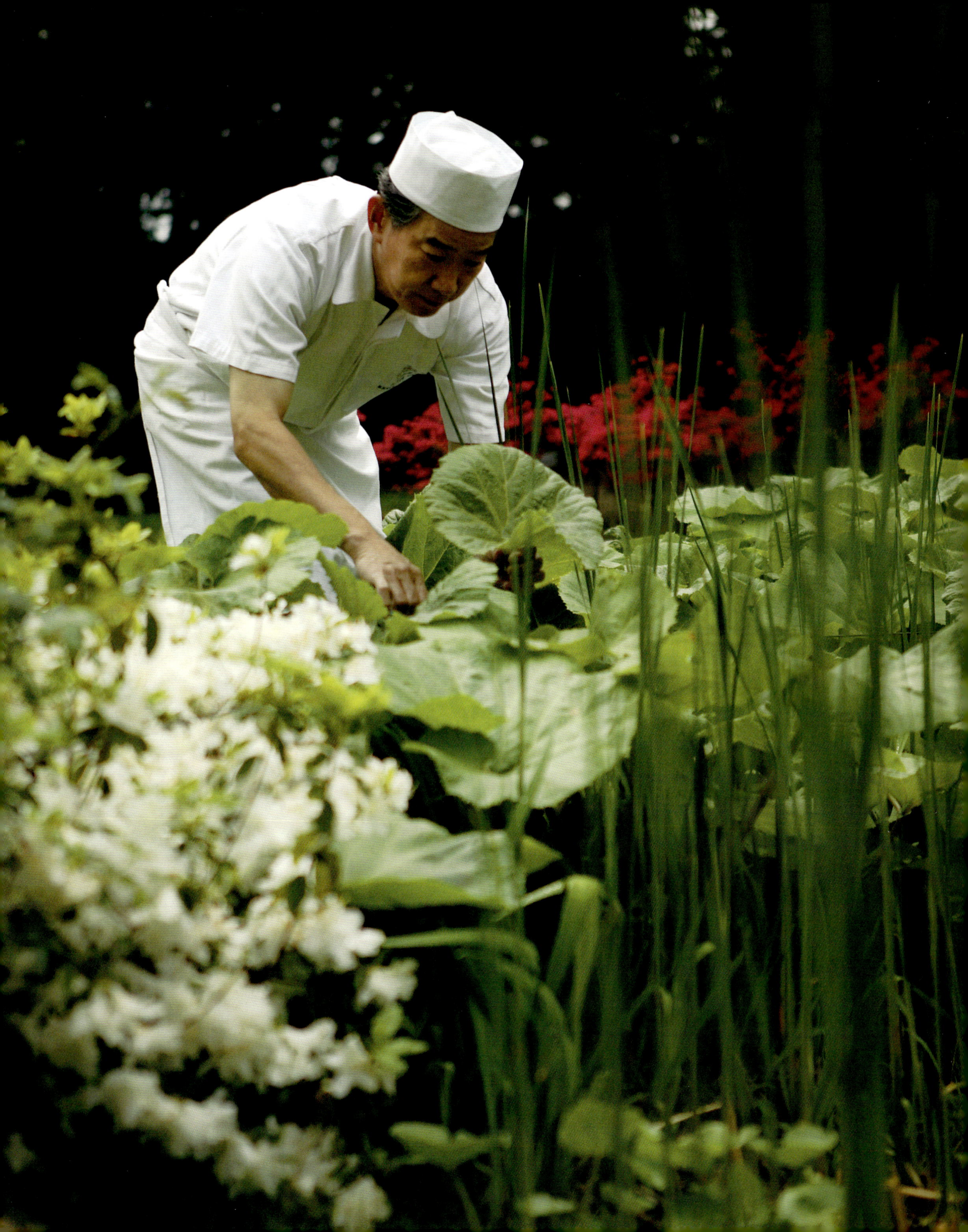

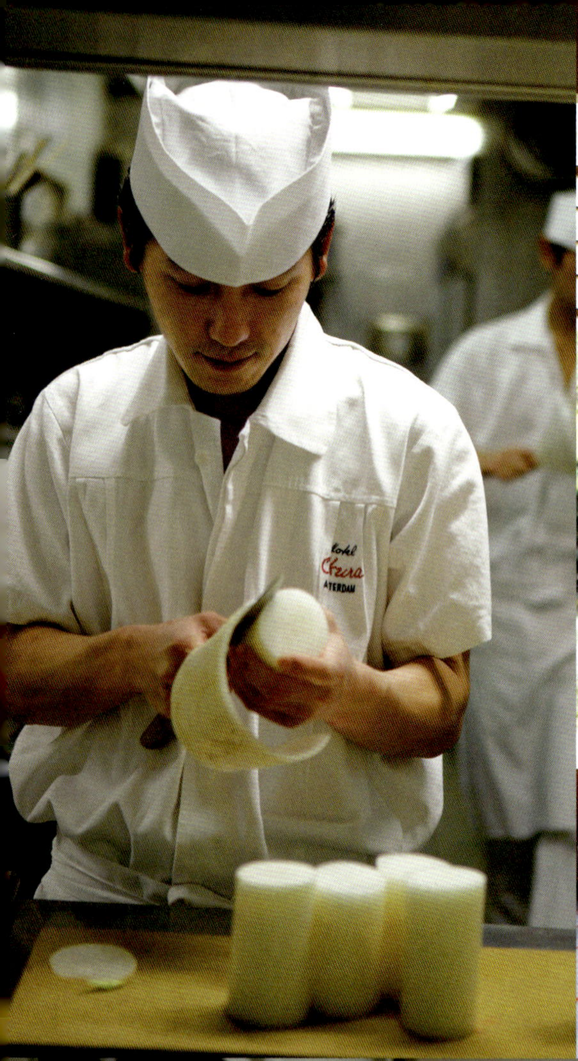
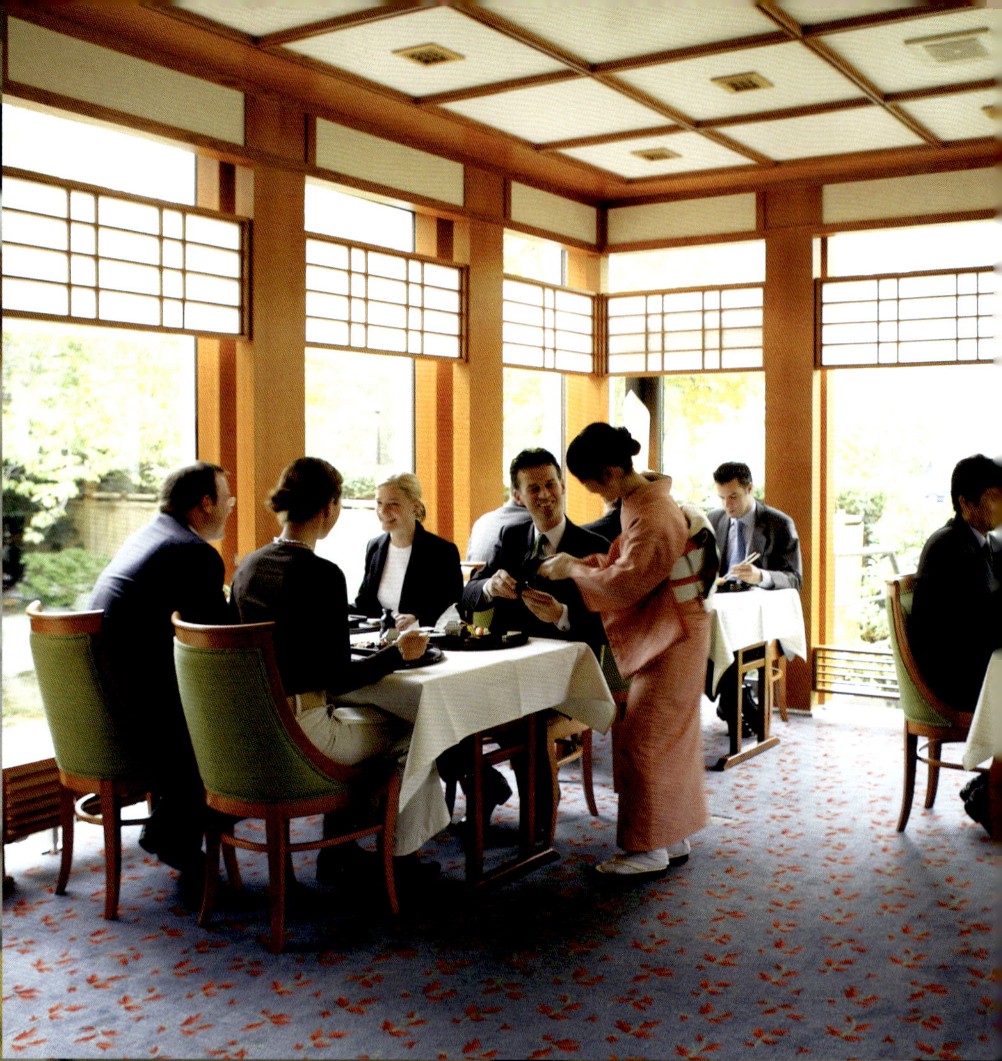
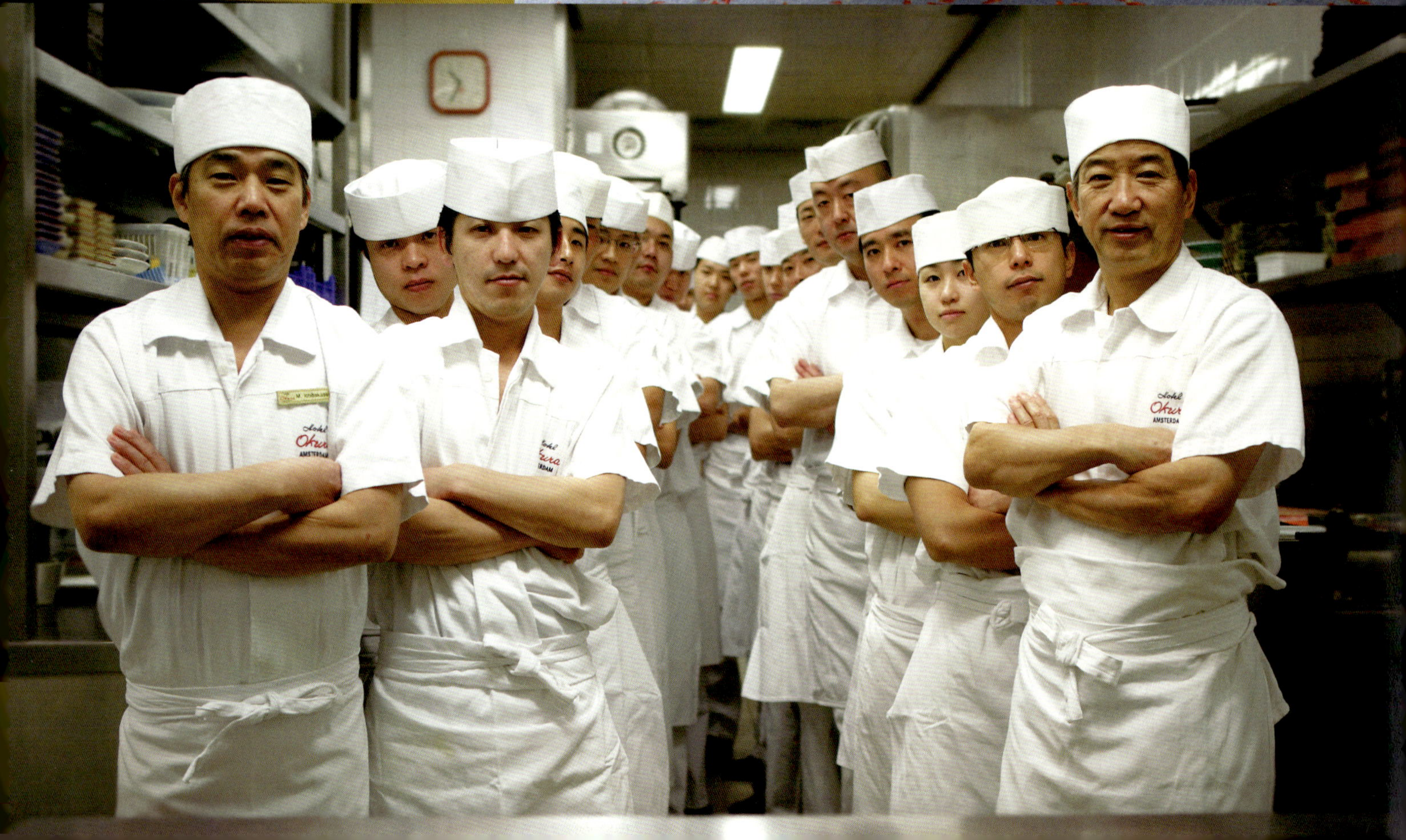

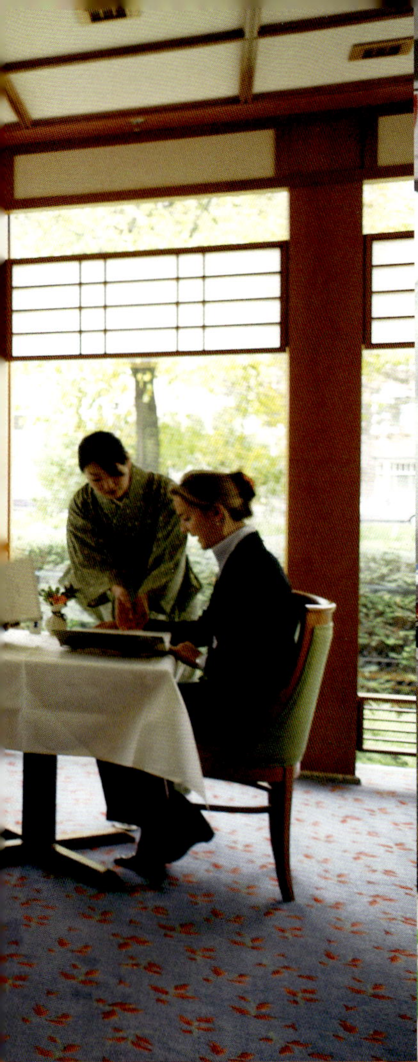
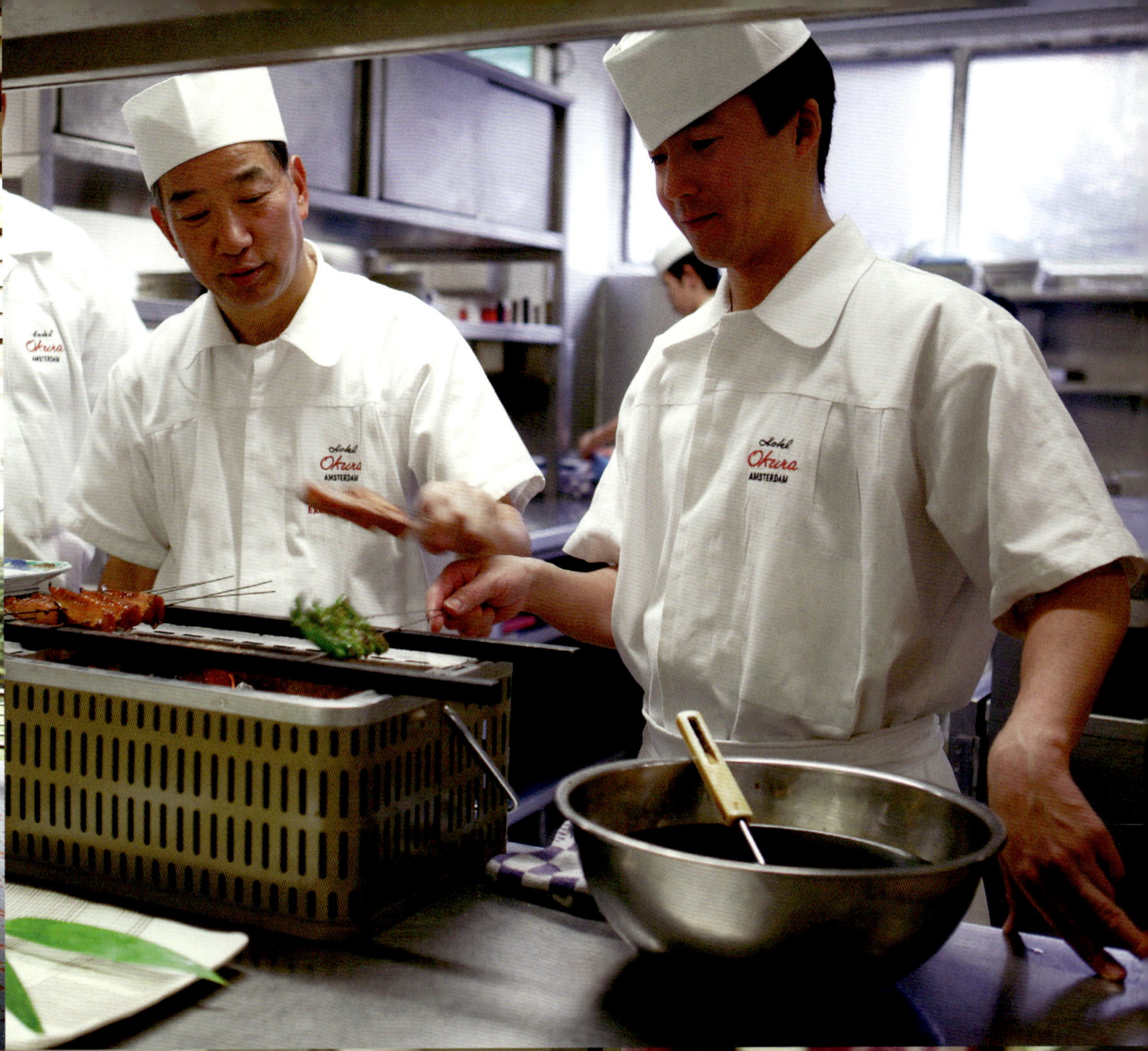
Hotel Okura
AMSTERDAM
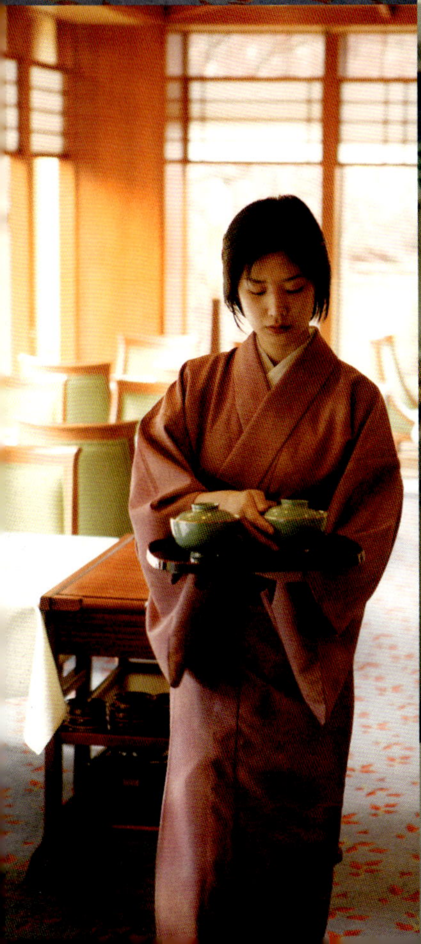
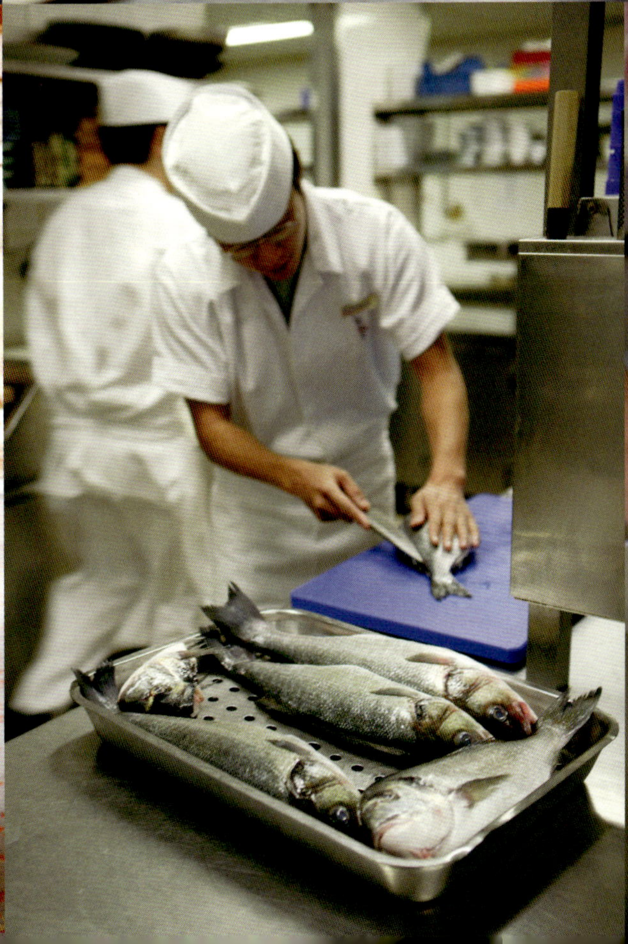
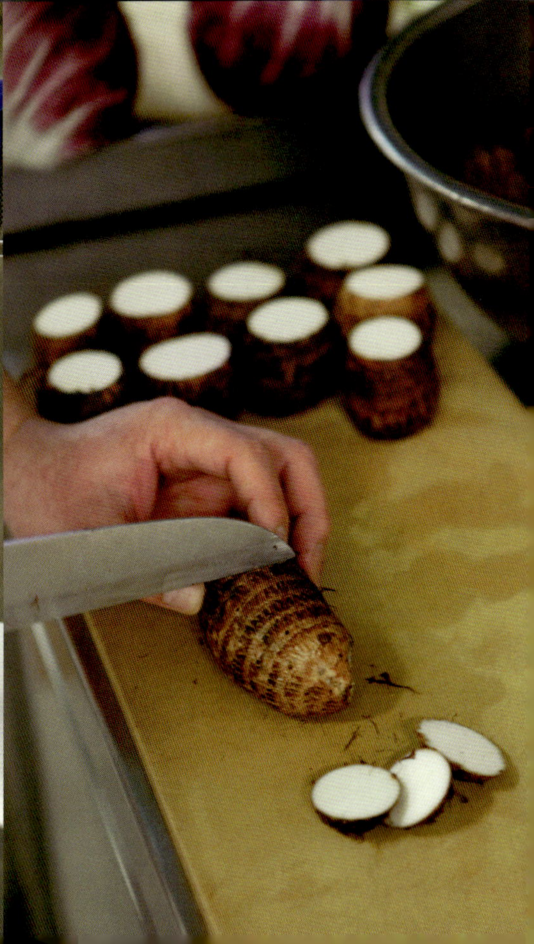

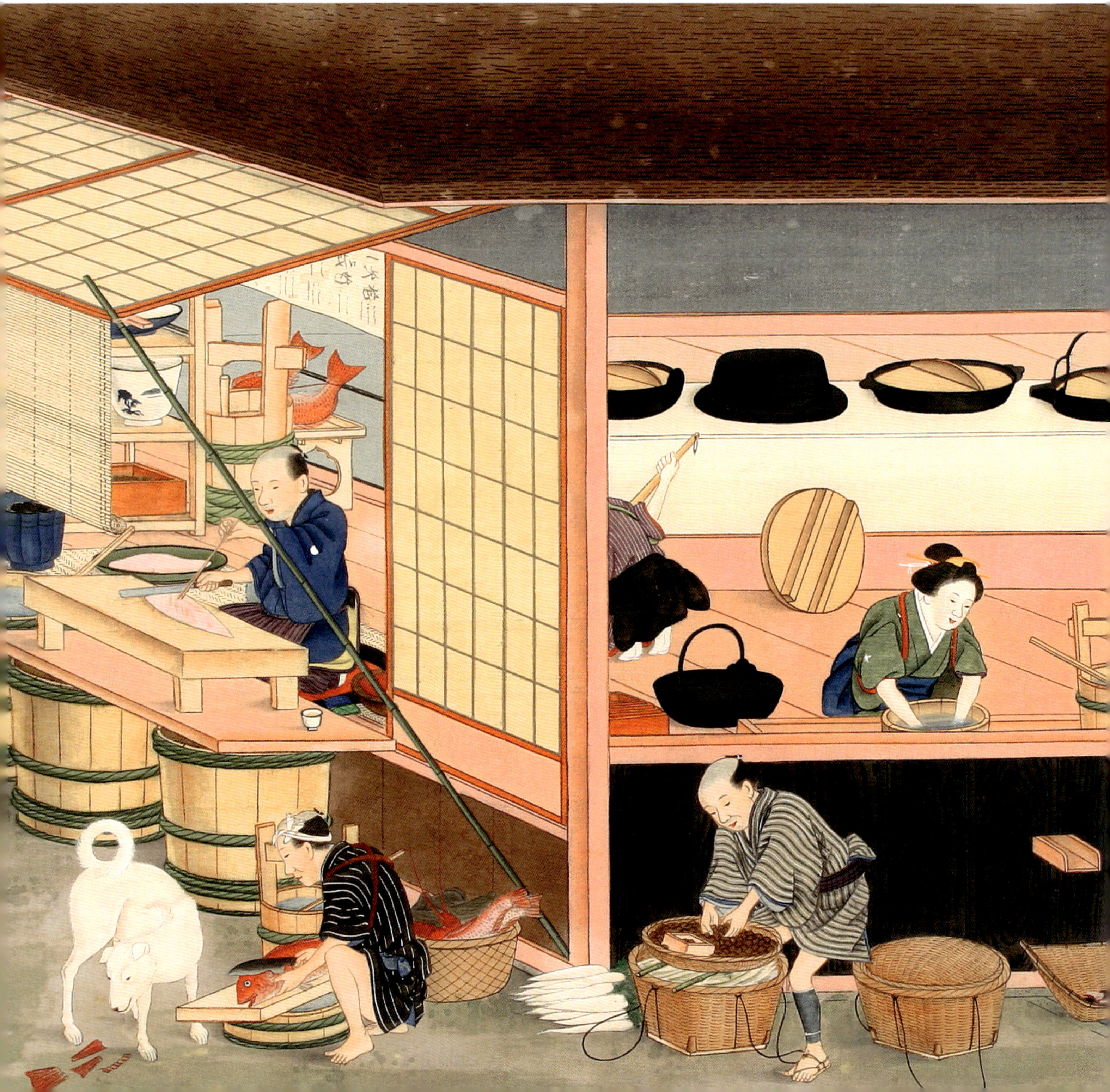

Change of climate

While Oshima came to Europe to introduce *kaiseki* cuisine in the early 1970s, the star French chef Paul Bocuse went to Japan to study Japanese cuisine. Back in Paris he revolutionized French cuisine by completely changing his style. *Nouvelle cuisine*, he called it. Bocuse often stressed how Japanese cooking had inspired him. He continued cooking with French ingredients, but rebelled against complicated and heavy sauces that smothered so many dishes at the time. He objected to the excessive use of cream and butter, for which he was much applauded by dieticians. He insisted on ultimate restraint with condiments, so the fare should taste only of itself. He demanded that cooking times be kept to a minimum to preserve some texture. He kept portions extremely small, but presented many dishes one after another, very much in the *kaiseki* tradition. He devoted himself entirely to the highest-quality ingredients and displayed them with great elegance.

Nouvelle cuisine took Europe and America by storm and the effect was noticed worldwide. Everywhere guests of the best restaurants suddenly complained that the vegetables were undercooked, and that they had to pay exorbitant prices for meals that did not satisfy their hunger. It was novel, and it was a real step forward. Elegant restraint in everything combined with a high appreciation of fish and vegetables are much better for the body than the outdated style of gorging fat and meat.

Nouvelle cuisine prepared the European public for Japanese cuisine, which caught on remarkably quickly afterwards. Within two decades *sushi* bars and *teppanyaki* restaurants popped up everywhere. Twenty-five years ago, very few westerners knew of the existence of *sushi* and *sashimi*, and the notion of eating raw fish might have horrified them. Nowadays you are just not with it if you are unfamiliar with these delights.

The importance of Japanese cuisine doesn't stop at *sushi* however. Its highest form, *kaiseki ryōri*, is worthy of a lot more investigation. For centuries, great masters have studied and refined its art, traditions and philosophy. *Kaiseki ryōri* originates partly from the meal eaten before the tea ceremony, that epitome of Zen-Buddhist aesthetics. Zen thinking may advocate restraint and minimalism, but *kaiseki* cuisine was also influenced by the rich tradition of the aristocratic *honzen* meals. This delicate mixture of luxury and restraint makes it such a relevant study for cooks all over the world.

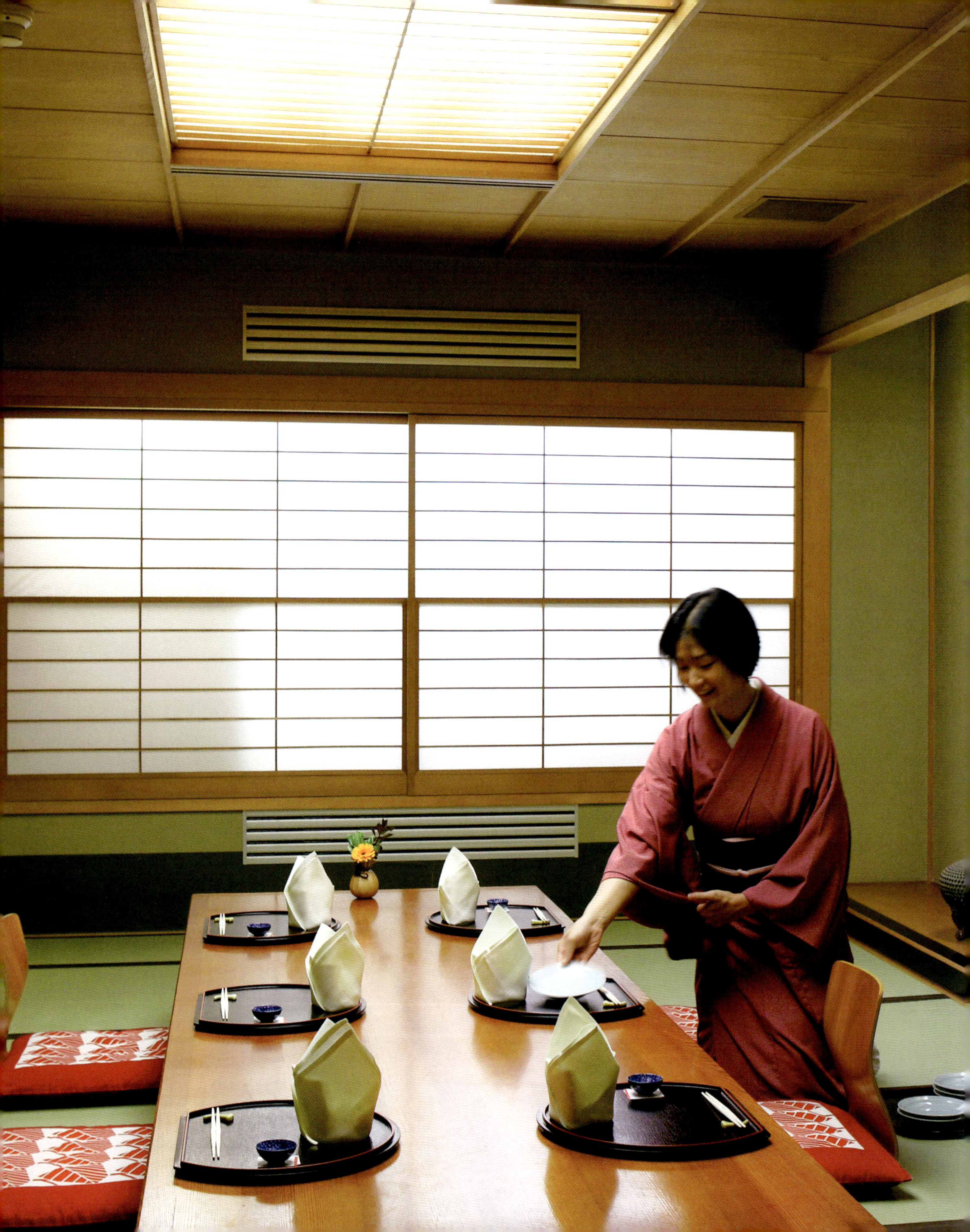

Origins of kaiseki

HONZEN BANQUETS (HONZEN RYŌRI)

The medieval aristocracy of Japan had grand ways of dining. During *honzen* banquets individual diners would be presented with a great number of dishes, which were displayed in front of them, on small portable tables (see p. 34) called *zen* (nothing to do with Zen Buddhism). The main *zen* (*honzen* in Japanese) bore a bowl of rice and seven side dishes, which may seem sufficient for a complete meal, but more tables with dishes were presented. The most elaborate dinner numbered 35 dishes, presented on seven tables per person, all at the same time. With so many tables each, guests naturally sat much farther apart than guests do around a modern western dinner table. *Honzen* banquets are still held on very formal occasions, such as weddings, but in a modified version with 'only' eight dishes on two tables per person. They still require much dining furniture.

The etiquette of *honzen ryōri*, influenced by the imperial court, was rather complicated. Court etiquette, for example, specified precisely which dishes were supposed to be eaten with chopsticks, which with a spoon and which with the hands.[1] Guests were supposed to take some of the food home.

Etiquette was somewhat difficult to master for those who had not grown up at court. The manners of the *samurai*, a class of warriors from the provinces, often clashed with those of the courtly elite in Kyoto. One courtier in the 10th century, Fujiwara no Hidesato, wanted to form an alliance with the *samurai* Taira no Masakado, leader of a powerful militia, and was invited to dinner. The meal was decent enough, but the table manners of the *samurai* were appalling. He took such clumsy bites that the rice fell out of his mouth, and he then wiped it off with his sleeve! The courtier was totally shocked and sided with Masakado's opponents. The *samurai* lost the battle and his life.

The culinary quality of *honzen* banquets has often been questioned. Originally foods were boiled, steamed, grilled, pickled or dried, but not flavoured. All the seasonings (salt, vinegar, *sake* and a condiment of fermented soya bean paste, similar to *miso*, called *hishio*) were on the table. Dishes began to be flavoured in the kitchen from the 14th century onward and condiments disappeared from the table.

PUBLIC TEA HOUSES

Just as 18th century middle-class citizens of Amsterdam and London met each other in coffee houses, so their contemporaries in Edo met up over a cup of tea. There were teahouses (*chaya* or *chamise*) of every kind. Some served only tea and snacks, others specialized in *sake*, which made them very popular. Many were found around temples, others catered for visitors to the theatre or *sumo* wrestling. Initially teahouses were not allowed to serve complete meals, since that was the prerogative of inns, but many served light snacks.

Edo was a very male-dominated city. The *shōgun* (head of the warrior class; ruler of Japan between the 12th and 19th century) controlled the provincial noblemen (*daimyō*) by requiring them to alternate their residence between Edo and their provincial home; one period in Edo, one period in the country and so forth. The *daimyō* built grand houses in Edo and resided there with their *samurai* soldiers. The workforce used to build the city (and rebuild it, after it was repeatedly destroyed by fire) was a migrant one, called in for specific tasks. Many also left their wives at home. Surveys from between 1710 and 1740 indicate there were about 58 women to every 100 civilian men in Edo – the military not included. With macho recklessness, workers would immediately spend all the day's earnings on food and drink, which gave a tremendous boost to the catering industry. Shops where quick snacks like noodles or *tempura* were served, popped up on every street corner. Tea-houses became very popular haunts indeed. In the early days of the Edo period (1600–1867), an affluent *samurai* might have turned up his nose at the fast-food culture, but by the 18th century many shops had refined their style. By then even highly placed officers discussed the best noodle shops.

The teahouse in Edo, where merchants and gentlemen met to talk business and politics, became what the coffee house was in London or Amsterdam, but tea in Japan was taken a lot more seriously. In Japan the drinking of tea had developed into a fine art.

Tables of *honzen ryōri*

Hosoda Eishi (inventor), *Party in a teahouse near Shinagawa bay*

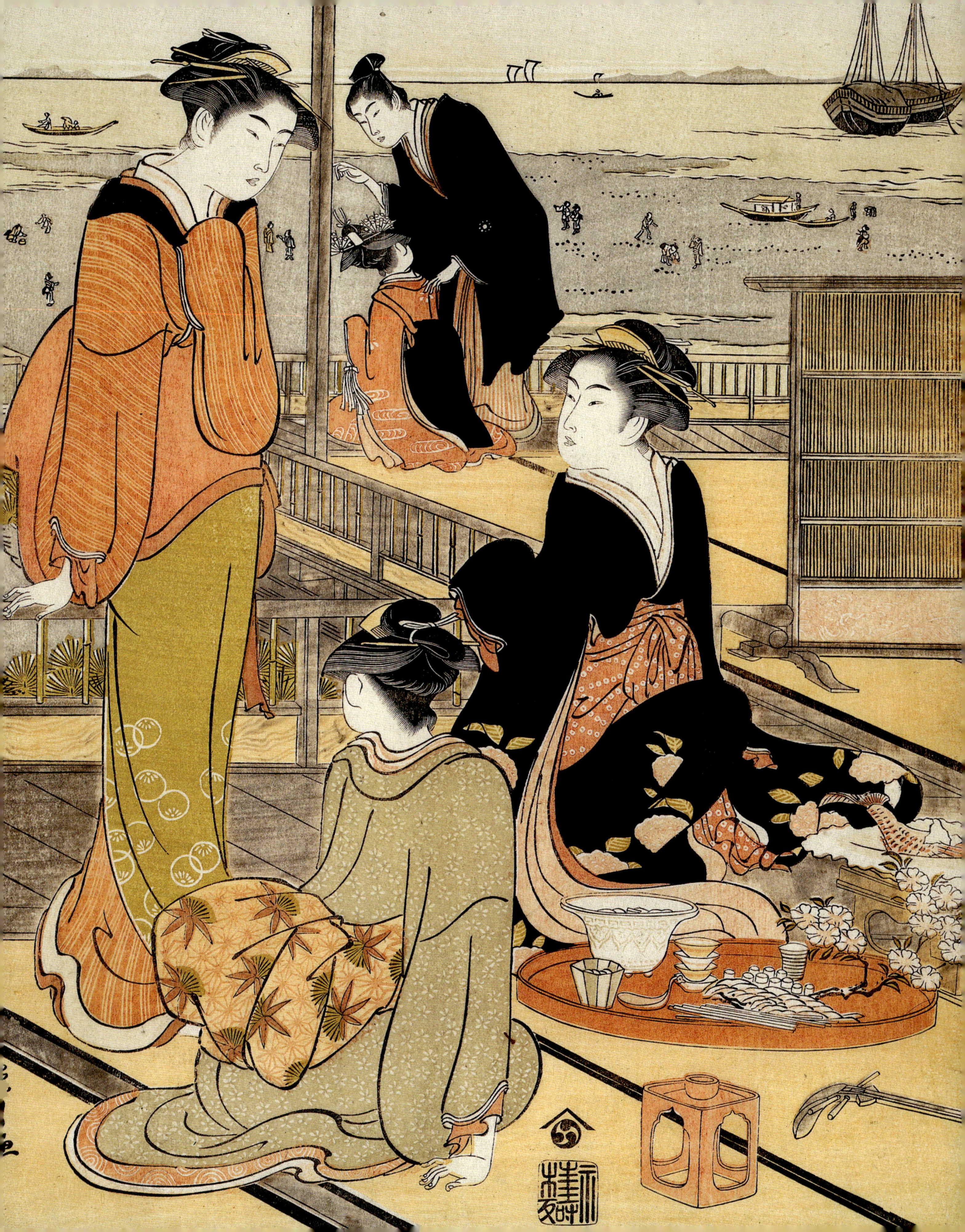

TEA CEREMONY (CHANOYU)

The art of making and drinking tea has been perfected to what is called the tea ceremony in English and *chanoyu* (hot water for tea), or more formally *sadō* (the way of tea), in Japanese.

Expression is given to a moral and aesthetic principle called *wabi*. This word is related to the verb *wabu* (to languish) and the adjective *wabishii* (lonely, uncomfortable) and refers to a serene state of mind, liberated from earthly pain and desire, somewhat comparable to the ancient Greek stoic ideal. In the course of the 12th to 14th century authors began emphasizing the pleasure that can be derived from simplicity and the beauty in minimalism. Tea masters embrace both these moral and the aethetic principles of *wabi*, which go a lot further than a superficial attraction to rusticity.

Several tea masters have contributed substancially to the developement of *wabicha* (*wabi* tea); Murata Jukō (1422–1502), Takeno Jōō (1502–1555), Sen no Rikyū (1522–1591), Furuta Oribe (1544–1615) and Kobori Enshū (1579–1647). Before the time of these masters tea receptions were usually held after copious *honzen* banquets and used to include plenty of *sake*, women and song, but now tea was simplified to the bare *wabi* essentials. In the stylized simplicity and cultivated minimalism of the tea house nobles, warriors and tradesmen could escape from the daily drag of life and share their love of *chanoyu*. However simple the action may be, the host makes a cup of tea for his guests, which they drink, every detail is reflected upon and has been studied by generations of great tea masters. The ceremony has been perfected for centuries but will never take its final form, since it lives and changes with life.

TEA KAISEKI (CHAKAISEKI RYŌRI)

The word *kaiseki* means 'pocket stone' and was a term monks used for their midday snack, which they named after the hot stones they held in their clothes during meditation on cold winter days. Sen no Rikyū used the term to describe the meal he designed to precede the tea ceremony.

The food of *chakaiseki* is supposed to be very simple and modest. It should reflect a sense of season and express sensitivity to human feelings, rather than show off the prestige and wealth of the host – as opposed to the opulent *honzen* banquets. In order to let the guest appreciate every detail, the meal was served in small courses, one after another. Every item was prepared by the host himself and served with the utmost care at the ideal time, and at the best temperature.

The ceremony of the *chakaiseki* is still performed today, even if the ideal of simplicity and sobriety have given way to some luxury. It is, now as always, an exclusive form of entertainment, which only those with sufficient resources and experience can really enjoy. But despite this elitist quality, the calm and restrained atmosphere of *wabi* still prevails.

Water features in many forms during the *chakaiseki*. Upon arrival guests may sometimes receive a cup of hot water, called *kumidashi*, ever so subtly flavoured with a seasonal herb. Lacquer bowls containing rice and *miso* soup are served at the beginning of the meal. No *sake* is served yet. The rice and soup are meant to line the stomach before any *sake* is drunk, and this is brought in only after the rice and soup have been eaten. On a tray behind these bowls stands the *mukōzuke* (put behind) dish, nearly always containing raw fish. The following course, *wanmori* or *nimonowan*, comes in another soup bowl and counts as the highlight of the meal – a range of delicacies briefly simmered in broth. Next come grilled foods, *yakimono*, and another dish

Mr Soujitsu Kobori
The 13th Grand Master of Enshū Sadō (Tea Ceremony) School

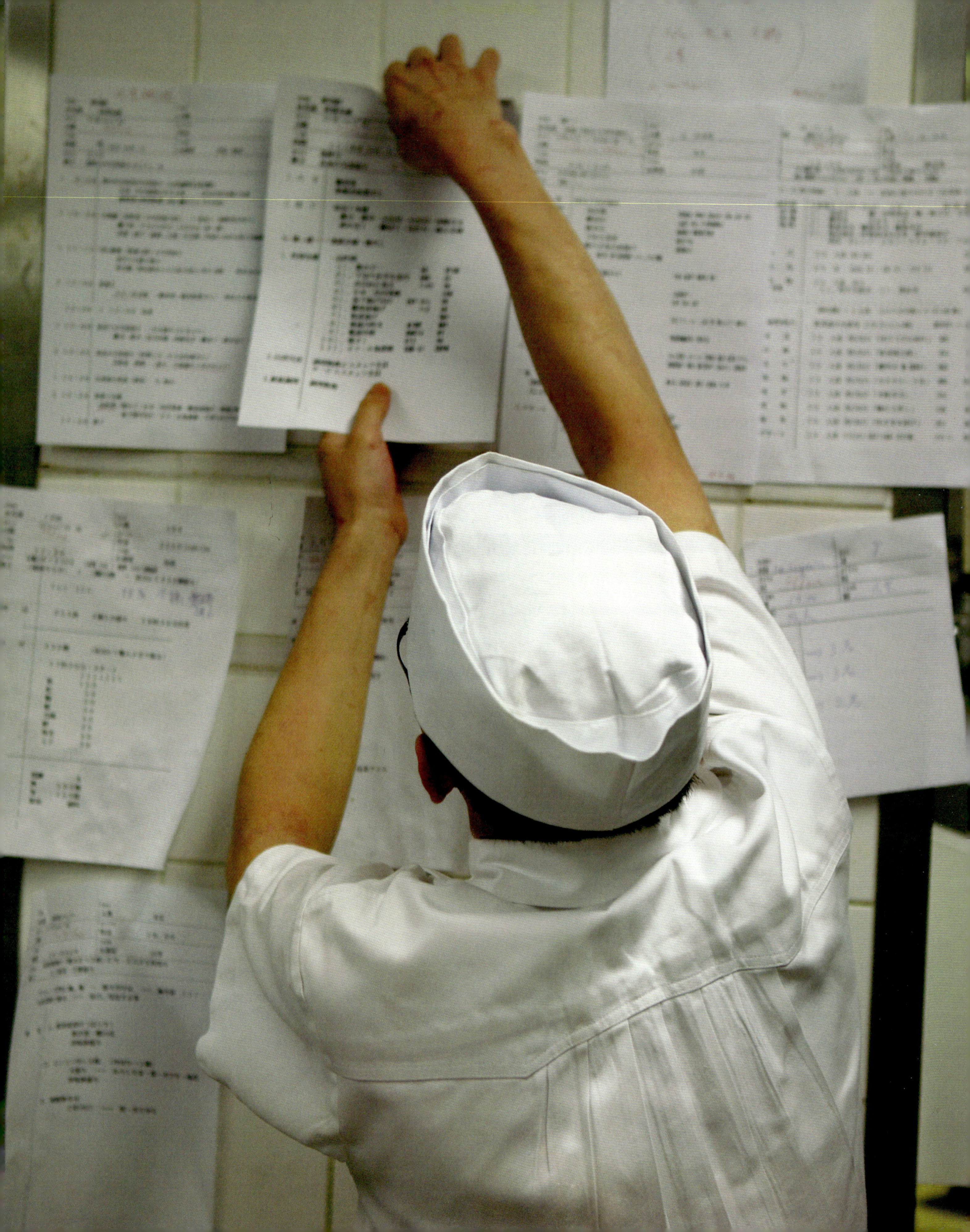

Courses of enkaiseki ryōri

In the art of *kaiseki* repetition is avoided. A dislike of repetition is characteristic of Zen. Buddhists believe lives come in cycles, and that everything in life comes in cycles too, but that a moment never comes around twice. Much in *kaiseki* pays homage to the season – that great cycle of food products – but acknowledges that still, every spring will be different. One year the spinach will be greener than the next. Not every year is a good vintage.

Avoiding repetition doesn't necessarily mean that an ingredient may not feature twice in a meal, quite the opposite. Respect and dedication to the product require that all of the animal or plant is used. A product may appear on the table in many different versions. A cook should make the most of the products and avoid waste. Rather than varying ingredients the Japanese cook creates variation by employing different cooking methods.

In Japan this notion has become part of any meal that is extended beyond the basic rice, pickles and soup. Different cooking methods are used for every course. One dish will be simmered; others will be raw, vinegary, steamed, grilled, or fried.

A basic meal consists of *ichijū sansai*, which means 'one soup and three side dishes.' Rice and pickles are served also, but the presence of rice is so evident, that it is not even mentioned. The 'three side dishes' are normally a *namasu* (*sashimi* or vinegary fish), a *nimono*, a softly poached dish and *yakimono* a grilled dish. Starters are served before these courses and fruit afterwards. The following series of courses, typical of a normal *kaiseki* meal distinguish themselves from one another primarily by the cooking method.

ZENSAI APPETIZERS

The *zensai* is a fun course for the chef. Three, five, seven, nine or eleven different kinds of cold delicacy are elegantly arranged on a tray. Holidays bring their own traditional foods, but even outside the feasts all the delicacies are seasonal *(shun)*, except for one. Just one of the foods will be chosen ahead of season *(hashiri)* to remind the diner of pleasures to come. One might serve a piece of eel in spring for instance, since eel is typical of summer.

OWAN SOUP

After the adventurous *zensai* comes a very solemn and traditional course, the soup. This course can also be called *suimono* and is the test of a good cook. If the soup is good, it means the chef knows how to make the basic stock – *dashi* (nearly always of bonito and kelp). A strictly vegetarian stock (of only kelp or with additional *shiitake*) is made on the Bon festival (All Souls Day) and in some cases the stock can be drawn from a main ingredient such as clams or chicken. The soup is filled with at least three softly simmered solid ingredients of complementing flavours and contrasting colours. A New Year's soup, for example, may contain brown slices of duck, green spinach leaves, orange slices of carrot, yellow rind of *yuzu* and a white radish. Most of the ingredients are sliced and cut, but traditionally one of them is left whole. When the bowl is empty the lid is replaced by each guest. Some people replace the lid upside down to show that they have finished, but (somewhat like turning an empty wine bottle up side down in the cooler) this is not done in the best restaurants.

TSUKURI RAW COURSE

Tsukuri, meaning 'creation', is the restaurant term for *sashimi* – cuts of raw fish. The word *sashimi* refers to cutting, which is an old and distinguished art in Japan. Each chef takes care of his knife like a knight does his sword, and indeed an old word for kitchen knife is *hōchōgatana*, the sword of the cook. As European aristocrats might once have entertained their guests by showing off their skills at the piano, Japanese aristocrats were entertained by the art of *shikibōchō*, the dextrously cutting of a fish into artistic shapes. The fish was not meant to be eaten, the pleasure was entirely in the aesthetics of skill. The cutting of *sashimi* is still considered a challenge; few housewives cut their own, but buy the fish ready sliced. *Ikizukuri*, (or *ikezukuri*) in which the flesh of the fish is cut while it is still alive, is especially difficult. The slices are served on the living (and often still moving) fish. This practice is not permitted in Europe, but according to Oshima, live cutting is the best for all white fish. Usually three, but sometimes two or five different kinds of fish are combined in a *sashimi* course. The choice of fish depends on which species are the best of the season, but variation will be made in taste, texture and colour. Thinly shredded *daikon* radish, seaweed and other edible decorations are added, as well as soy sauce for dipping, into which the diners can mix grated *wasabi*.

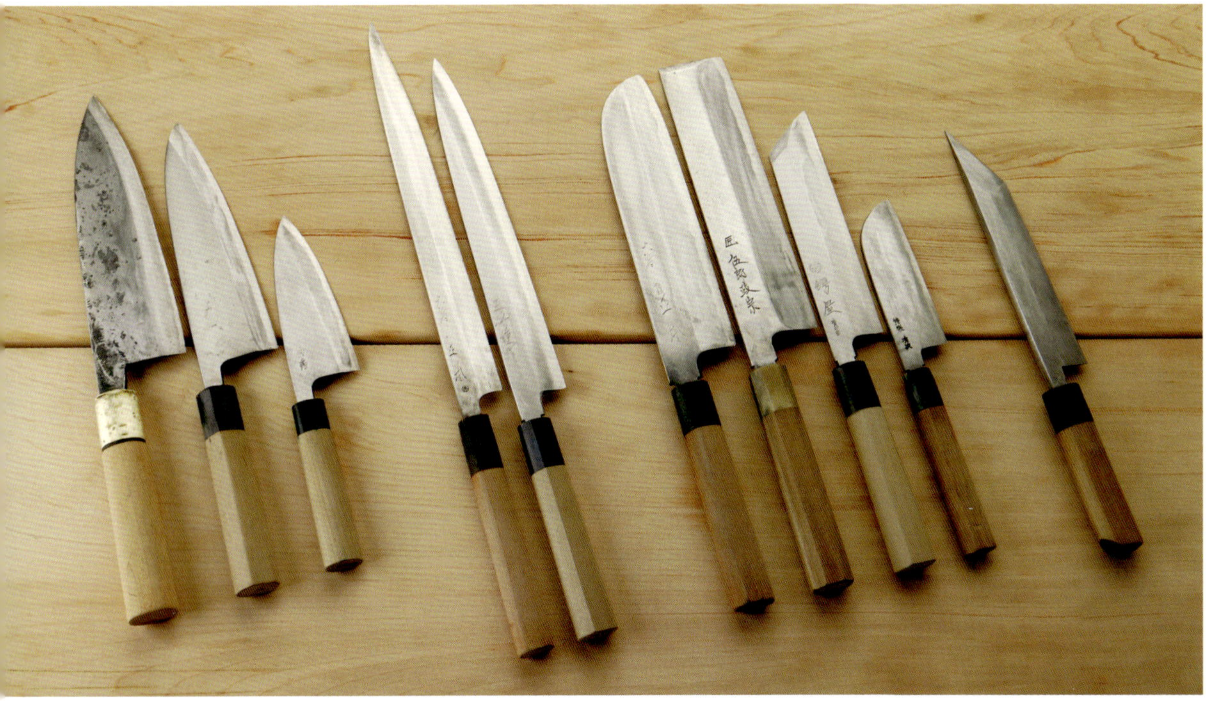

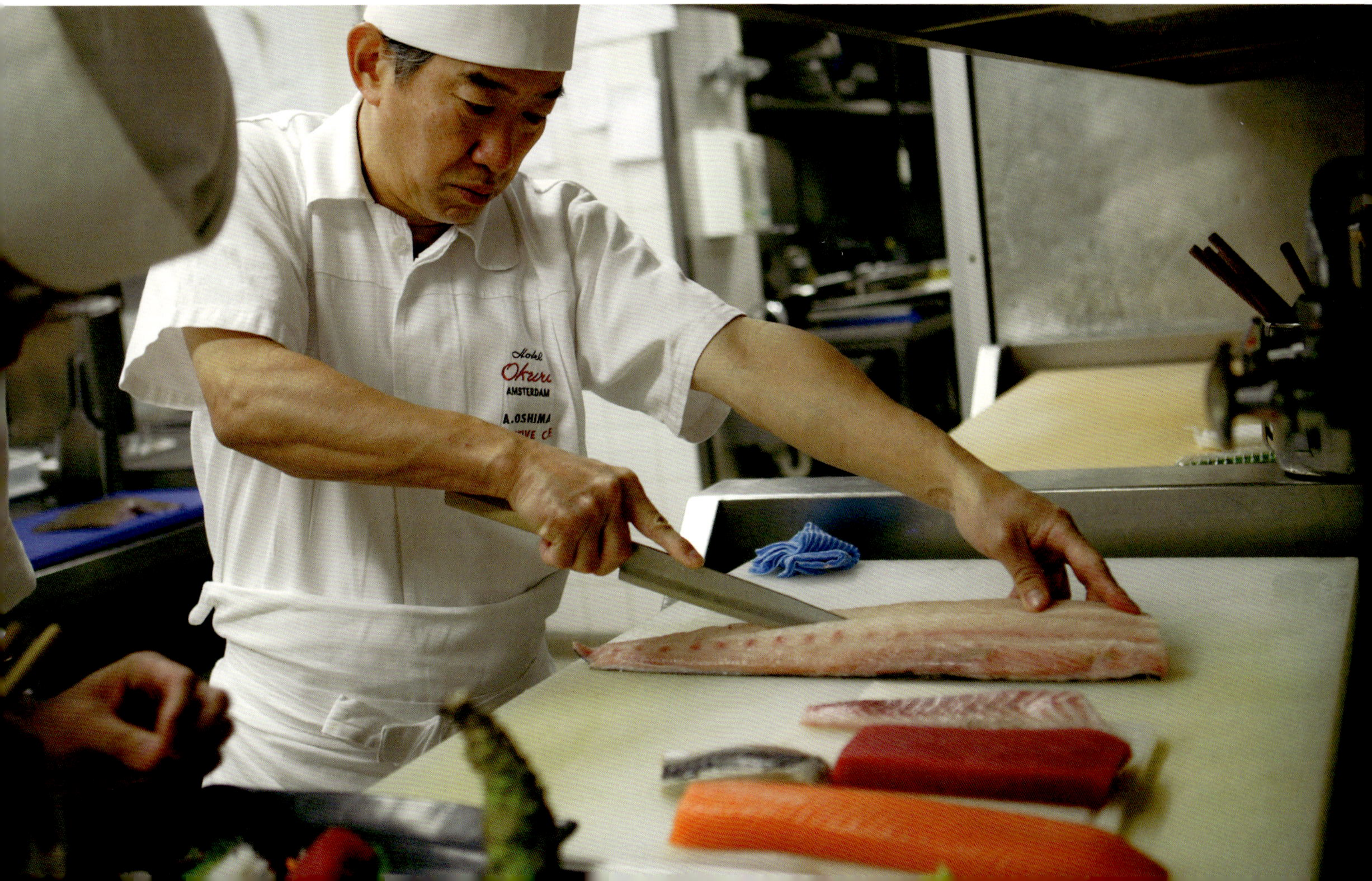
AMSTERDAM
A.OSHIMA

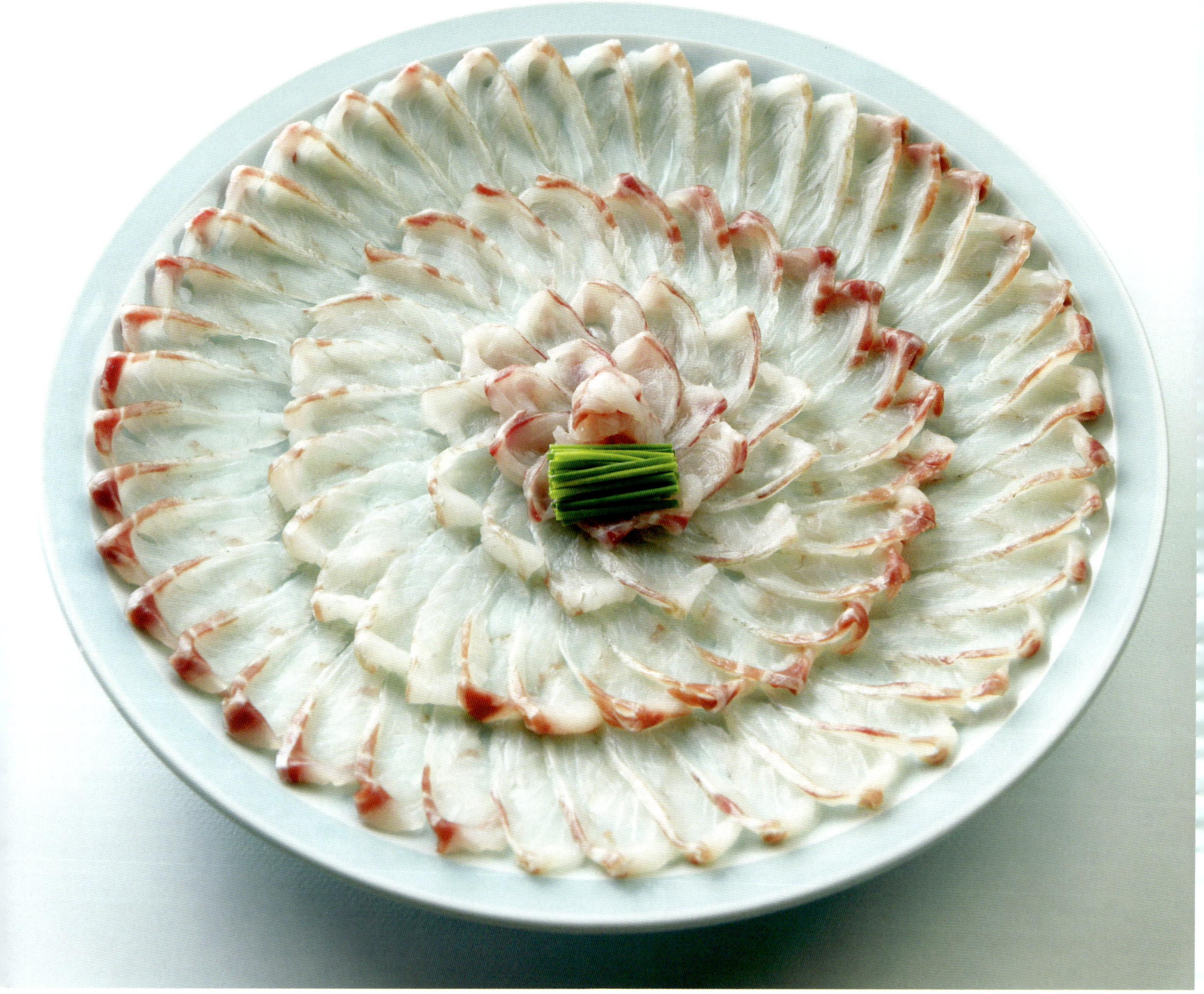

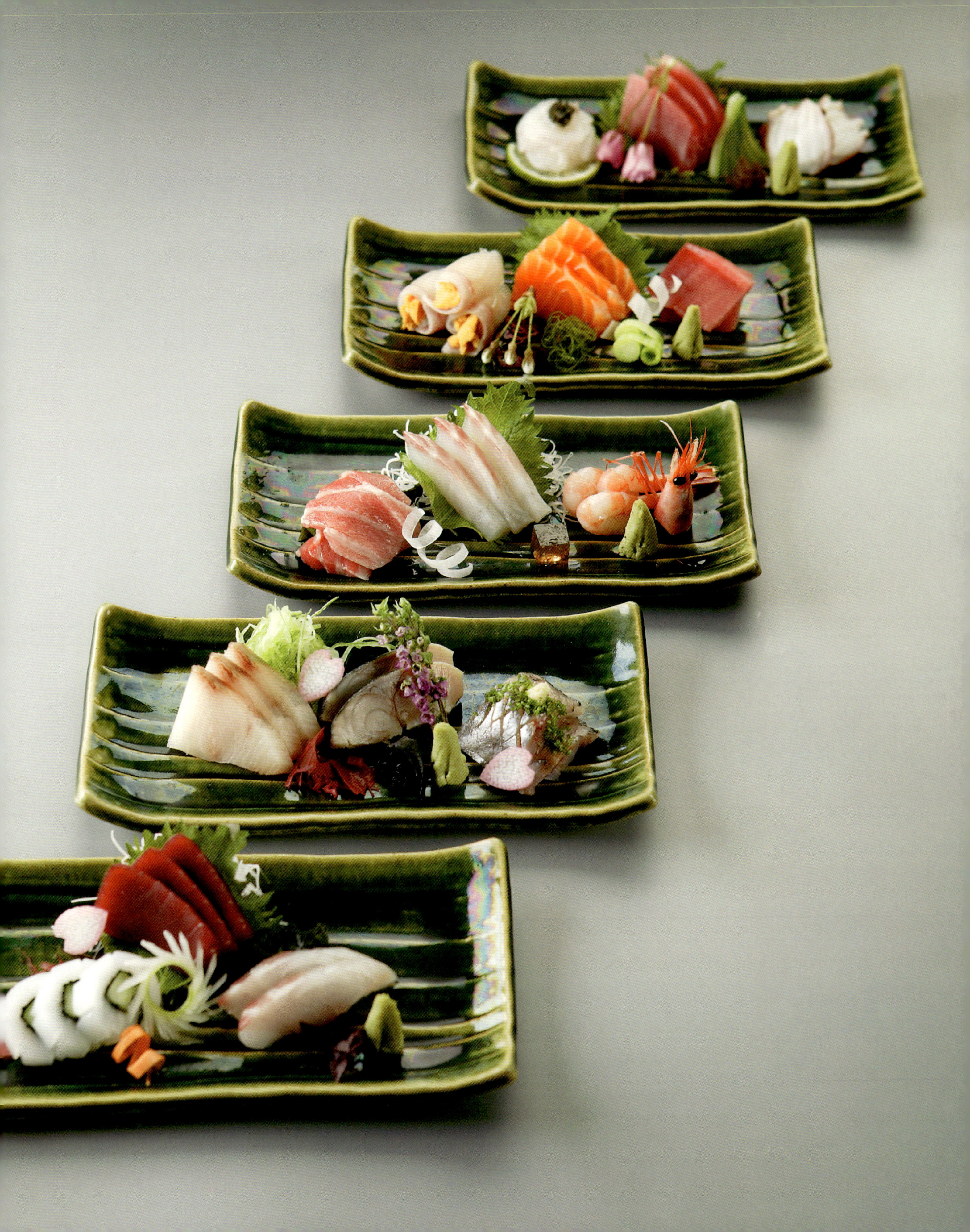

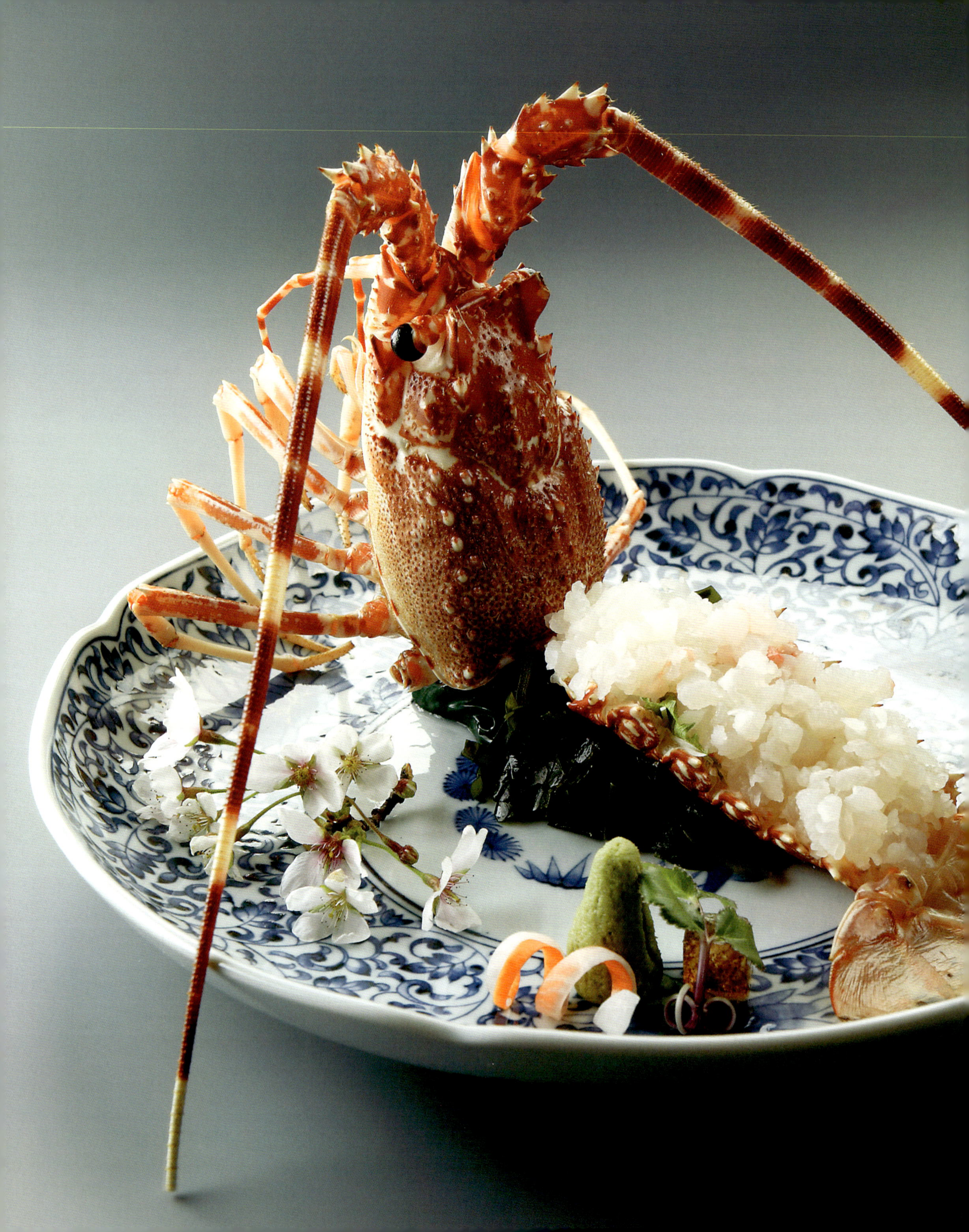

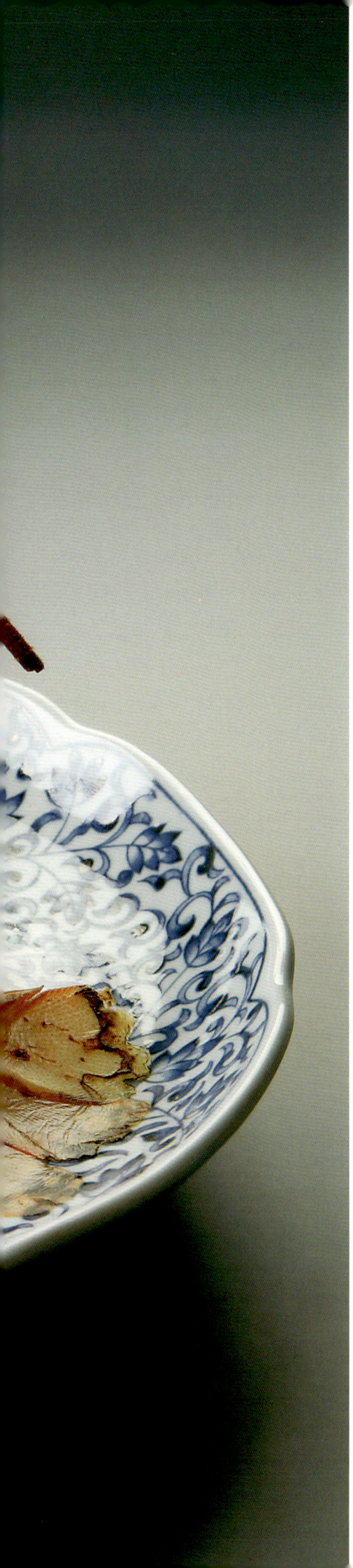

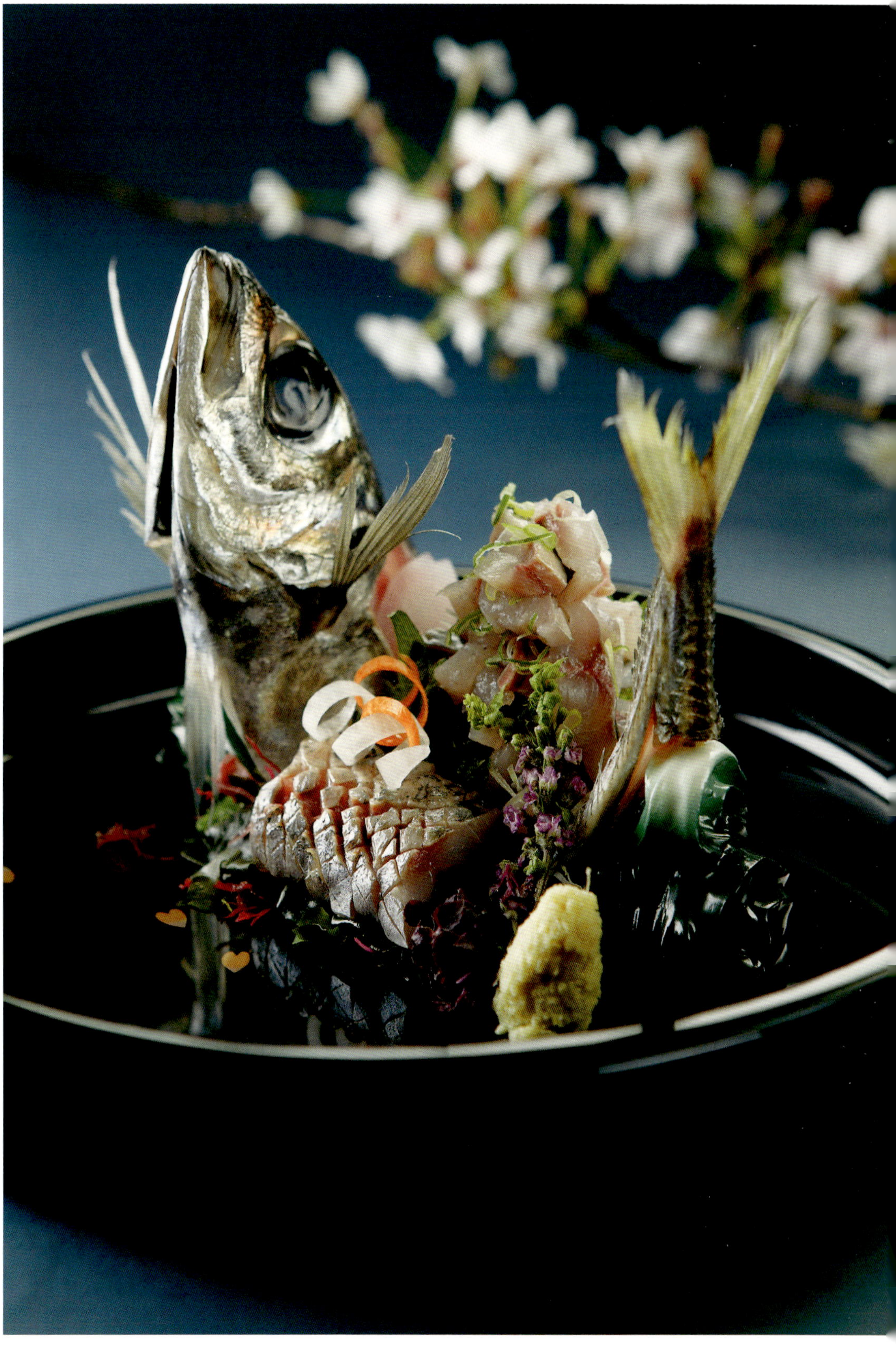

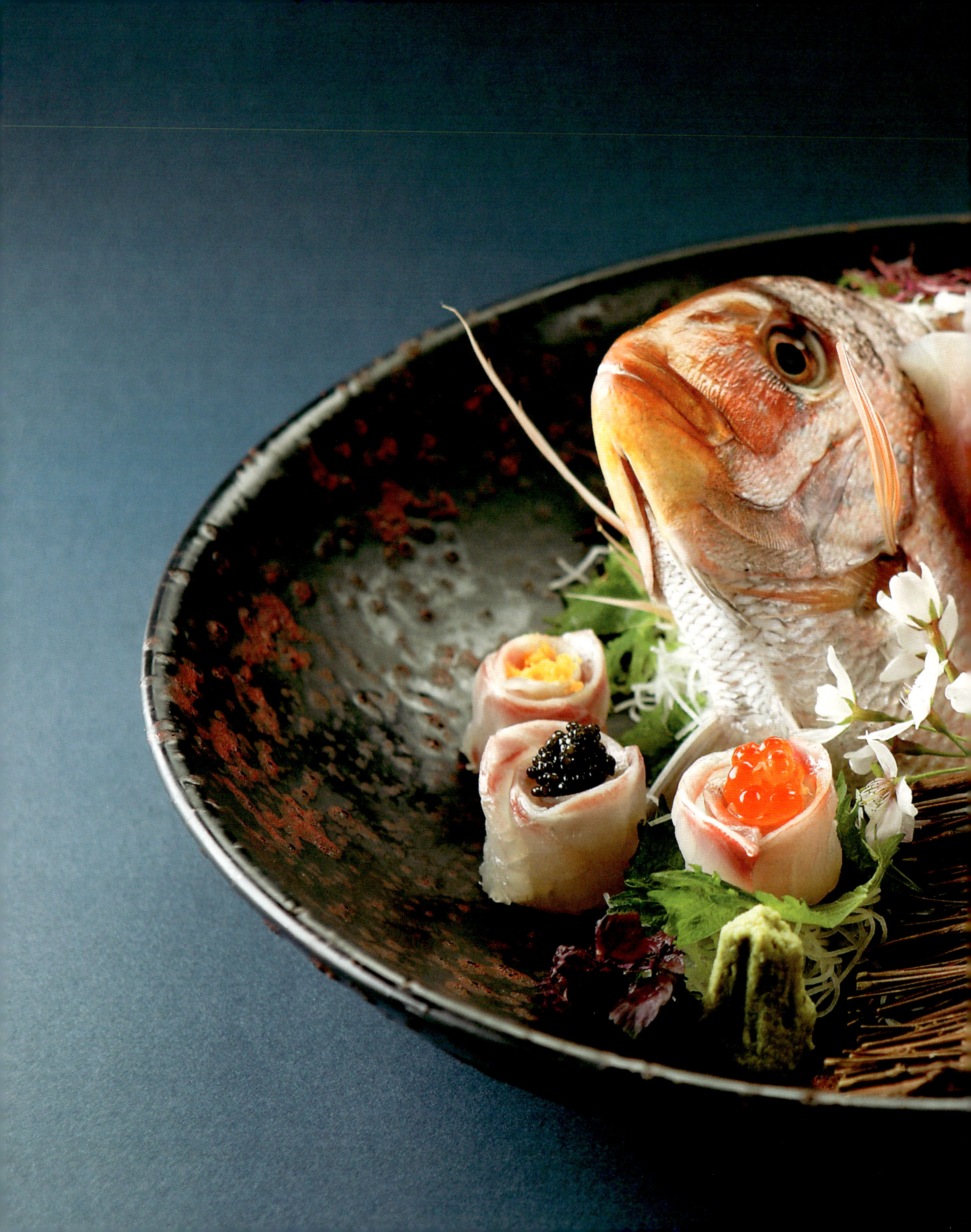

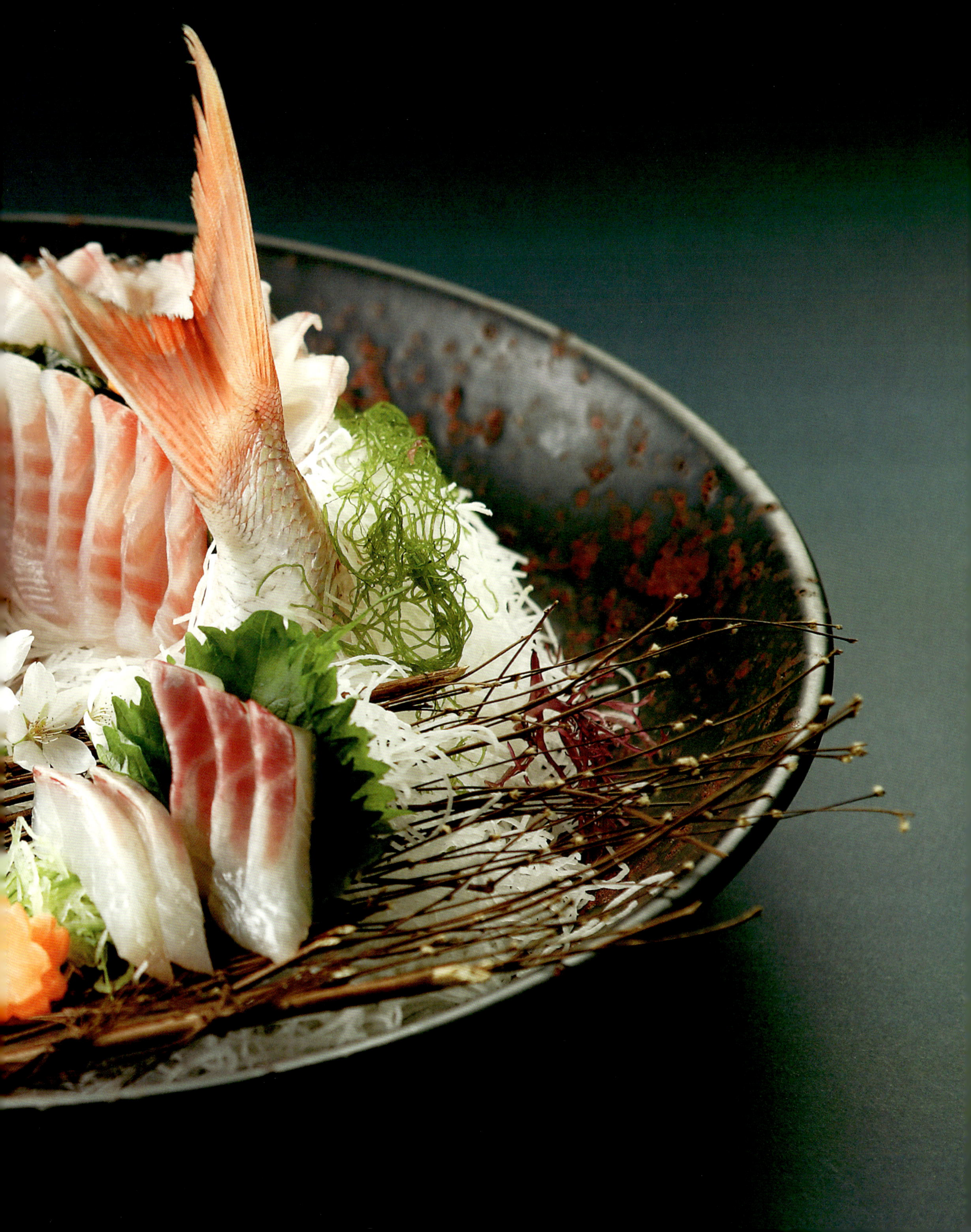

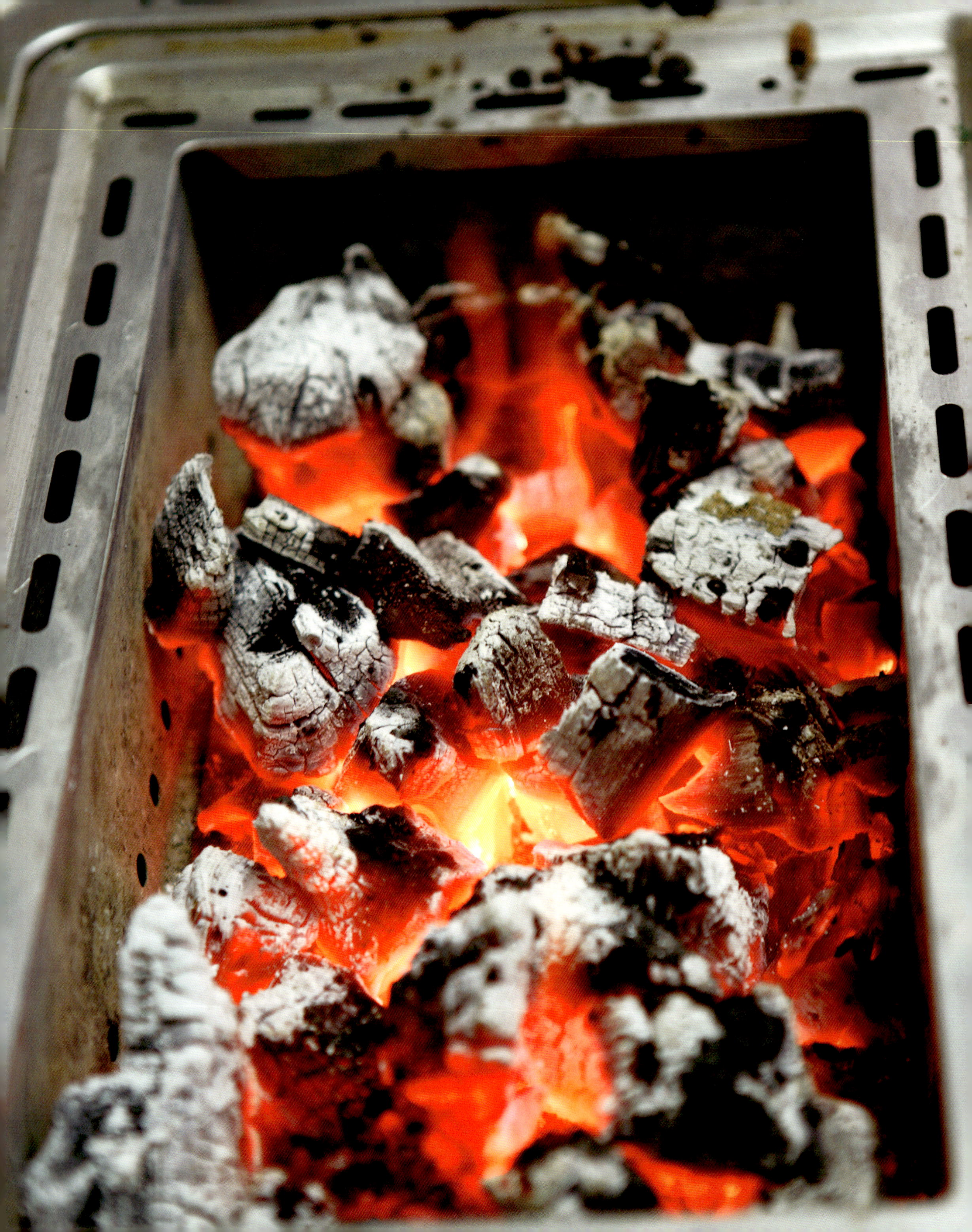

YAKIMONO GRILLED COURSE

Originally *yakimono* was made of the trimmings and lesser parts of ingredients left over from cooking other courses. To compensate for their second-rate nature, the grilled foods were served on exceptionally elaborate and decorative receptacles. Nowadays *yakimono* is no longer made with scraps – quite the opposite. Vegetables, fish, crustaceans, shell fish and poultry can be grilled in a variety of ways. Hot plates of stone or pottery can be used, but grilling over hot smokeless *binchō* charcoal is most popular. Food can be grilled on stakes, normally two per morsel, so the pieces can be easily turned over the fire. The skewers are removed before serving. Otherwise *kushiyaki* (bamboo skewers) are used – of these *yakitori* (chicken satay) is most well-known. Salt grilling, *shioyaki*, is the most simple type of *yakimono* and chiefly suitable for fish, but grilled food is often marinated and basted, as in *teriyaki* ('lustre grilling'), which involves a sauce of reduced soy sauce, reduced *mirin*, *sake* and sometimes sugar; or *kabayaki* (with a thicker sauce), which is the classic for eel. The *yakimono* course comes to the table without any complementing dishes or condiments – though a little *sanshō* pepper may be scattered over it.

36

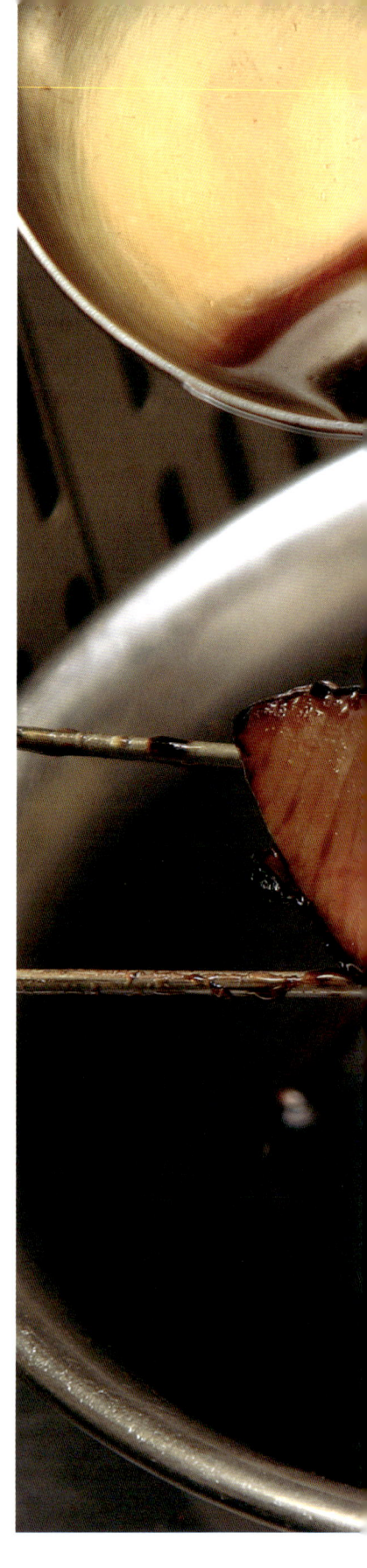

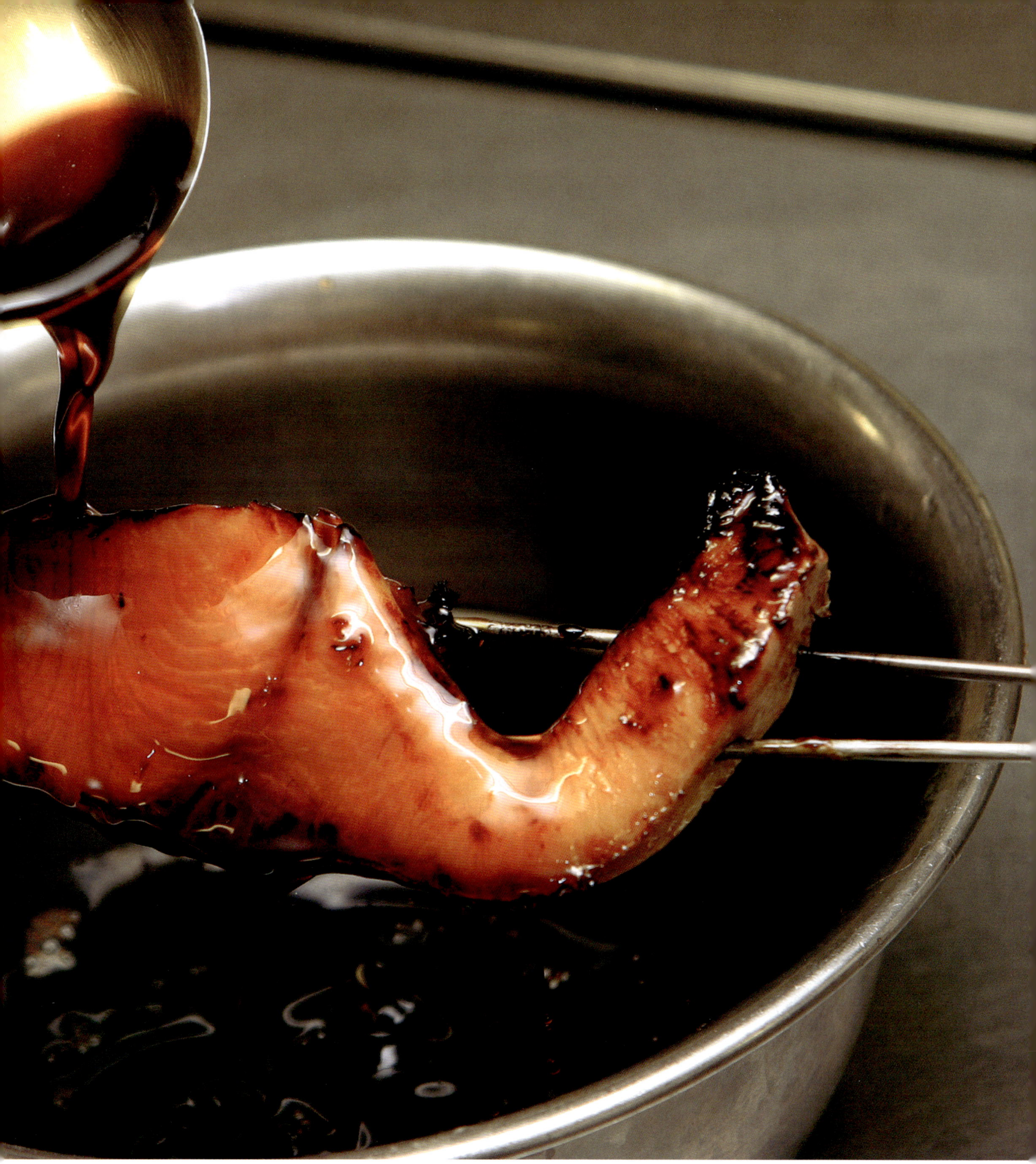

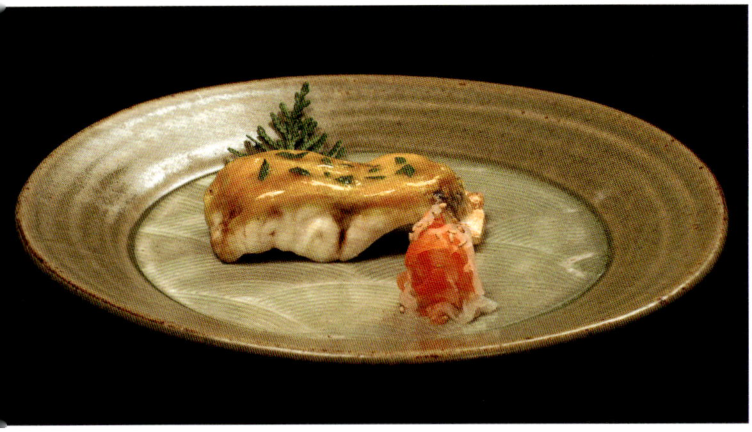
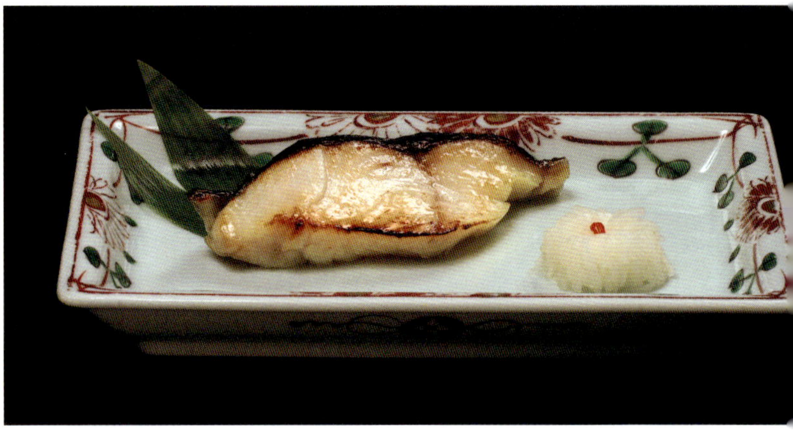
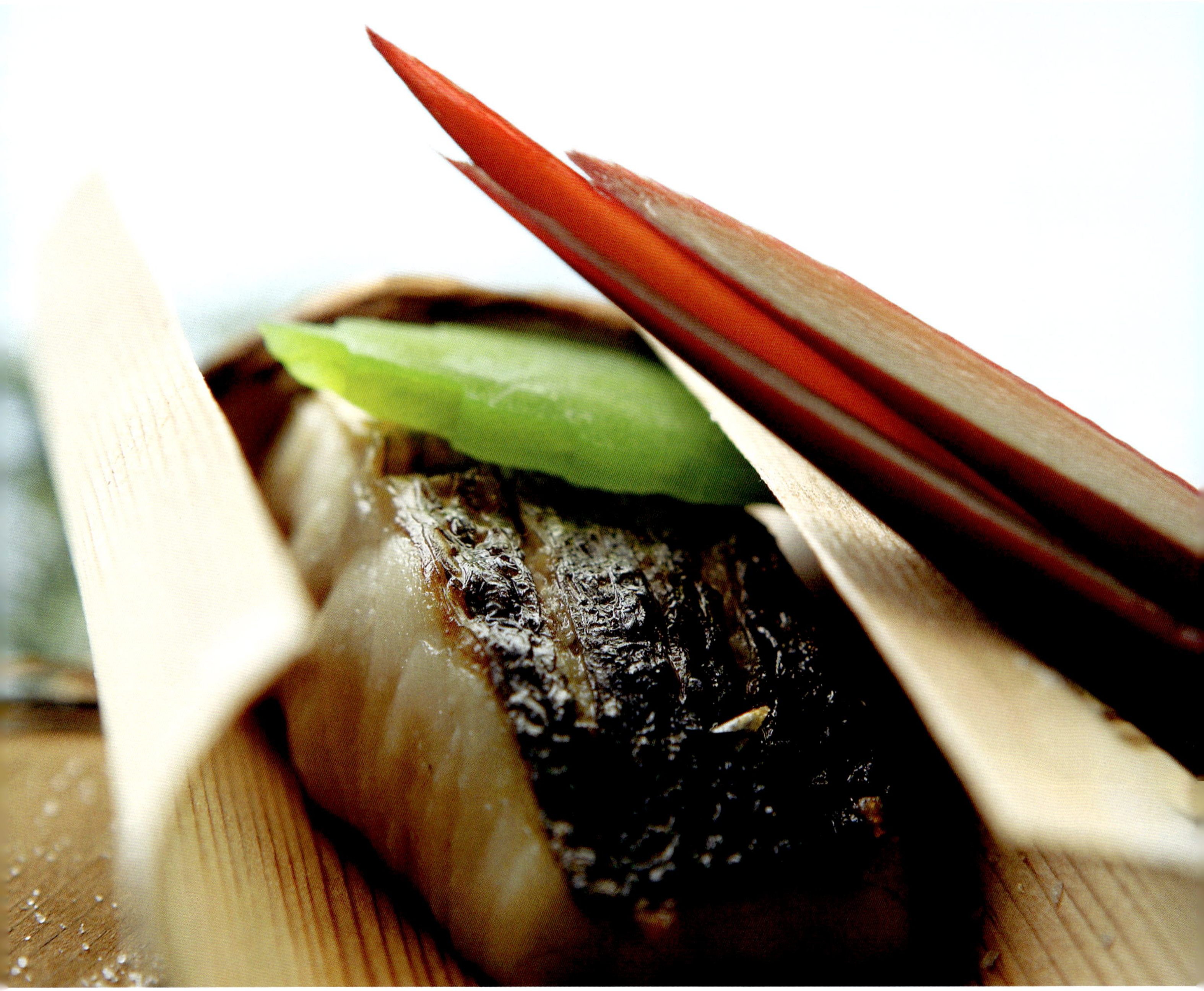

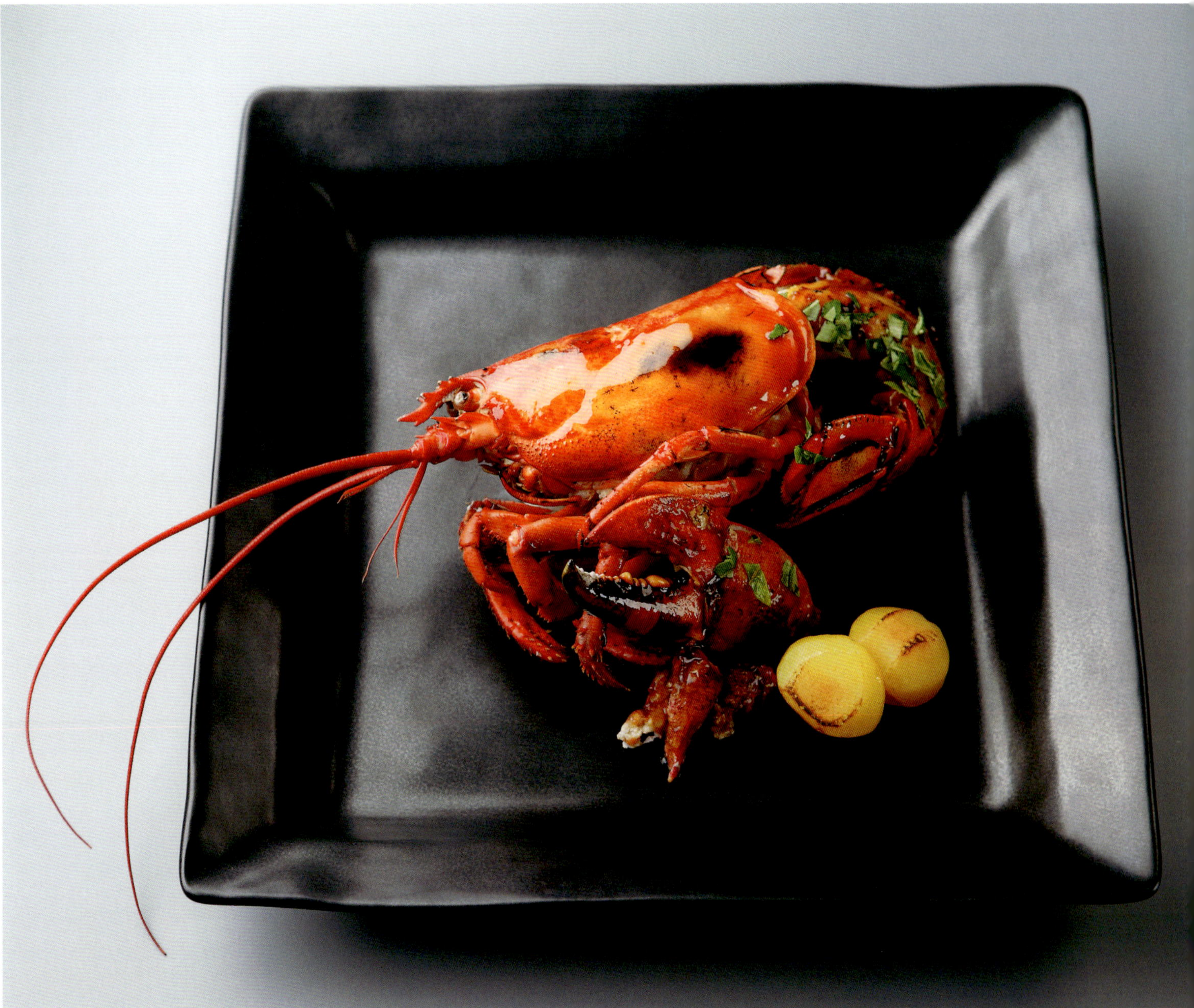

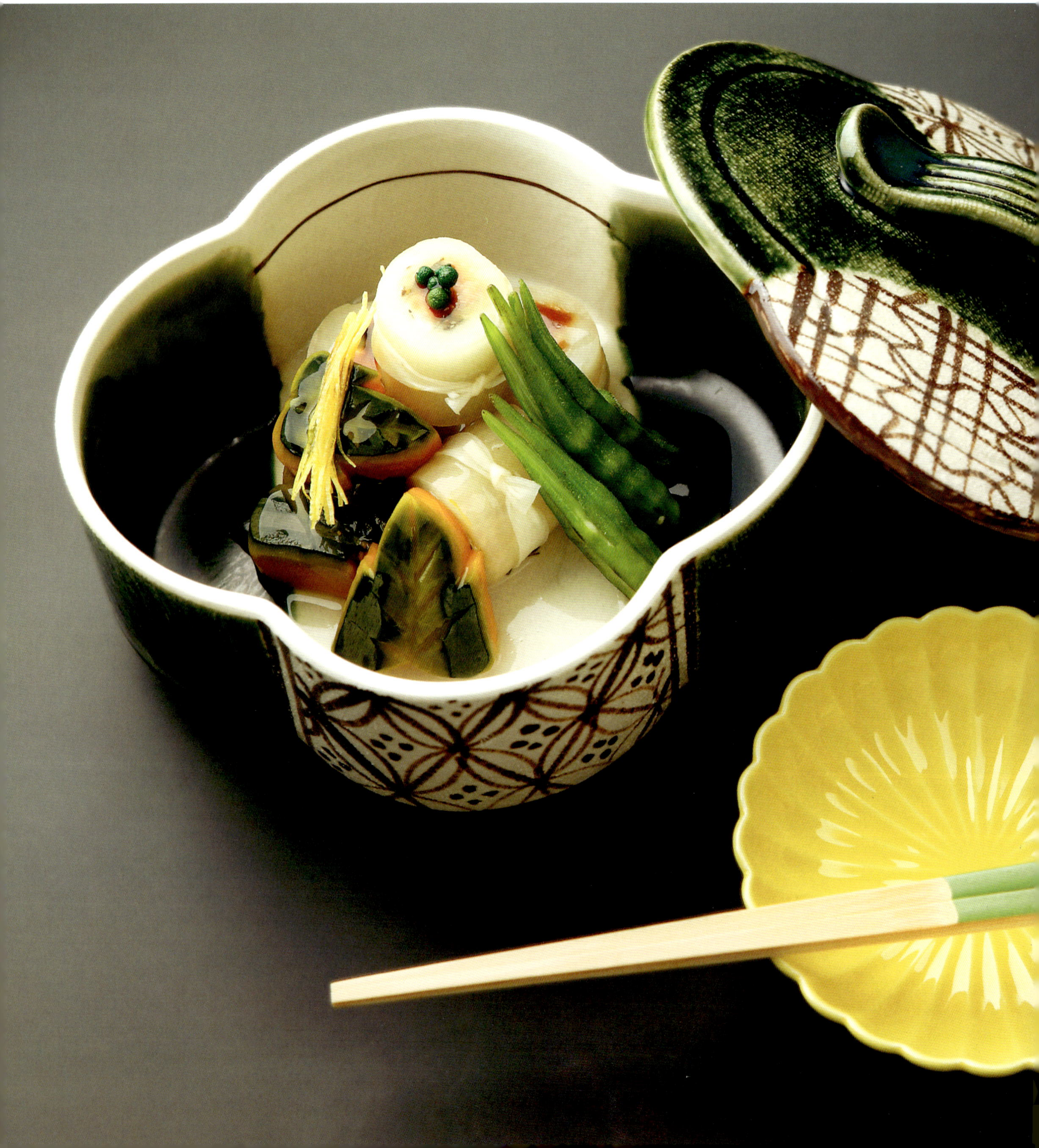

NIMONO SIMMERED COURSE

Simmering may sound like a lengthy process, but restraint in cooking times is so important that even dishes called 'simmered for 10,000 years' can be prepared in a few hours. Fish is simmered so briefly that it never encounters a boiling bubble and most vegetables are done in a matter of seconds. *Dashi* is used as a simmering stock, often flavoured with soy sauce or *miso*. The morsels are carefully composed in a bowl, which often has a lid. One ingredient will be slightly more prominent than others and they balance each other in texture shape and origin. If one ingredient is in season, the other will be ahead of season.

SUNOMONO SALAD COURSE

Sunomono (see p. 58) is often translated as salad, but salads normally consist of raw vegetables, while the ingredients of *sunomono* are lightly cooked (except for cucumber and shellfish) by pouring some boiling water over them. Fish and vegetables are dressed with vinegar, often slightly sweetened and sometimes softened with *dashi*. Soy sauce, salt and sugar are also used for flavouring. *Aemono* is a type of *sunomono* with a dressing that is made thicker with crushed sesame seeds, *miso* or *tōfu* that has been rubbed through a strainer, which changes its consistency into that of yoghurt.

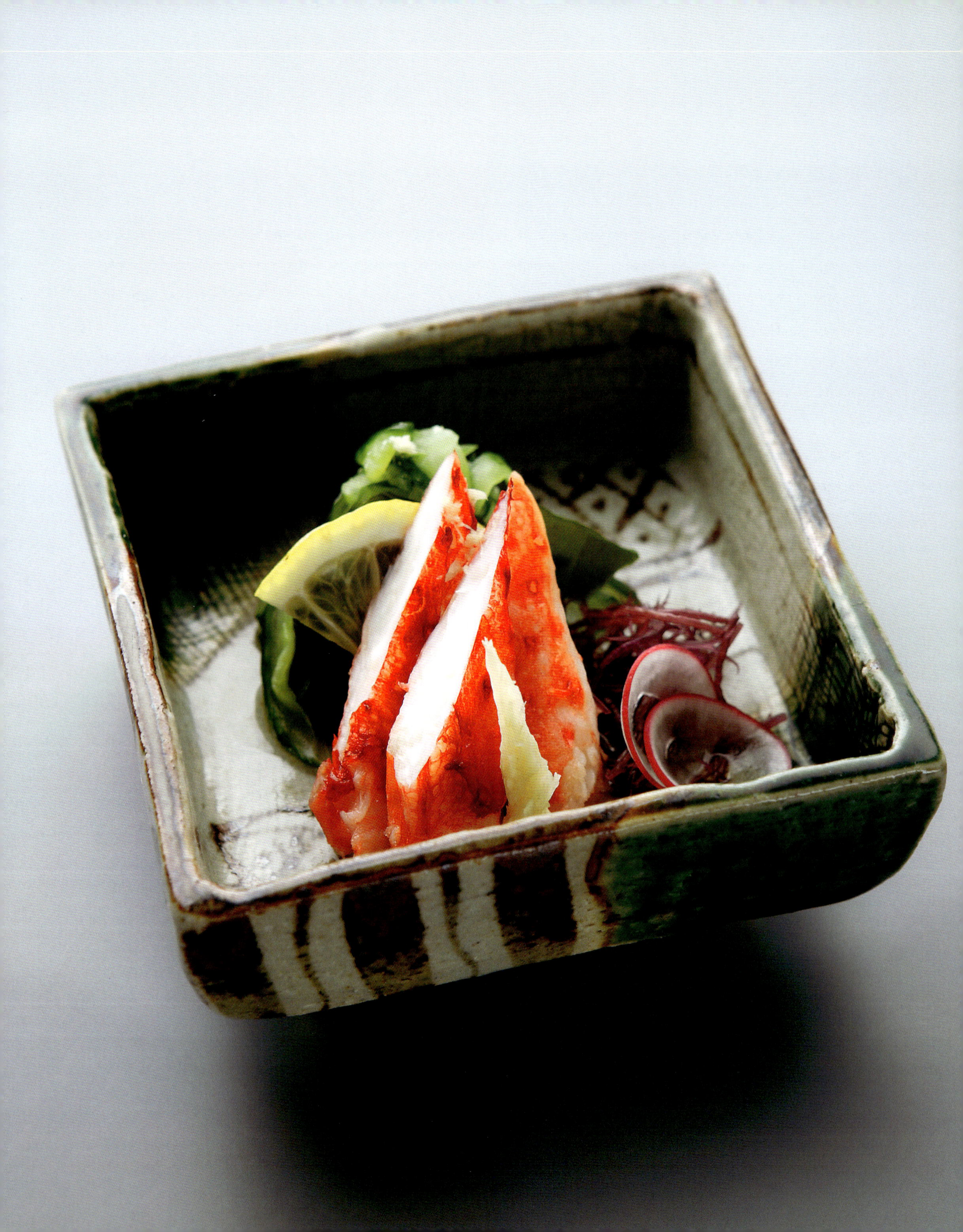

SHOKUJI THE MEAL

Rice, soup and pickles – the holy trinity that forms the basis of the Japanese meal – are served at the end in the banqueting *kaiseki*. The Japanese know and appreciate this, but many non-Japanese guests feel awkward about eating soup at the end of a meal, so it can be skipped in the Yamazato restaurant. Rice cannot be omitted. It is polite to eat all of it, down to the last grain if possible – portions are never large. After a meal of so many courses, few still feel hungry and this last bowl of rice certainly shows the difference between the tea *kaiseki* and the banqueting *kaiseki* – the latter totally satisfies all hunger. The rice may be flavoured with blossom, peas, beans, herbs or mushrooms, according to season.

Pickles, called *kōnomono* (or *tsukemono* to use a less formal word), are an important part of Japanese cuisine. Many families make their own. Vegetables are pickled in a number of ways. The simplest way to do this is overnight: vegetables are peeled, salted and pressed down with a weight. The next day they are sliced and eaten. Pickling in rice bran, *nukazuke*, takes a matter of days to a week. In addition vegetables can be pickled in *sake* lees or in *miso*. Every village and town in Japan has its own regional pickles, which are sold in shops and at train stations and are often taken home by visitors as a souvenir.

KASHI DESSERT

Traditionally no dessert is served with a Japanese meal, even though the Western custom of finishing off with some fresh fruit has now also become widespread in Japan, especially in restaurants. Japanese sweets *(wagashi)* and Western style patisserie *(yōgashi)* are more often eaten as a day-time snack, than as the end to a meal. Japanese sweets have always had their role in the tea ceremony, compensating for the bitterness of the tea. In that sense they fit at the end of a meal with the tea that is served, but they seem somewhat meagre in comparison to European equivalents, so Oshima has invented Western style desserts in the spirit of *kaiseki*, such as soufflé of green tea with ice cream of cherry blossom.

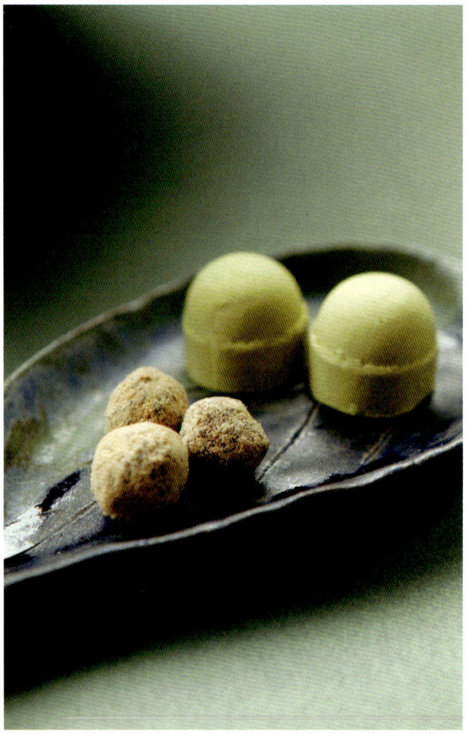
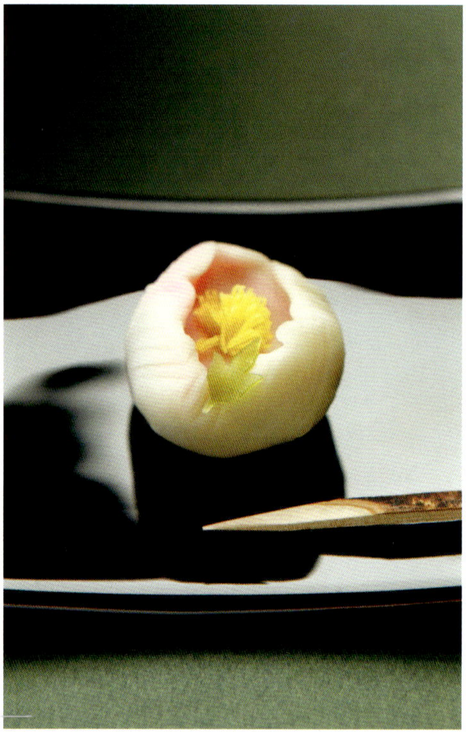
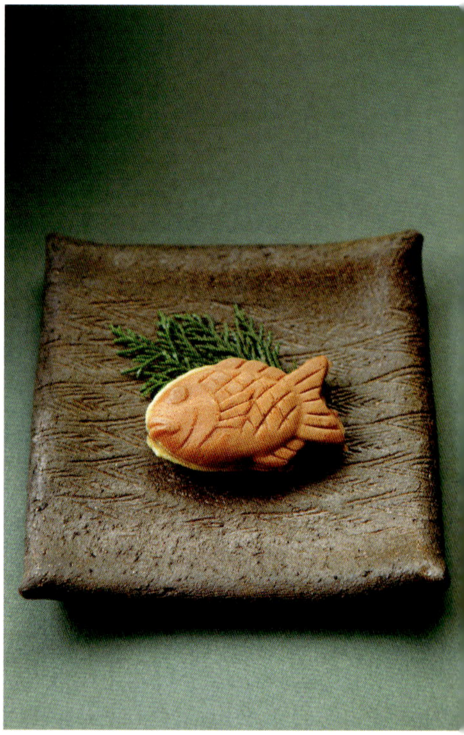
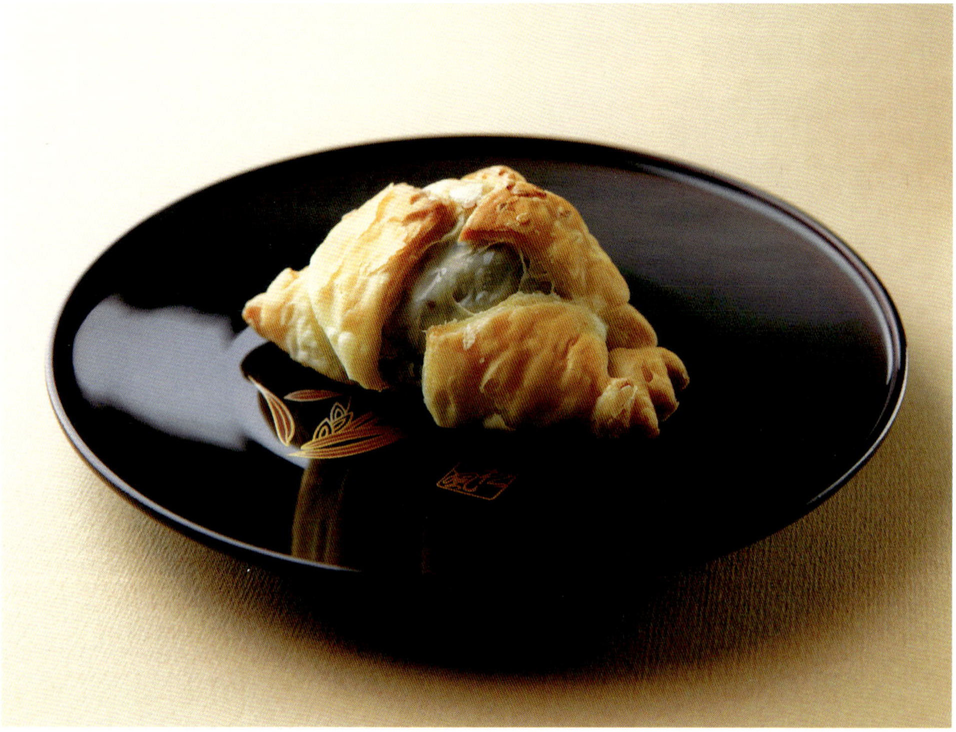
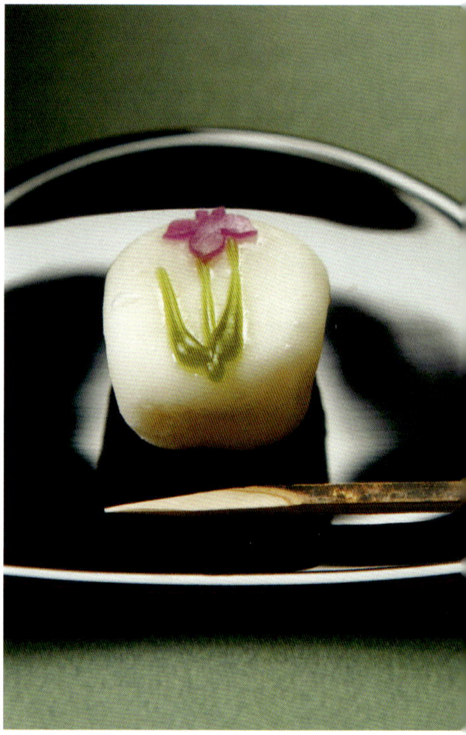

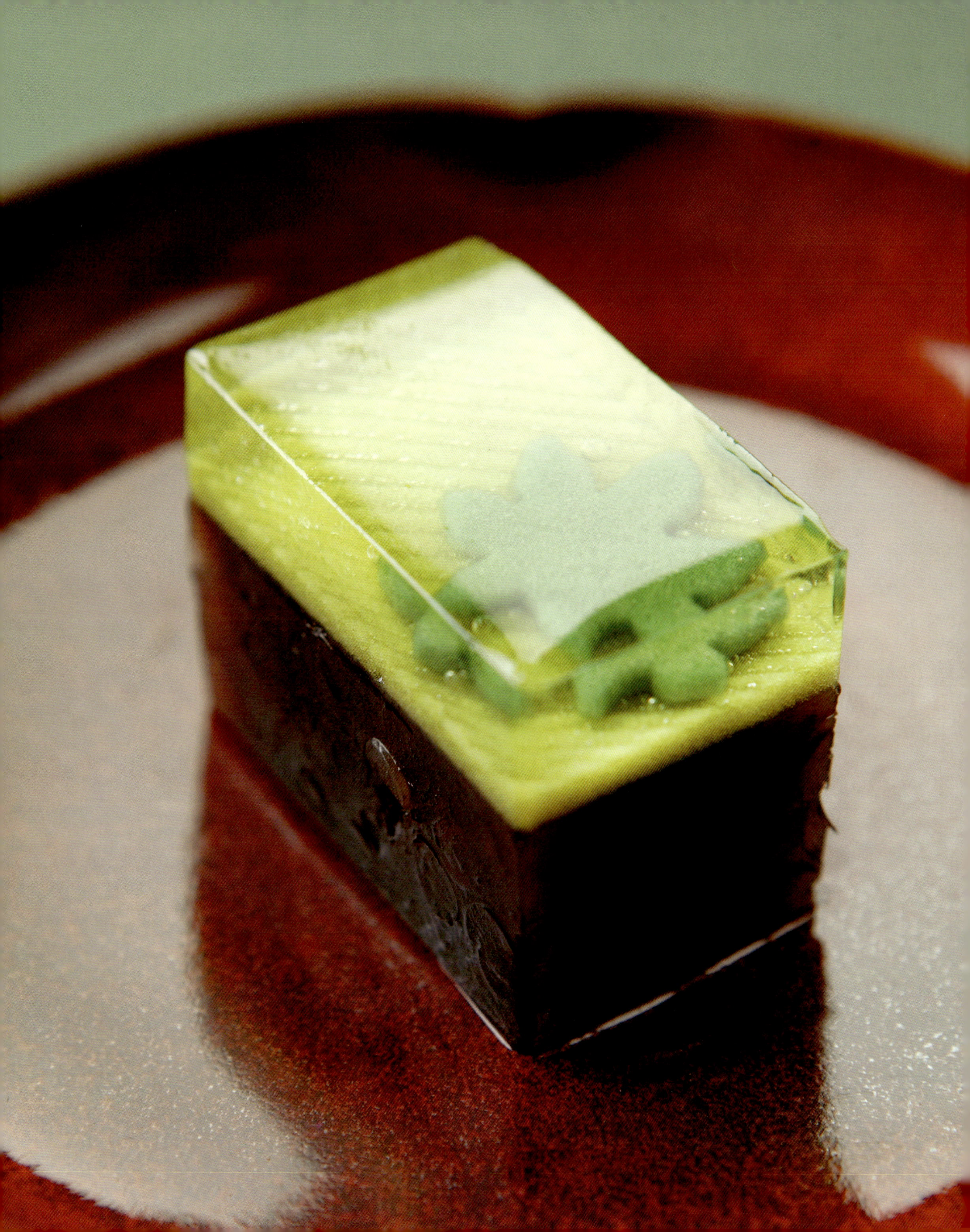

The courses mentioned above constitute a normal *kaiseki* meal, but it can be (and usually is) extended with many more courses, such as the following.

SAKIZUKE AMUSE

Just like the popular *amuse* served in Western restaurants before guests have ordered anything, the *sakizuke* is not really part of the meal, but an optional opening to the evening. The word means 'what comes first' and the dish usually consists of two types of food – one very ordinary and common, the other rare and special.

MUSHIMONO STEAMED COURSE

A dish of steamed food may serve to extend the meal by one more cooking method. Steaming is considered healthy, both according to modern dieticians, because no nutrients are lost into the cooking water, as well as according to East Asian traditional medicine. Many foods may be steamed, from vegetables and fish, to chicken and shellfish, or the much loved *chawan mushi* – savoury custards with ingredients like *ginko* nuts, *mitsuba*, chicken and shrimp. Another popular steamed dish is *sakamushi*, in which *sake* is poured over the ingredients before steaming.

TEMPURA DEEP-FRIED COURSE

Tempura is a dish of deep-fried vegetables, fish, shellfish or mushrooms. The ingredients are first coated with flour and then dipped in a batter of wheat flour, egg yolk and ice-cold water, which has been mixed quickly so that it still contains pockets of dry flour and air. These increase the lightness of the final product. The ingredients are then dipped in hot vegetable oil (at 180 °C), often mixed with some sesame oil for a nutty flavour. The Japanese are said to have adopted this method from the Portuguese in the 16th century, and the word *tempura* to derive from the Portuguese *tempuras*, the Roman Catholic 'Ember Days'. These are days of abstinence on which the eating of meat is forbidden. It is possible that Portuguese missionaries would have eaten deep-fried fish and vegetables on these days, but there is no proof of that. It is also possible that the word and the method came from the Dutch in Nagasaki. In a Dutch cookbook dating from 1514 *(Een Notabel Boecxken van Cokeryen)* the verb *temperen* is the normal culinary term for mixing liquids and solids, such as flour, with water (or milk) and eggs, as required for *tempura*. For the following two centuries, *temper* was the normal Dutch word for a thin batter – like the one, for instance, from which waffles were made. In addition, it may be noted that deep-frying is far more common a practice in northern Europe than in the south. But whatever the origin, it took quite a while before this cooking method became part of Japanese cuisine. Not until the second half of the 18th century did little street stalls preparing and selling *tempura* dishes became a normal feature in the city of Edo. The adoption of *tempura* in the *haute cuisine* of *kaiseki* was a slow process, taking another 200 years. *Tempura* is eaten with *tentsuyu*, a sauce of hot *dashi* with *mirin* and soy sauce. Grated ginger and *daikon* can be mixed into the sauce at the table. Osakans eat *tempura* dipping it in salt.

Karaage is a deep-fry technique in which the ingredients are not coated at all, or only dusted with flour and salt. *Furai* (from the English word 'fry') results in a heavy coating, by dipping the foods into beaten egg first and then in breadcrumbs or rice noodles, which puff up when deep-fried. Many Japanese are fond of *furai*, but it is rarely seen as part of a *kaiseki* meal.

48

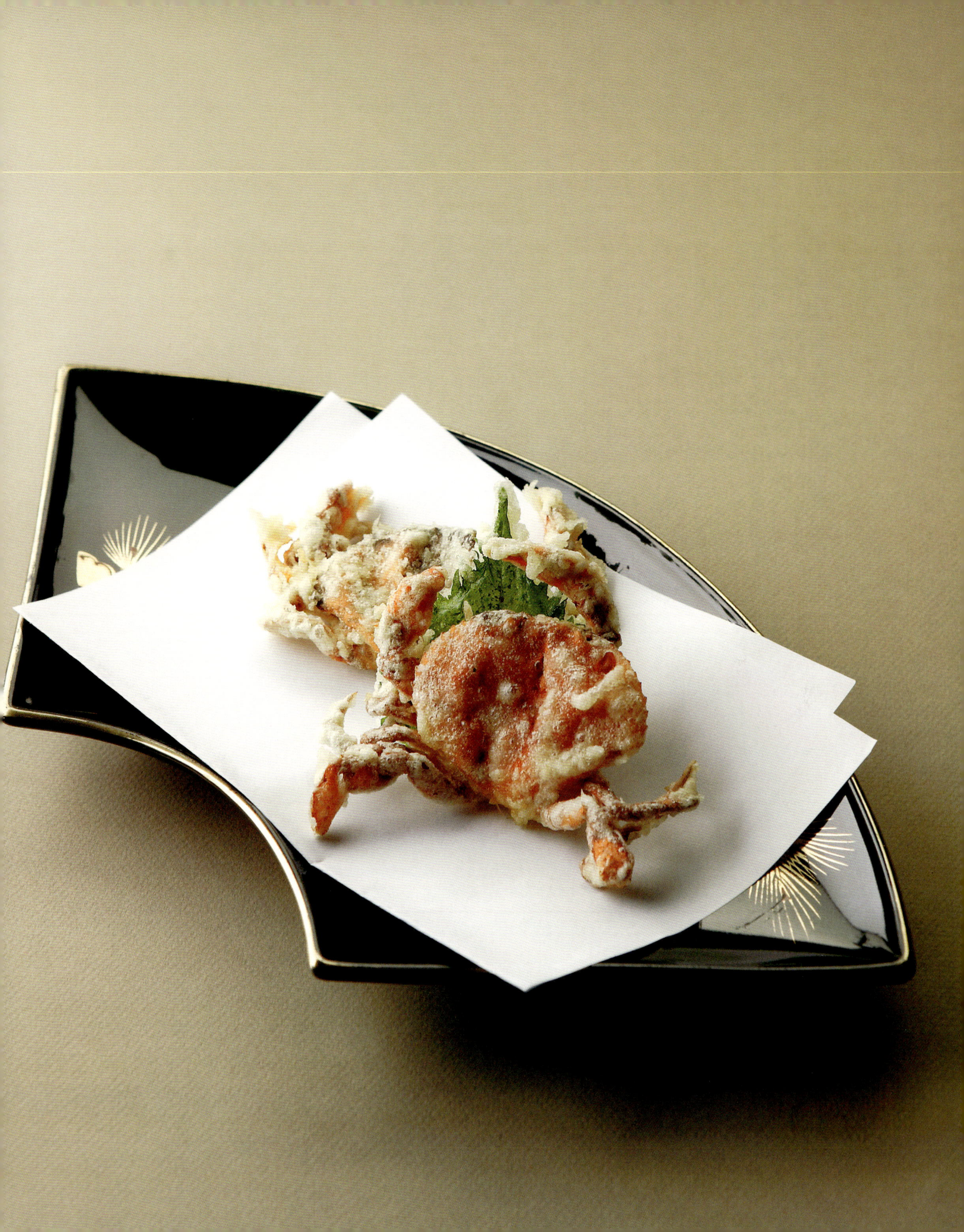

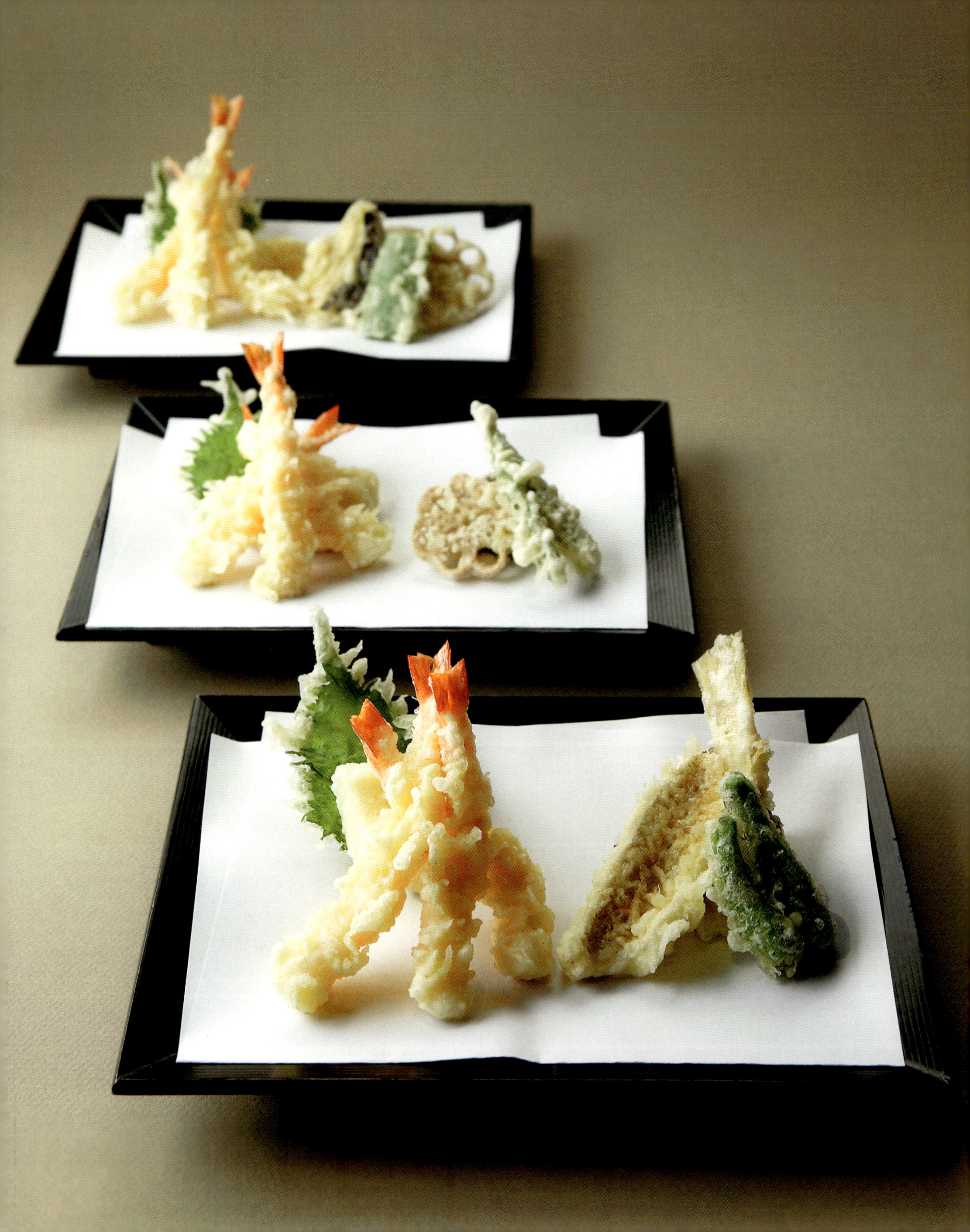

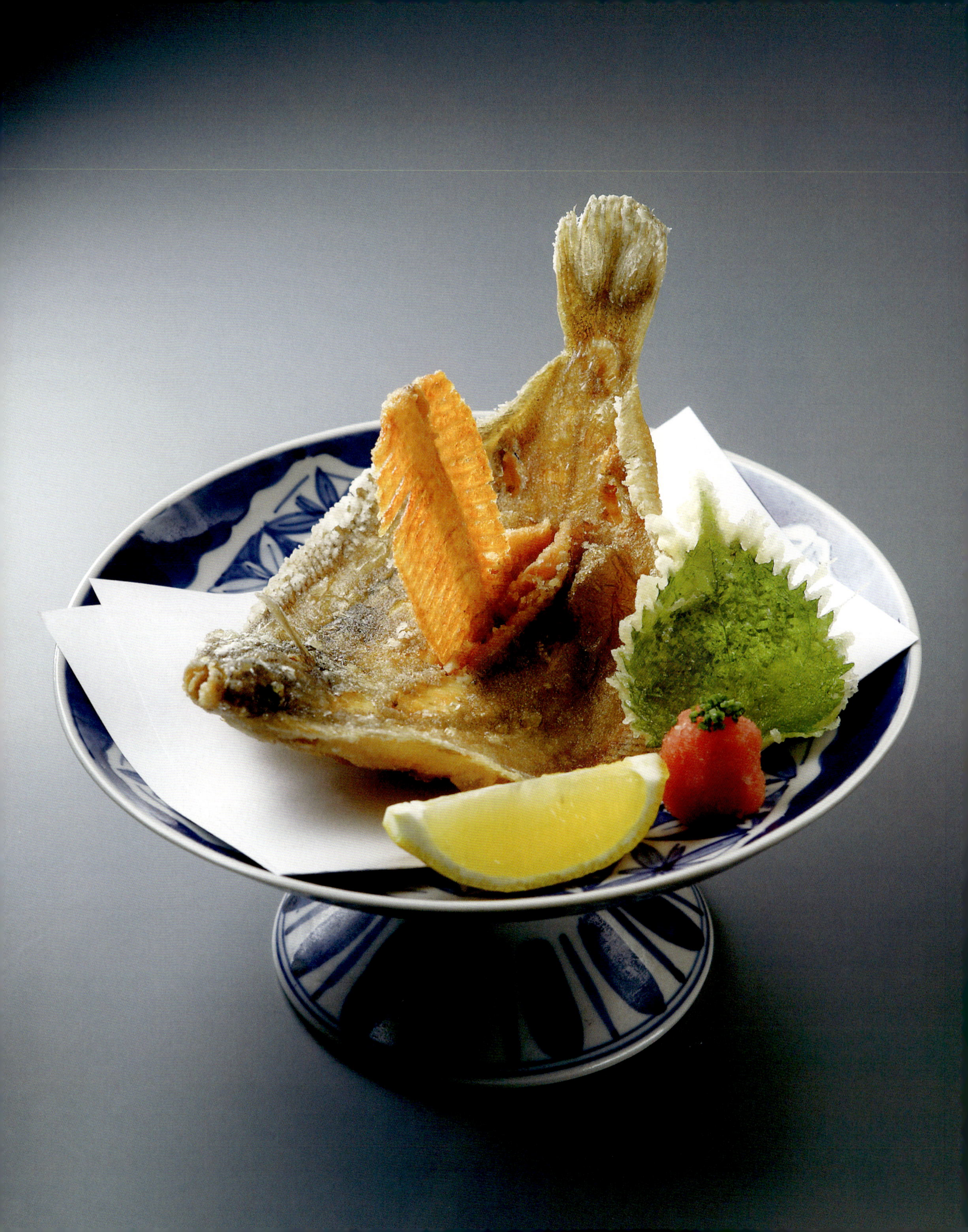

SHIIZAKANA STRONGLY RECOMMENDED COURSE

Sakana means 'drinking snack' and is to be eaten next to a cup of *sake*. A dish that is not served with *sake*, but with rice is called a 'side dish' *(osai)*. The fact that only one course in a *kaiseki* meal includes rice, reduces all the other courses to the 'drinking snacks' they truly are, and according to that status they can be added or omitted. *Shiizakana* ('strong drinking dish') can be anything the chef fancies. At the Yamazato restaurant it may well consist of a meat dish, out of consideration for non-Japanese consumers.

NABEMONO ONE-POT STEW

Yosenabe means 'hotchpotch' and the same dish can also be called *tanoshiminabe*, which means; 'joyful pot.' Cooking different ingredients in a simple pot has been known for thousands of years all over the world. The Japanese, however, have turned this simple peasants' dish into a fine art through their dedication in finding the best ingredients and by avoiding overcooking them. The stock in which they are simmered is usually *dashi* of *konbu* seaweed and flakes of *katsuobushi*.

In restaurants guests don't have to worry about spoiling the precious delights, since a waiter or waitress will cook each individual item for them. Before the 20th century, when the Japanese adopted the Western style of eating around a central table, each guest had his little individual *nabe*, but since then the pots have become bigger again, and now the Japanese enjoy the snugness of all sharing the same pot.

As the name implies, *yosenabe* can contain all kinds of ingredients, but there are certain *nabe* that refer to a specific ingredient, such as *ankōnabe*, made of *ankō* (monk fish). In *mizutaki,* which means cooked in water, water rather than *dashi* is used, because the main ingredient is chicken, which will by itself turn any liquid to soup.

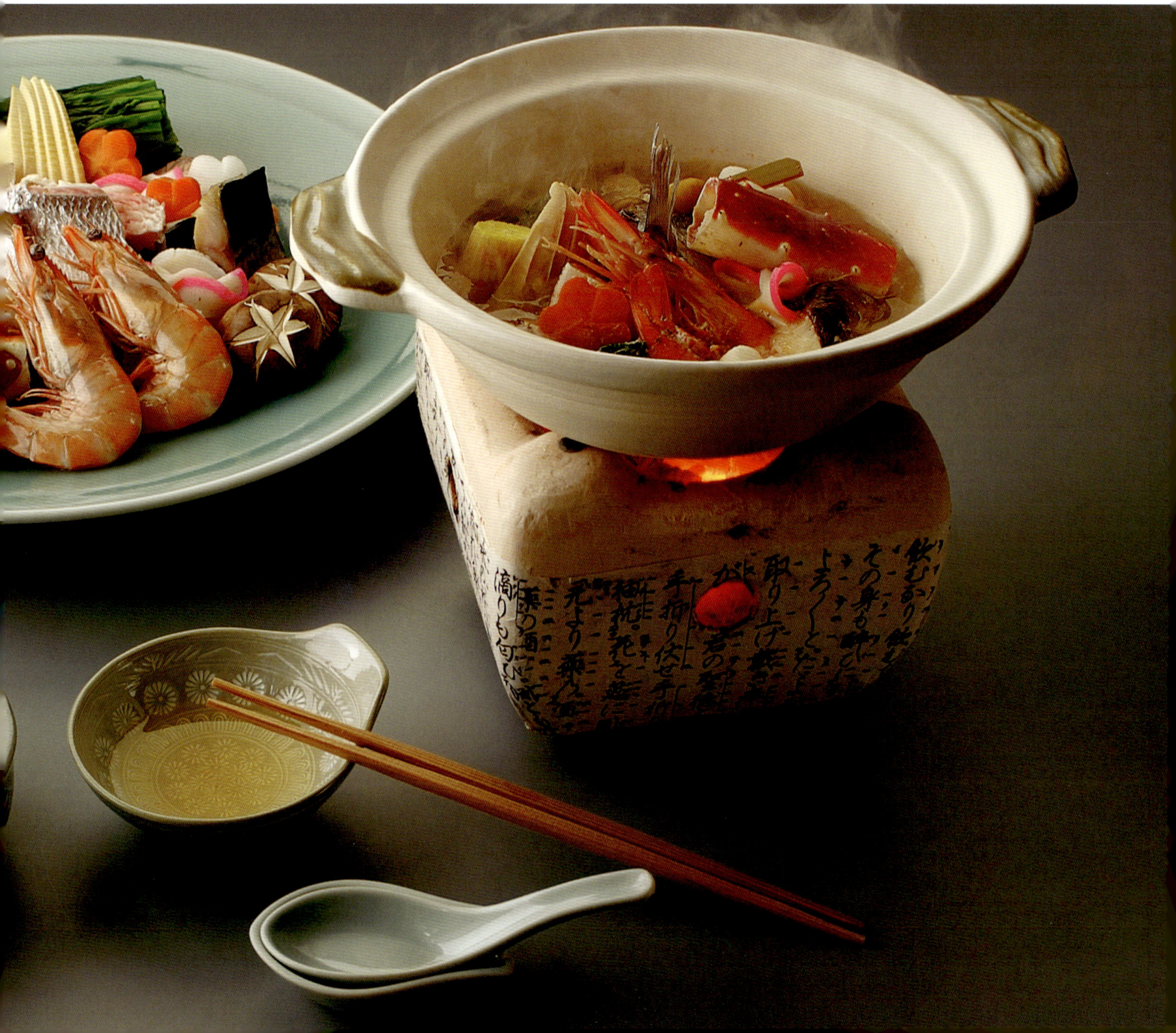

SUKIYAKI MEAT STEW

Since Emperor Temmu forbade the eating of cattle, horses, monkeys and chickens in 675, consumption of meat has been fairly restricted in Japan. No animals were reared for the table. The taboo on eating mammals (except for whales, which were classified as fish) lasted until 1872 when it was officially announced that emperor Meiji ate beef dishes. At the imperial court, French meat dishes were cooked, but the people, lacking the services of French chefs, prepared beef in a Japanese way – simmered with *miso* or soy sauce, in the fashion game was eaten.

From the late 19th century onward, the dish became known as *gyūnabe* and in western Japan as *sukiyaki nabe*. *Nabe* is the cooking pot and the word *sukiyaki* would derive from *suki* 'spade' and *yaki* 'frying' because farmers would fry game on their spades. It became the dish we now know of thinly sliced beef, seasoned with soy sauce and sugar, and served with *tōfu* and vegetables. The meat is cooked very briefly and removed from the pan while still red. Then the *tōfu* and vegetables are cooked, after which the meat is returned to be arranged for presentation. Each guest has a bowl with beaten egg as a dip.

Although breeding animals for the table is not an old tradition in Japan, the country does produce the most expensive beef known; the *wagyū* cattle from Kobe are the world famous. The animals graze on herbs between the volcanoes, and are fed additional straw and malt from the beer and *sake* factories. They are massaged daily to make sure the fat blends into the flesh evenly to produce finely marbled beef. The fat melts into the meat after very short cooking periods, which makes it very suitable for Japanese cooking.

For the moment the Hotel Okura Amsterdam is the only place in Europe where *wagyū* beef, presently imported from the US, is always on the menu, but thanks to guarantees of the Hotel Okura Amsterdam this cattle is now also reared in Europe. More *wagyū* beef from European soil can be expected in the near future.

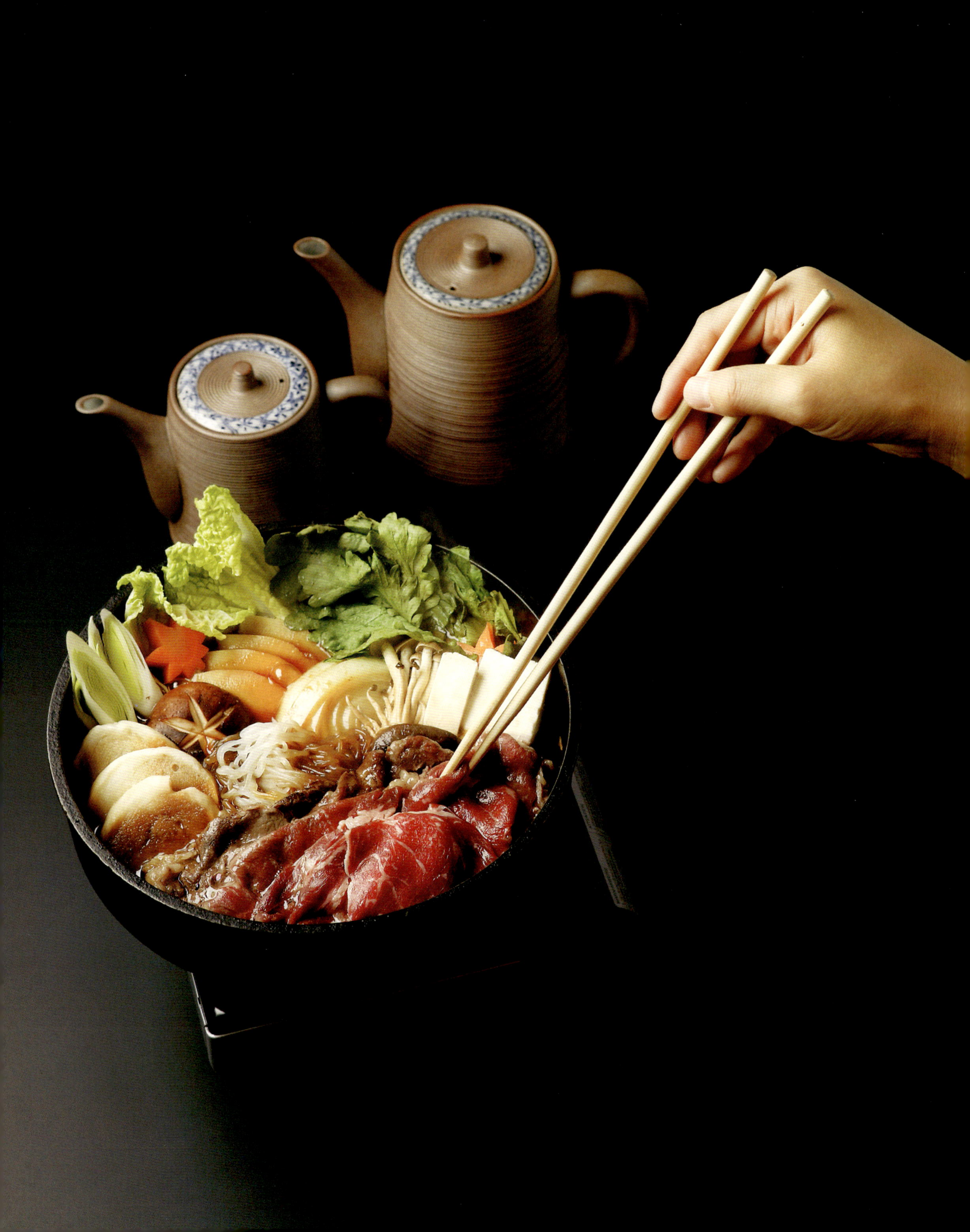

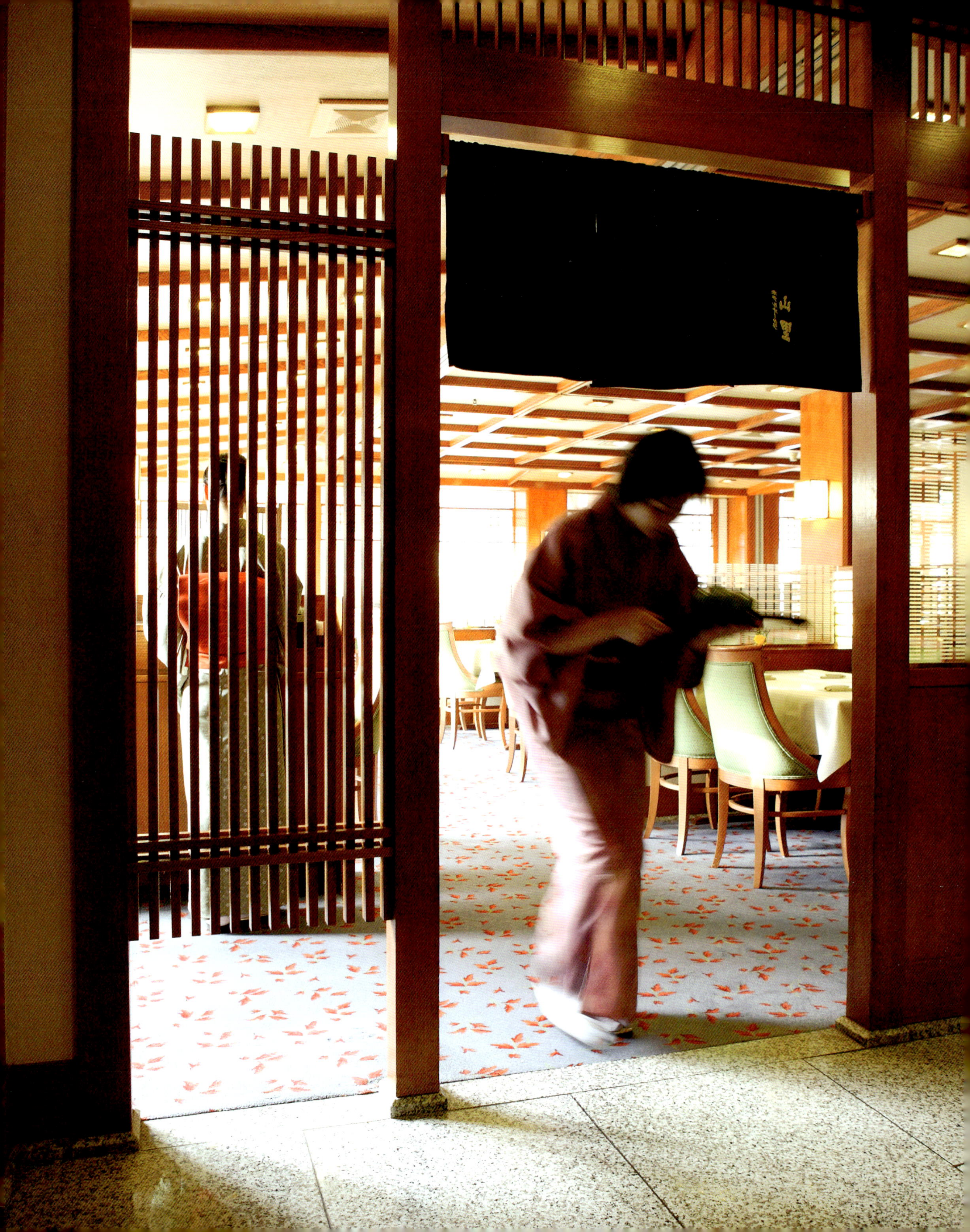
山里

Kaiseki art

Balance is sought after in everything. East Asian tradition distinguishes five elements that make up the universe: wood, fire, earth, metal and water (or earth, water, fire, wind and space). The theory is remarkably similar to the ancient Greek theory, which remained the basis for Western science until the 18th century, but which recognized only four elements. In accordance with the five-element theory, many principles are divided into five. Europeans split these into four, but in both traditions a balance between these elements is considered the best way to health and happiness.

Five principle colours are recognised: yellow, red, white, black, and blue/green. In the same way as flavours ought to be carefully balanced, so should colours. This does not mean that cooks always have to produce loud multi-coloured dishes. *Kaiseki* cooks balance colours very carefully, each used according to its strength, in the same way as they balance flavours. Five senses have to be stirred: sight, touch, and sound are as important as smell and taste.

VISUAL ART

With its roots in *wabi* aesthetics, *kaiseki* doesn't lend itself to gigantic displays, as are familiar from aesthetic movements throughout European history. Instead utmost care is given to the smallest detail. Great masters have set examples, but these are only guidelines to the cook, since every situation differs somewhat from another. The artist is always challenged by three varying factors:

kikai occasion
kisetsu season
ki container

Oshima: 'Three aspects are crucial in *kaiseki* cooking: serving the food at exactly the right temperature, in the appropriate tableware, and, most importantly, in absolute harmony with the season. The connection with nature is very important, and this is why we don't use only traditional Japanese ingredients, but also try to incorporate Dutch seasonal food into our menus – such as white asparagus in our spring menu.'

Kikai

The occasion refers to the circumstances of the meal. A meal for a frail old lady will be different from a meal for hungry *samurai*. Nor do the monk and the merchant eat the same. In restaurants, the occasion is not always known, since the guests choose the reason for the gathering. A restaurant chef can only take the occasion into account if he is informed beforehand, which many people only do with grand occasions such as weddings.

Kikai refers to the importance of a single moment that will not return, and to timing. Precise orchestration of the meal helps to get the best out of every dish and for the cook timing is everything. A dish should be cooked at the precisely the right moment, and for exactly the right time. In the kitchens of the Yamazato every minute counts.

Kisestsu

The seasonal aspect is all-pervasive. Flower arrangements in dining rooms change according to season: pine for New Year, in February plum blossom, peach blossom in March, in March or April cherry blossom, in May irises and azaleas, in June hydrangeas, in July bamboo leaves, in August water lilies, in September chrysanthemums, and in October maple leaves. In the winter evergreen or branches with fruits are sometimes used.

The hangings at the entrance of restaurants change in colour and design with the seasons, as do the waitresses' *kimono*. That food served in restaurants should be seasonal is not the prerogative of Japan. Everywhere in the world, cuisines change with the seasons, since they are dependant on the products available. Festive food often shows a seasonal aspect – in Europe game for Christmas, eggs for Easter; in Japan herring roe for New Year and carp for Boys' Day. In *kaiseki* cuisine slight adjustments in the seasoning are made with the passing of the year; slightly more sweetness is appropriate in winter and more salt in summer, since we need the energy when it is cold and the salt when the sun dehydrates us.

Ki

Ki refers to bowls, plates, dishes, and other receptacles. In many Japanese store rooms extensive collections of porcelain, lacquer ware, wooden, bamboo, stone and earthenware receptacles for food will be found. Some, like the ships for displaying *sashimi*, are very grand, others are small and simple, but designed with refinement and extreme restraint. Much of the pottery used in *kaiseki* is so simple that it is difficult for the untrained eye to see the difference between a dish worth € 20 and one worth € 200.000. The difference is in extremely subtle beauty, and in the consequential reputation of the artist.

Japanese *urushi* (lacquer ware) and pottery are world famous. The oldest example of lacquer work dates from 7000 BC, and consists of six red lacquered decorations excavated in Hokkaido. Lacquer is harvested in a similar way as rubber, but from the lacquer tree, which is very vulnerable and produces the substance to protect itself when cut. It has disinfecting properties. When it dries, it does not shrink like paint, but expands in contact with oxygen. This is what causes its hardness. Sometimes decorated with gold dust or mother of pearl, lacquer ware in Japan is considered even more prestigious than porcelain or earthenware.

NOREN

The cotton hangings in the doors of Japanese restaurants change in colour and design according to the seasons. Short hangings are used inside a building, but long ones at an outside door. The word noren *is spelled with the characters for 'warm' and 'screen,' which clearly indicates that they were once intended to keep out the cold. In the 13th and 14th centuries, first temples and later other public places, such as shops and workshops, adopted the hangings following the Chinese example. They served as banners, advertising the shop and indicating the location of the entrance. As a result of westernisation during the latter half of the 19th century,* noren *have disappeared from regular shops. Nowadays, only restaurants and traditional establishments, such as Japanese confection workshops, feature* noren.

Metal cutlery and serving dishes made of silver, gold, copper, tin or stainless steel are quite normal in the West, but not in Japan. In the 7th century, the Chinese custom of using a set of metal chopsticks and a spoon was adopted at the Japanese court. In the long run, however, neither the spoon, nor the use of metal chopsticks became rooted in Japan. Historians have thus far found no explanation for the Japanese rejection of the spoon, but they argue that practical reasons were responsible for choosing wood rather than metal as the primary material for making chopsticks. Metal was relatively scarce in Japan, and could therefore be put to better use for making other objects, such as weapons. Bowls of cut glass, which the Europeans introduced, were keenly adopted into the range of Japanese tableware. The water-clear appearance makes glass very suitable for carrying refreshing food in summer.

Other than the bowls for rice and soup, which are always made of black or red lacquer, receptacles change with the seasons. Hard glazes and fresh colours fit the summer, rougher textures and darker colours are called for in colder weather.

Japanese cuisine does not require large selections of matching sets, as does Chinese and European *haute cuisine*. The host is expected to make elegant compositions with different shapes and materials. There are round and square dishes and a variety of other shapes, but also round, square and crescent trays. Square trays are suitable for round dishes and vice versa, but most of the time a variety of shapes will be juxtaposed on a tray. Parallel lines are often avoided, since they seem unnatural and contrived. One always looks for elegant but 'natural' looking compositions.

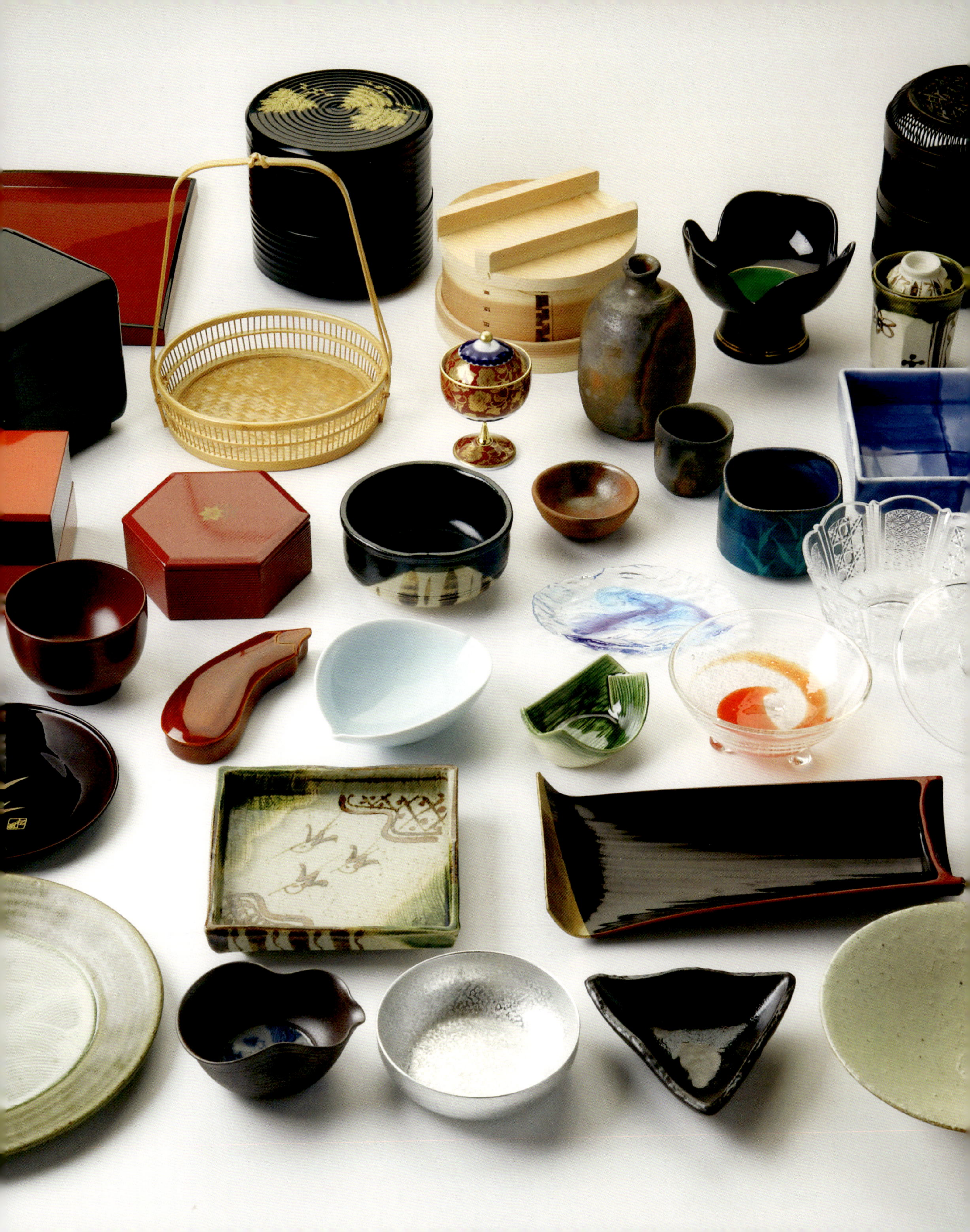

MORITSUKE FOOD ARRANGEMENT

As with the art of Japanese flower arrangement, *ikebana*, there are several schools of teaching, but all pay homage to certain overall principles and recognize some basic styles:

[1] *Sugimori:* strips of food slanting in a pile; cedar-tree style
[2] *Kasanemori:* slices overlapping; piled-up style
[3] *Tawaramori:* blocks in neat pyramids; rice-bale style
[4] *Hiramori:* vertical chunks of sashimi in a row; flat style
[5] *Mazemori:* pile of different coloured strips; mixed style
[6] *Yosemori:* different items piled in mountains leaning together; nestled style
[7] *Chirashimori:* different items spaced out; scattered style

Three terms, taken from calligraphy, express the level of formality with which food is displayed:

[A] *Shin:* 'basic', neat as a printed letter, refers to food presented and piled with architectural formality. *Tawaramori* and *hiramori* are typically *shin*.

[B] *Gyō:* 'going,' comparable to handwriting, individual but legible. Many styles qualify as *gyō*. *Kasanemori*, for example, is used for fairly large pieces of food, that could be piled as neatly as in rice-bale style, but that are more irregular and therefore call for a looser presentation. *Gyō* allows high levels of poetry. References are made to nature and to the landscape. *Yosemori* of two or three ingredients piled separately but leaning together can evoke dramatic scenes. On an island built of soya skin, with trees of rape blossom, a simmered shrimp may look like a stranded whale.

[C] *Sō:* 'grass,' running wild and spontaneous like graffiti, and possibly illegible like a signature, but when done with skill and talent, of great 'natural' beauty. A little aromatic garnish, like chrysanthemum leaves, *shiso*, or other herbs might add a wild touch to a dish, but that hardly means it is haphazardly plonked on top. Every wild sprig is intentional.

The levels of *shin, gyō* and *sō* depend on the occasion. More formality requires slightly more *shin*, and *sō* is always used fairly sparingly, but a balance between the three is attempted. However the food is piled, guests never have to dismantle complicated structures before they can start eating.

If a single ingredient is intended for a bowl it should never be placed in the dead centre, but slightly to the rear of the bowl, away from the diner. There should be more space in front, which gives the diner a better perspective of the food. In addition, it should be stressed that empty space is of great importance. Food should not touch the sides of the bowl.

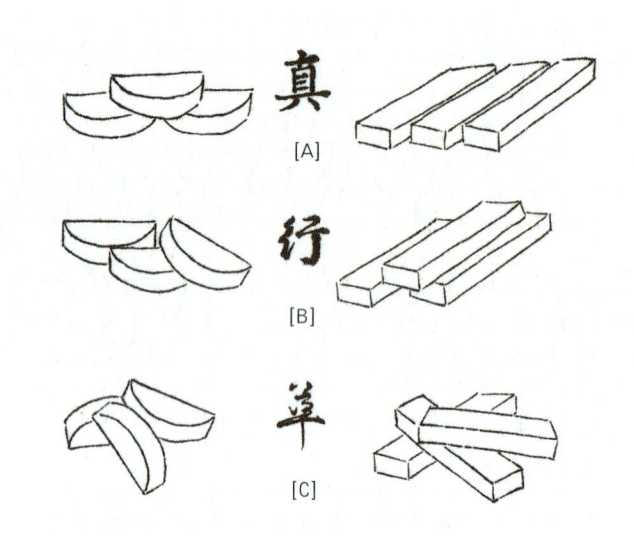

This love of the empty is crucial to Zen aesthetics. Space, or empty space, called *ma* is part of the design. If European aesthetics has long been ruled by a *horror vacui* (fear of vacuums, i.e. the need to fill up every bit of open space), then Zen aesthetics does the opposite. In drawing or calligraphy, the untouched white rice paper is as much part of the design as the black ink. Japanese love a landscape of an endless empty sea, from which a single mountain rises in the distance. All this emptiness emphasises the importance of even the smallest things. It is in this Zen tradition that food is decorated with empty space.

When more than one ingredient is to be displayed (normally in threes, fives, or sevens, since uneven numbers are considered luckier in East-Asian tradition) symmetry is avoided. In classical Europe (as in China) symmetry was considered the epitome of beauty. The symmetry of the human body was pointed to for reference. However, Zen thinkers did not refer to the human body, but to the natural landscape. And in that they saw no symmetry.

In *kaiseki* cuisine, too, the natural landscape is the point of reference and consequently symmetry is avoided. So when you do have two ingredients, one should be a little more voluminous than the other and they should complement each other in colour, texture, shape, origin, smell and taste. They should never be in a straight line, since that would not reflect a natural landscape. Likewise, when five foods are to be placed on a plate, they are not spaced out evenly, which might look contrived, but some of them are clustered, like mountains in the sea.

When food is placed in boxes it lacks that celebrated open space, but the three levels of *shin, gyō* and *sō* are still taken into account. Putting food in boxes, such as lunch boxes *(bentōbako)*, is no less of an art in Japan than other

65

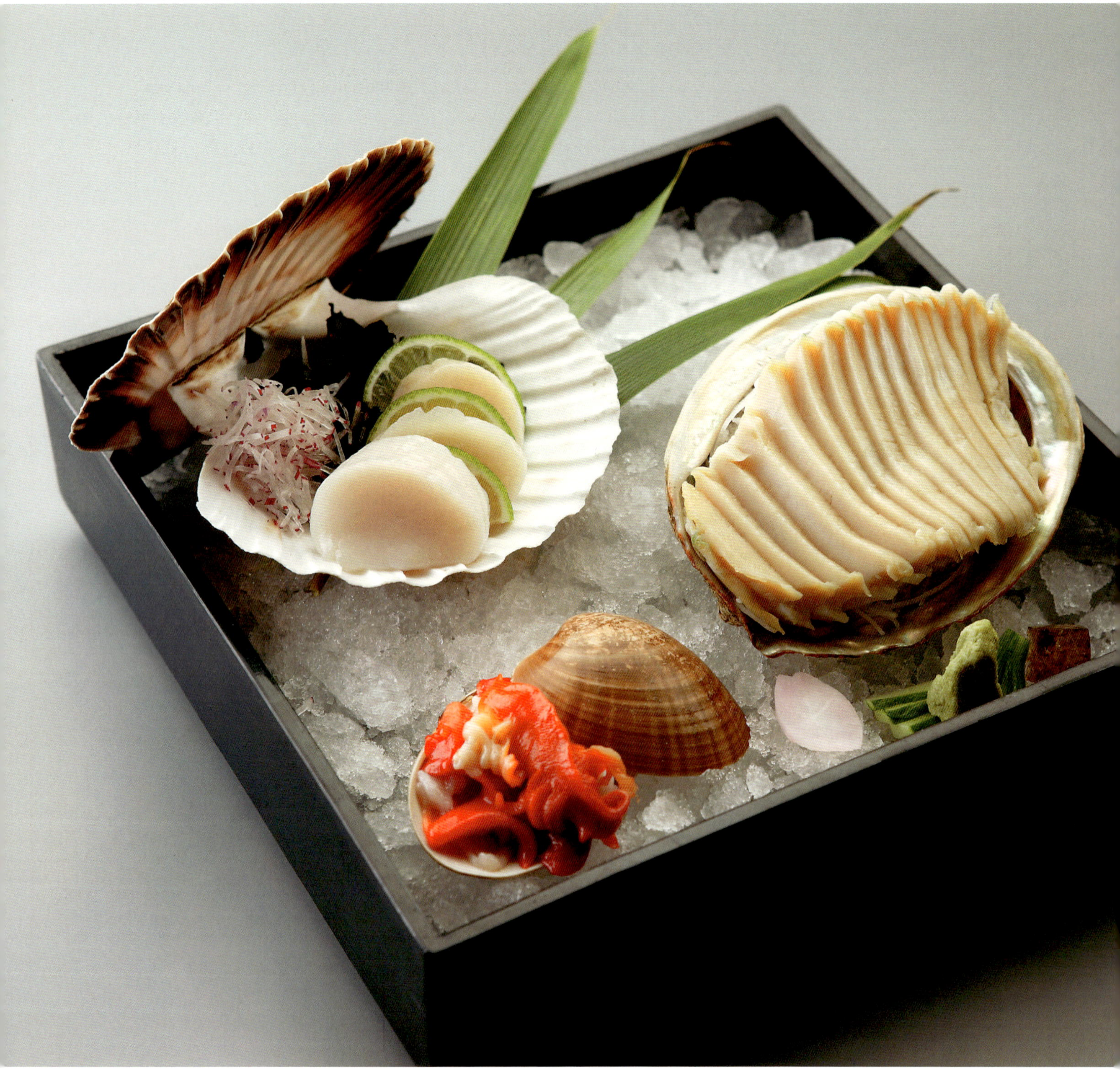

food arrangement, even if it makes fewer references to the natural landscape. *Kaiseki ryōri*, however, originated in the garden teahouse; it involves grooming nature and being groomed by nature.

TASTE

Europe recognises four flavours – sweet, sour, salty, and bitter – but East Asians count five. The Japanese call the fifth *umami*. In pursuit of a chemical analysis of this fifth flavour Kikunae Ikeda stumbled on monosodium glutamate (MSG) in 1908. This amino acid has flavour intensifying properties, and occurs naturally in many foods, in particular in *miso* paste, green tea, dried *shiitake* mushrooms and kelp, but is not restricted to Japanese foods. Parmesan cheese and fresh tomatoes, for example, are rich in MSG.

Chemical MSG is now used worldwide. It is administered extensively by food producers, who refer to it as a 'flavour enhancer'. The employees of the Anglo-Dutch company Unilever have already started speaking of five flavours. They call the fifth *(umami)* 'savoury', which implies the presence of MSG. As a main ingredient of stock cubes MSG has found its way into soups and sauces all over the world. There is hardly a modern meal anywhere without it.

Salt may be used for saltiness and sugar for sweetness, but at the Yamazato restaurant no MSG is used in pursuit of a *umami* flavour. Since its immense popularity in the 20th century it has been somewhat overused. An overdose of MSG is referred to as 'Chinese restaurant syndrome.' The best cooks stay well away from it and traditional cuisines, like that of the Yamazato, don't need it. They have evolved over centuries and include sweet, salt, sour, bitter and savoury flavours without MSG.

SMELL

To a great extent cooking consists of perfuming food; giving it the right smell. Most herbs, spices and condiments are appreciated because of their aroma. Food tends to be more aromatic in warmer climates, possibly because people are used to smelling more in the warmer air. Japan's cuisine is singularly subtle in its use of aromatics, though since Japan stretches from sub-polar to subtropical regions, climate cannot be a cause of this.

It is something of a cliché, and one to which many cooks take offence, that strong aromatic sauces are used to mask the inferior quality of products, but the opposite is nevertheless true: if you don't use those aromatics, the quality of the products has to be perfect. Fish and vegetables have to be very fresh. Although meat-eating is not traditional in Japan, meat when eaten has to be properly cured. Oshima assures us that tuna, red like beef, should be fresh, but cannot be turned into *sashimi* straight after it has been caught. The fish has to rest first so amino acids will develop. Many other foods are purposely fermented – such as turning rice and soya beans into *nattō, miso* and soy sauce. Vegetables are pickled and acquire strong aromas. The Japanese like elements of very strong flavour as a part their meals, such as ginger, or the aromatic and searingly hot *wasabi* that is eaten with the subtle flavours of raw fish.

Soup, rice and simmered dishes are served in bowl with a cover, so the room remains odour free until the lid is removed and the aromas hit you in the face. Sometimes people fan the vapours towards them with a hand to increase the pleasure.

SOUND

The sound of food is no issue in the West. With the possible exception of 'crunch,' sounds are not appreciated. Westerners don't want to hear other people munching and slurping. To make the slightest sound while eating is considered a breach of etiquette. To avoid irritation many Western meals are accompanied by music, drowning any eating noises.

Not so in Japan. Originating partly in the tranquillity of the Japanese teahouse, where guests carefully listen to the boiling of the water, which should sound like the rushing of wind through pine trees, *kaiseki* cuisine is best dressed with silence so the trickle of a stream and the song of a distant bird are audible. The snap of chopsticks being broken apart announces the beginning of a meal, and the ticking of these chopsticks against the rice bowl will be a pleasure to the ear, as well as the mushy sound of the rice they pick up. The music of saliva running through the mouth, lips smacking and teeth chewing, accompanied by the dance of the tongue are all part of that pleasure. The loud crack of something hard or crunchy is perfectly sensational.

This notion gets somewhat exaggerated in everyday eating. Soup with noodles has been sold in simple street stalls for centuries. The soup is served very hot, but Japanese don't blow on it. The Western tradition of blowing on soup seems questionable, since the aromas are blown away from the diner. When the Japanese eat in a street stall they slurp the soup and the noodles, inhaling the aromas with the air that cools the soup. During the *chakaiseki* it is also customary to slurp the *miso* soup, which is served before the *sake* is presented, as mentioned earlier. This is done so the host knows when to enter with the alcohol. In classy restaurants however, no eating noises are made and the Japanese do not smack their lips or chew with an open mouth as is acceptable in China.

TOUCH

Texture is totally underestimated in the West, but it is taken very much into account in East Asia. Despite the general acceptance of Japanese and Chinese cuisine in the West, Westerners still have difficulty in understanding texture. European tourists still find it difficult to appreciate certain textures they encounter in authentic cuisines of East Asia. They are continuously surprised by the astronomical prices Japanese, Chinese and Koreans will pay for delicacies that have practically no flavour, but that are solely enjoyed for their texture.

When talking about food, texture is rarely mentioned in the West. Yet the Japanese often speak of *kuchiatari;* feel of the mouth, *shitazawari;* touch of the tongue, *hagotae;* resistance to the tooth, *nodogoshi;* slide through the throat.

European children eat liquorice and sweets in a great variety of textures, including tough, rubbery and rock-hard.

These delights are produced to amuse young mouths with entertaining textures, but for some reason adults forsake such diversions. Adults have taken some interest in texture, since the *nouvelle cuisine* revolution, when vegetables were boiled for shorter periods and retained some bite; and also since the popularisation of Italian pasta, which is supposed to be served *al dente*. But the careful balancing of textures during every course of the meal, as in *kaiseki ryōri*, remains yet to be experienced in European cuisine.

Sticky and syrupy substances are mostly associated with sugar in the West and restricted to dessert. The Japanese enjoy all kinds of stickiness, which make flavours linger in the mouth. Sticky *mochi* rice cake chews like gum.

When fish and vegetables are meticulously cut into artistic shapes by Asian chefs, Europeans and Americans may appreciate them for their visual beauty, but often don't realise that this can also be done for reasons of tactile pleasure. A European cook may slice a squid into bite size rings, but when the Japanese cook turns the squid into a pine cone, it serves to entertain the tongue. *Kakushibōchō*, the Japanese chef's 'hidden knife', often passes unnoticed by Western guests. This entails the making of incisions that cannot be seen, but which improve the feel of the food.

Gelatinous qualities, again, are appreciated for their visual appeal in the West, but for their texture in the Far East. Ever since the Renaissance, when refrigeration techniques improved, European chefs have created beautiful displays of aspics and jellies, with gelatine extracted from animal bones. These jellies retain their shape at room temperature, but immediately turn to the liquid, whether soup or juice, in the mouth. In Asia, jellies are made with *kanten* drawn from red alga (called *tengusa*). Asian jellies retain their texture in the mouth and give the teeth something to play with. *Kanten* can be used for greater variety in 'tooth resistance.'

Slimy and slippery qualities are not very highly regarded in the West, and there are no words with positive connotations to describe them. Sigmund Freud noticed the intense dislike in Western society for viscous substances. We are dealing with a typical example of a Freudian taboo: slimy things are too dirty to touch, let alone to put in your mouth. In East Asia, however, the perception of slimy and slippery qualities is quite different; they are often part of a well-balanced meal and are said to be beneficial to health, strength and virility.

Oshima is quite aware of the preferences of the Dutch: 'When they have the choice between something grilled, deep-fried, poached or steamed they will always choose from the first two categories. Chicken or fish dusted with flour and then simmered in broth is much disliked by the Dutch, because of the gooey coating, but this happens to be a texture Japanese like very much.' A careful balance has to be struck between what is acceptable to Europeans on one hand, yet authentic enough for the Japanese on the other. This balance was found, it appears, in the Yamazato restaurant. Oshima noticed how Chinese restaurants with Michelin stars are visited mostly by Europeans, while restaurants frequented by Chinese seem to lack European guests. The difference in perception of texture and touch may partly be responsible for this cultural gap. The Yamazato restaurant however is visited and praised by both European and Japanese guests alike.

The twelve animals of the Japanese zodiac. Every year, every month and (before the introduction of the biblical week) every day was dedicated to one of these signs.

Japanese festivals

Festivals can be devided in two groups; matsuri and *nenchū gyōji* (often pronounced as *nenjū gyōji*). Matsuri are the original festivals of the *Shintō* religion and are celebrated locally. The most prominent festivals belong to the *nenchū gyōji*. They are closely tied to the season and changes of season and have a Chinese or at any rate Buddhist [1] origin. They form the basic structure of the yearly calender, to which the *matsuri* have been connected. The imperial court adopted the lunar calendar and its festivals from the Chinese at the beginning of the 7th century. The festivals celebrated by the imperial court slowly spread through the rest of the population and became influenced by the *samurai*, the warrior class who began to dominate Japanese culture from the 15th century onwards. The culture was further enriched by many folk traditions and spread through a wider range of the population during the Edo period. The present-day cycle of seasonal festivals derives from these combinations.

The most important festivals in Japan are the New Year Festival (*Oshōgatsu*), the Bon Festival (or *Obon*) and the five seasonal *sekku*. The term *sekku* was first applied to offerings *(ku)* of food made to mark changes of season *(sechi)*. In time, the term came to refer to actual days.

The seventh day of the first month:
    Seven Herb Festival *(Nanakusa no Sekku)*.
The third day of the third month:
    Dolls' Festival *(Hina no Sekku)*.
The fifth day of the fifth month:
    Boys' Festival *(Tango no Sekku)*.
The seventh day of the seventh month:
    Tanabata Festival *(Tanabata no Sekku)* [2].
The ninth day of the ninth month:
    Chrysanthemum Festival *(Kiku no Sekku)*.

After 1873, when the modern Japanese government adopted the Gregorian calendar, January, March, May, July, and September were conveniently substituted for the first, third, fifth, seventh and ninth months. However, the actual time of celebration shifted, as there is approximately a one-month difference between the lunar and the solar calendars.

The biblical seven-day week has now been adopted, with the Sunday as a day of rest, and this has initiated in a new rhythm of work and leisure. After the adoption of the Gregorian calendar, many old feasts were no longer celebrated, but new ones appeared, such as the Snow Festival *(Yuki Matsuri)* in Sapporo; or old customs took on a new meaning – Buddha's Birthday for instance, on April 8th, which became the Flower Festival *(Hana Matsuri)*. Countless subtle and more obvious references are made to the festivals in the menus of the Yamazato Restaurant. The appetisers, especially, are full of symbols.

1 — Buddhism came to Japan from China via Korea in the 6th century.
2 — Nowadays the festival is usually referred to simply as *Tanabata*.

'One of my fondest childhood memories is of my mother preparing her treasured ojūbako. *The food was simple, but I always looked forward to it on New Year's Day. Later, in the Japanese Traditional Restaurant Tsuruya, I learned how to prepare the dishes in a more formal way. Composing the contents of the boxes is quite an ordeal, since each box takes twelve hours to prepare. It is also an artistic challenge. On the one hand I want to be innovative, but on the other a menu without black beans, herring roe or sardines, would not feel like* Oshōgatsu. *Every year I try to balance between creativity and tradition, and after thirty years of experience it hasn't become any easier.'*

— Oshima —

New Year is Japan's most important and widespread festival. The whole country celebrates the first three days of the New Year. All government offices and most commercial ones are closed, and most workers return to their hometowns. Children are treated to envelopes with money (*otoshidama*). Traditional games to play are *hagoita*, somewhat similar to badminton, a card game called '*karuta*', and kite flying.

In the past, distinction was made between Major New Year, which ended on the Seven Herb Festival (*Nanakusa no Sekku*) and Minor New Year, which continued until the 15th of January, but most people nowadays go back to work after three days.

The Seven Herb Festival is no longer celebrated, but the Winter *Kaiseki* Menu contains several elements of this festival. Rice with herbs, for example, relates to the ancient custom of eating seven-herb rice gruel on January 7th, to ensure good health.

Preparations for New Year start with cleaning and decorating the house. A sacred straw rope (*shimenawa*) is hung in the front door to prevent malevolent spirits from entering. A special altar with offerings to the *Toshigami* (God of the Year) is set up. The most important offering is *kagamimochi*, a rounded rice cake. Usually, there are several *kagamimochi* stacked one on top of the other. Even in the smallest apartments little shrines are erected, and a bamboo decoration called *kadomatsu* (gate pine) is placed near the door, as much part of the Japanese New Year as the Christmas tree is in the West.

On the first day of the New Year a visit to the temple is made, where the temple bells are sounded. For many women this is the only occasion on which they would wear a kimono. Hundreds of silhouettes dressed in kimono can be seen in the streets on New Year's Day.

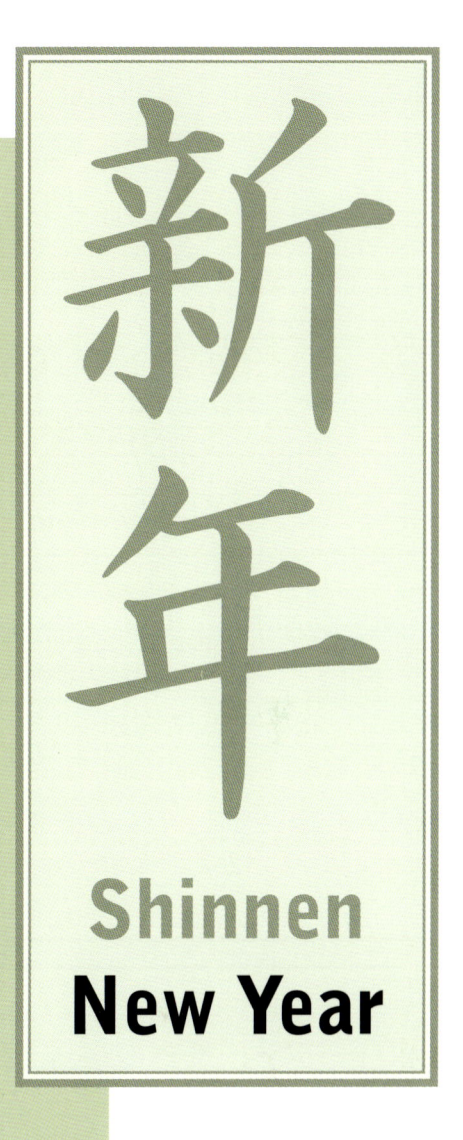

Shinnen
New Year

Speciality New Year's dishes, called *osechi*, are an indispensable part of the celebrations. In the ancient times, the term *osechi* denoted the food served at *sechie* – banquets given by the imperial court to celebrate changes of season. Since no cooking is done on New Year they are all prepared in advance and placed in lacquer boxes, *jūbako*, which can be stacked.

Osechi dishes are eaten with spiced sake *(otoso)* and accompanied by a New Year's soup called *zōni (or ozōni)*. The taste and ingredients of the soup differ very much according to the region; different families may even each have special recipes. Nevertheless, what they all have in common is a piece of cake *(mochi)*, which has been made by steaming and pounding rice.

The content of the boxes varies depending on local custom and individual taste – nowadays, Western-style or Chinese-style New Year's boxes are also widely available. However the following items are always included, since they are as connected to *Oshōgatsu*, as eggs to Easter.

Kuromame are black soya beans cooked in sugar syrup. The name of the dish sounds similar to the word *mamemameshii*, which means 'to work hard'. Eating *kuromame* implies a promise to do one's best all year. In addition a connection is made to *mame ni*, which means 'healthy'.

Kazunoko is salted or dried and cured herring roe, which has been rinsed and softly poached in *sake, mirin, dashi* and soy sauce. The words *kazu* (number) and *ko* (children) indicate the significance of this dish; it expresses the wish for many children.

Tatsukuri are very small dried sardines simmered in soy sauce and *mirin*. Sardines swim in large shoals and the delicacy also refers to numerous offspring. Farmers needed many children to help them in planting new rice fields, hence the name which means 'making the rice field'.

Kobumaki are poached rolls of kelp, called *konbu* or *kobu*, which sounds like the verb *yorokobu*, 'to be happy'.

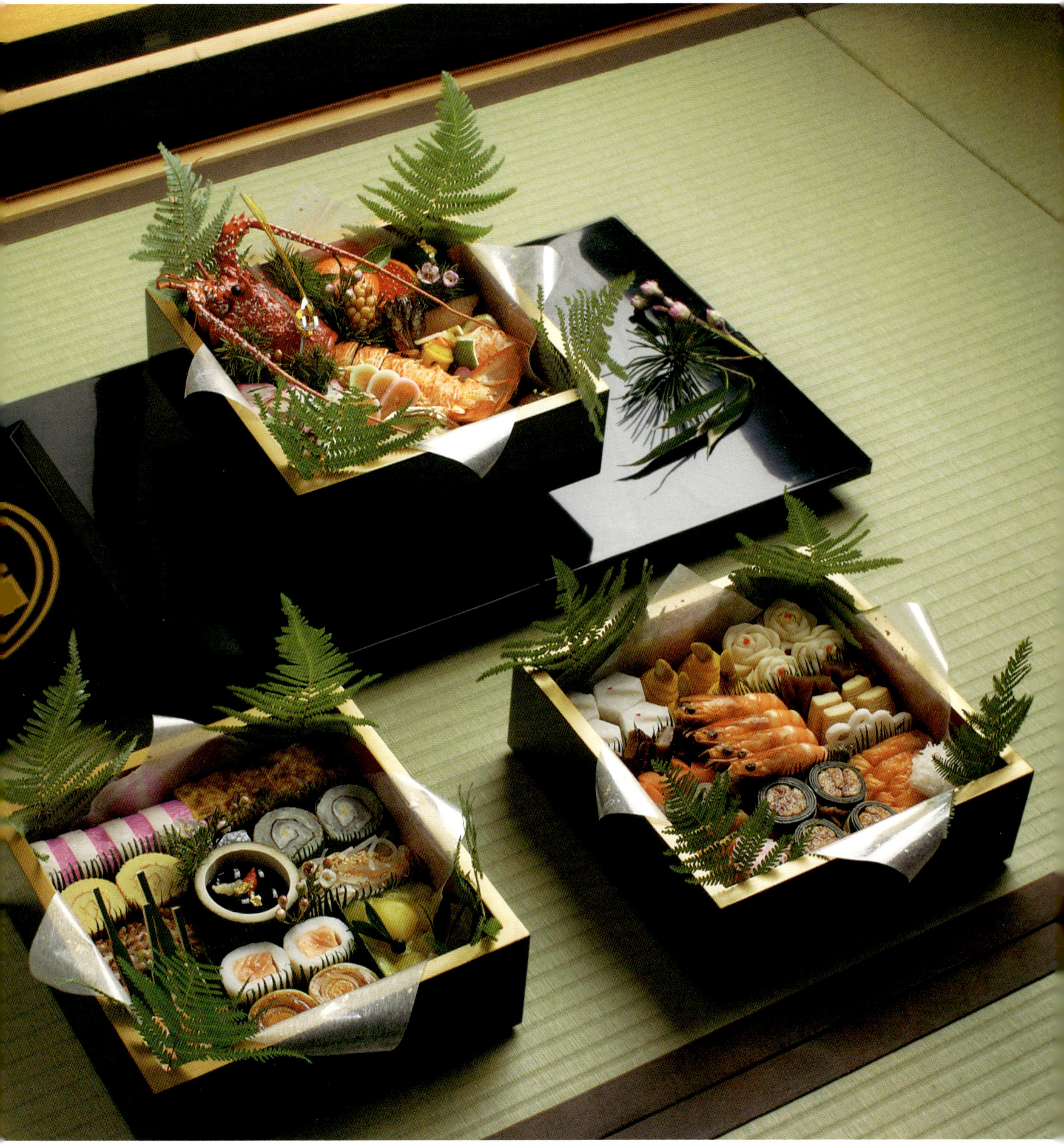

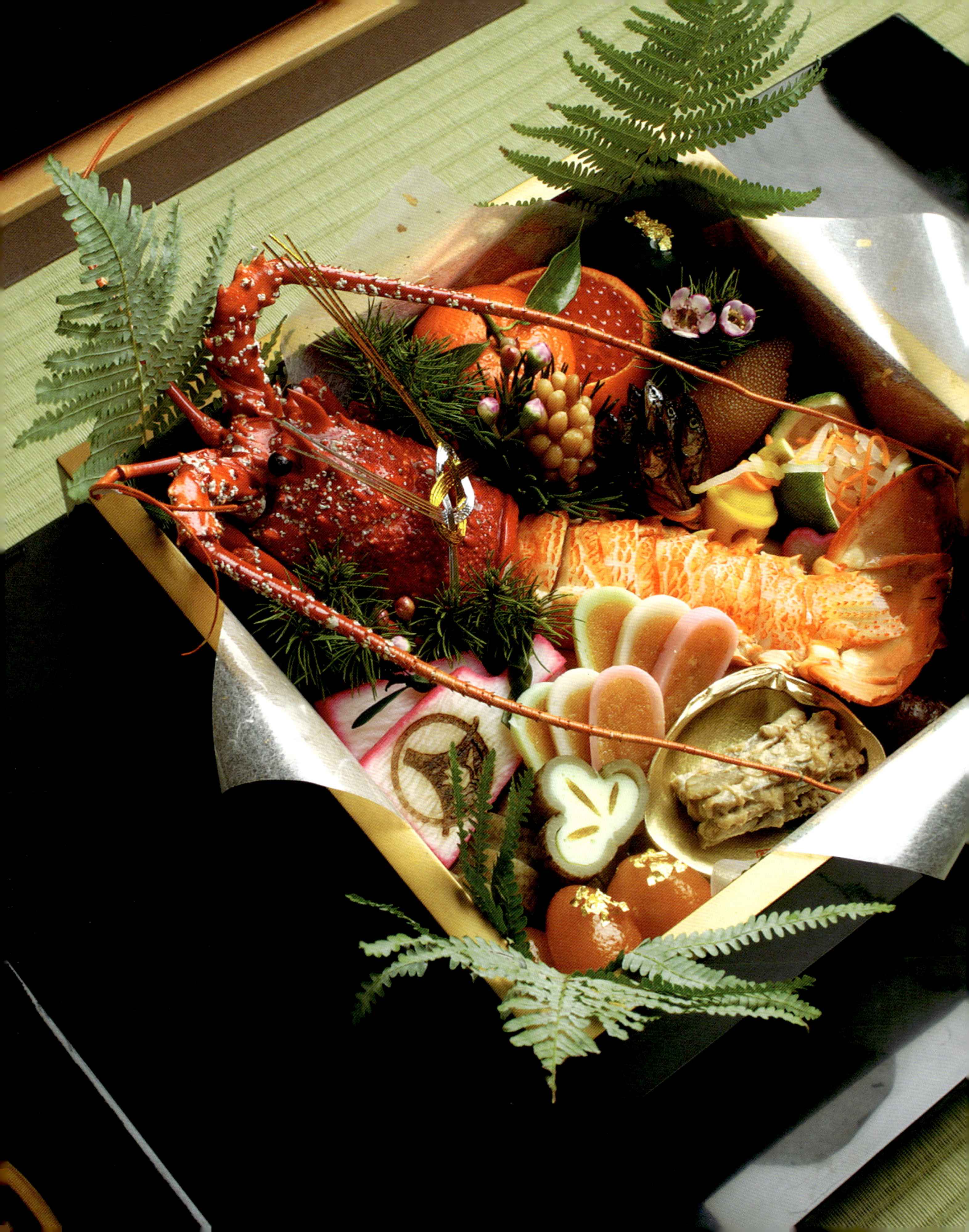

Ojūzume

New Year's boxes

ICHI NO JŪ	BOX 1
Iwaizakana	Festive drinking snacks
Iseebi sugatani	Spiny lobster
Ikura	Salmon caviar in mandarin
Aoume	Green *ume* apricot simmered in syrup
Kazunoko	Cured herring roe
Tatsukuri	Simmered sardines
Suzu kuwai	Temple bell of arrowhead root
Matsukasa hotate	Pine cone of scallop
Tai kobujime	Salted sea bream with cod roe in cup of lime peel
Shibukawa kuri	Sweet chestnuts with skin
Tataki gobō	Burdock root with white sesame sauce in clam shell
Kōban karasumi	'Coins' of sea bream paté filled with cured grey mullet roe
Matsu gobō	'Pine trees' of fishcake in burdock root
Kinkan	Candied kumquat
Hagoita nagaimo	'*Hagoita* racket' made of yam

お重づめ

New Year's boxes

Ojūzume

NI NO JŪ — BOX 2
Kuchitori — New Year's treats

Tori matsukaze	Chicken and duck paté with pine-kernel topping
Hirame ryūhimaki	Vinegary brill rolled up with kelp
Kōhaku namasu	Salad of thinly sliced *daikon* and carrot
Kuri kinton	Chestnut and purée of sweet potato
Kujaku tamago	'Peacock' of simmered fillets of eel around quail eggs
Ogawa kunsei	Smoked salmon in cod fish-cake
Ebi hagoita	'*Hagoita* rackets' of shrimp and yam paté
Kamo rōsuni	Seared breast of duck in sweetened soy sauce
Kuromame	Black soya beans simmered in sugar syrup with Japanese artichoke
Datemaki	Rolls of omelette mixed with shrimp paté
Kosode	Pink and white cod fish-cakes

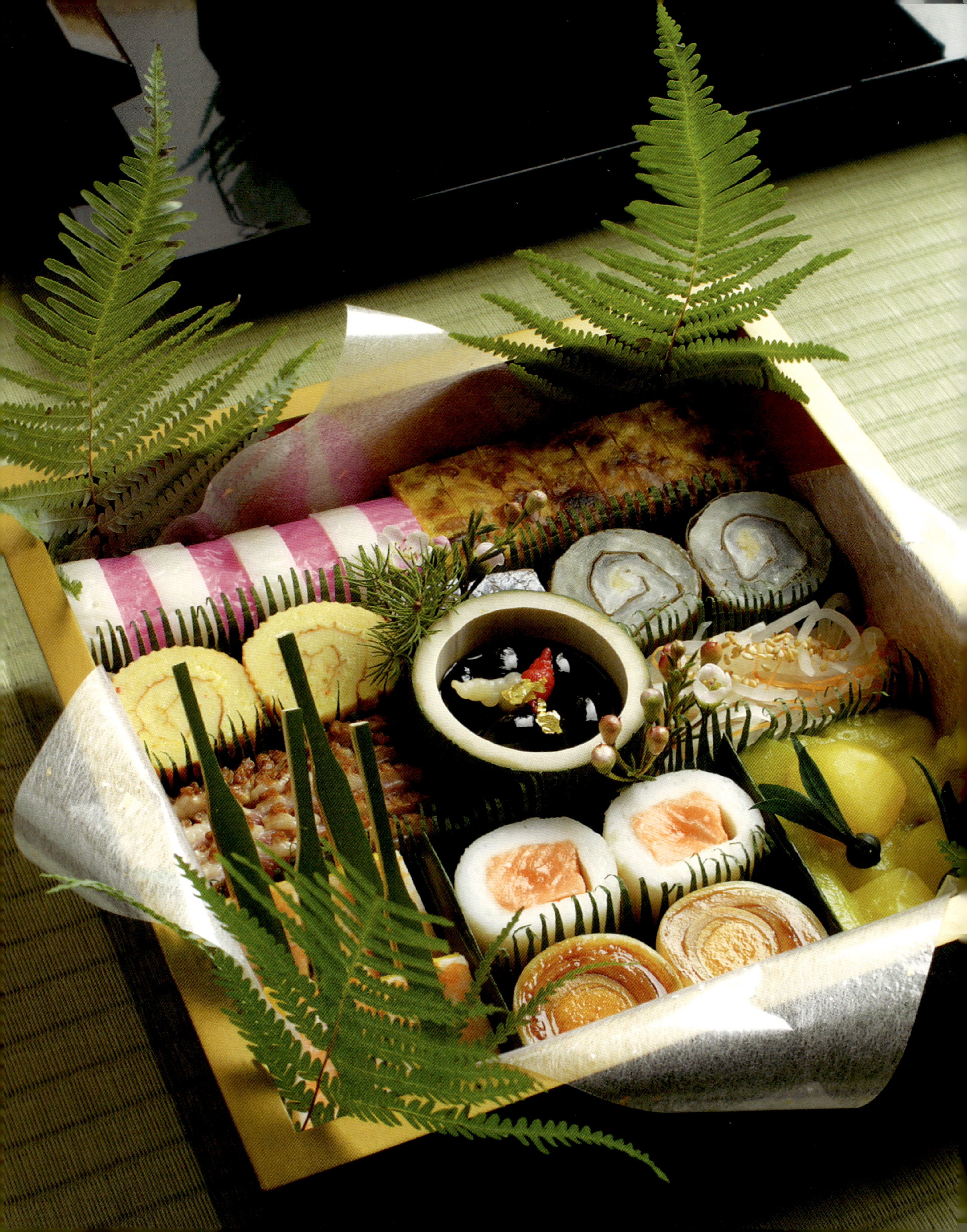

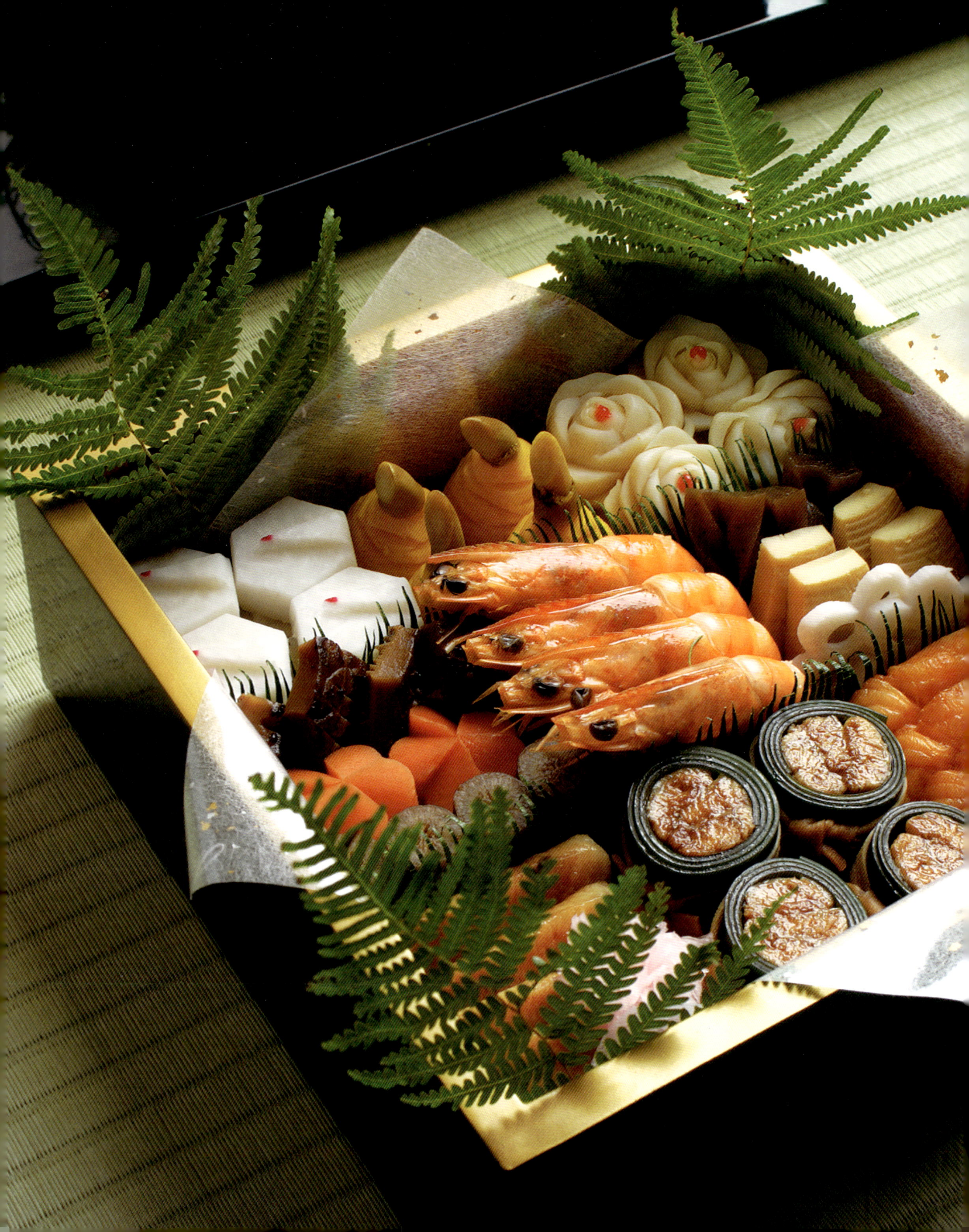

Ojūzume — New Year's boxes

SAN NO JŪ	BOX 3
Shukō	Snacks to accompany *sake*
Hana yurine	'Flowers' of simmered lily bulbs
Musubi konnyaku	'Knots' of *konnyaku* jelly
Takenoko	Simmered bamboo shoots
Hana renkon	'Flowers' of dressed lotus root
Aramakizake	Salted, semi-dried and grilled salmon
Unagi kobumaki	Slowly simmered rolls of kelp around eel
Buri teriyaki	*Teriyaki* of yellowtail
Gobō	Simmered burdock
Ume ninjin	'Apricot flowers' cut from carrot
Kikkō shiitake	'Turtles' of dried and simmered *shiitake*
Tsuru satoimo	'Cranes' of taro
Matsukasa kuwai	'Pine cones' of arrowhead
Ebi shibani	Prawns lightly simmered in *sake*
Kikuka kabu	Pink and white 'chrysanthemum flowers' of turnip

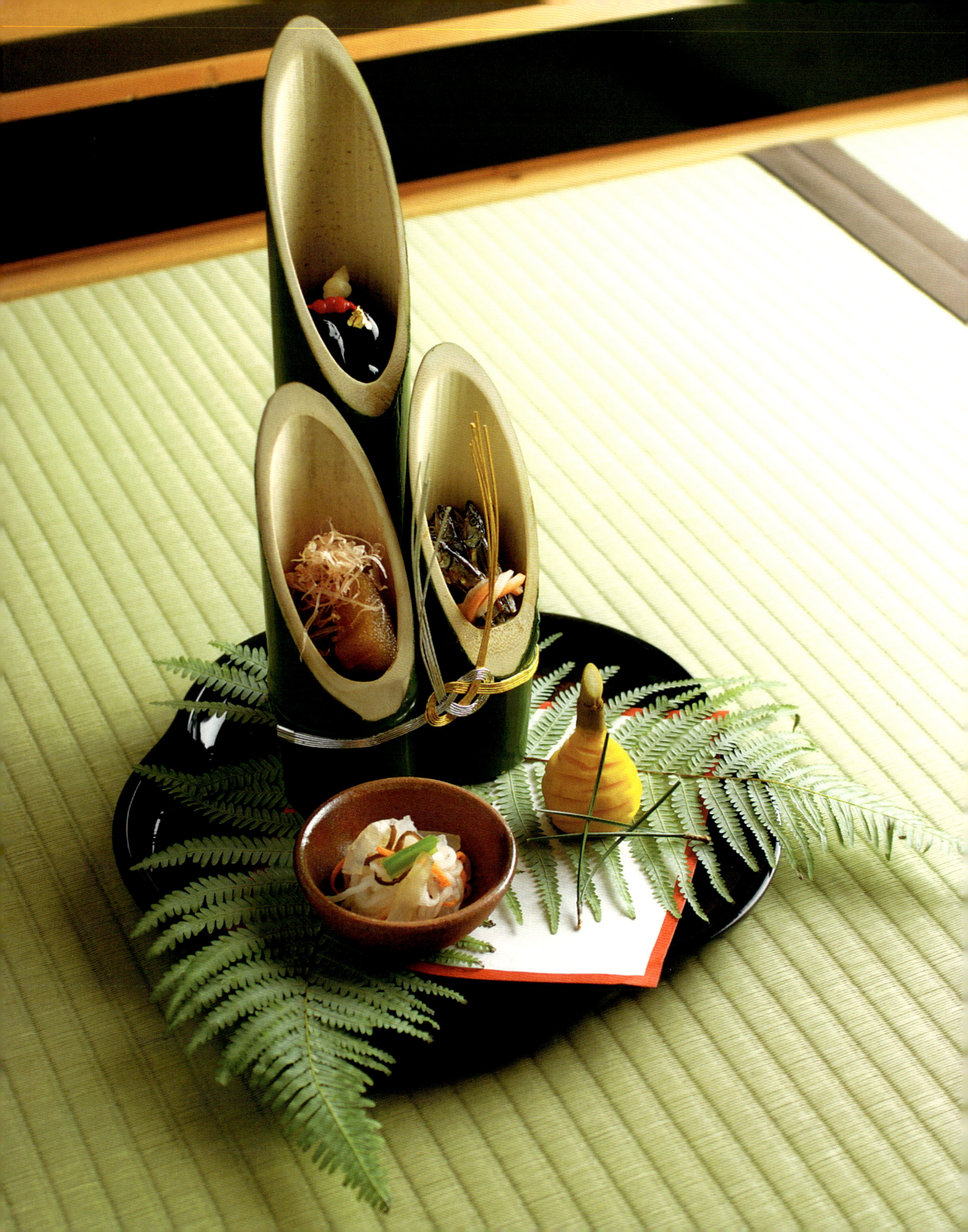

Hatsuharu

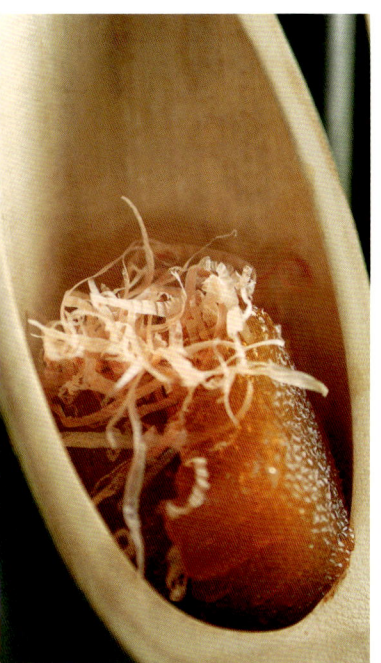

EARLY SPRING MENU

初春の会席

ZENSAI	**APPETISERS**
Kadomatsumori	Three delicacies of the New Year served in *kadomatsu* bamboo
Kazunoko	Cured herring roe
Kuromame	Black soya beans simmered in sugar syrup
Tatsukuri	Dried and simmered sardines
Goshiki namasu	New Year's salad in five colours, of *daikon* radish, carrot, *suizenji nori, mitsuba* and brill
Matsukasa kuwai	'Pine cone' cut from arrowhead

EARLY SPRING MENU

Hatsuharu

OWAN
Kamo zōni

SOUP
New Year's soup of duck with sticky *mochi*, *daikon*, *shiitake*, carrot, taro root and *daidai* orange peel

TSUKURI
Iwaimori

RAW FISH COURSE
Sashimi of lobster and sea bream

YAKIMONO
*Aramakizake,
kanburi teriyaki,
matsunami renkon,
kinkan suzuko*

GRILLED COURSE
Grilled semi-dried salmon and *teriyaki* of yellowtail

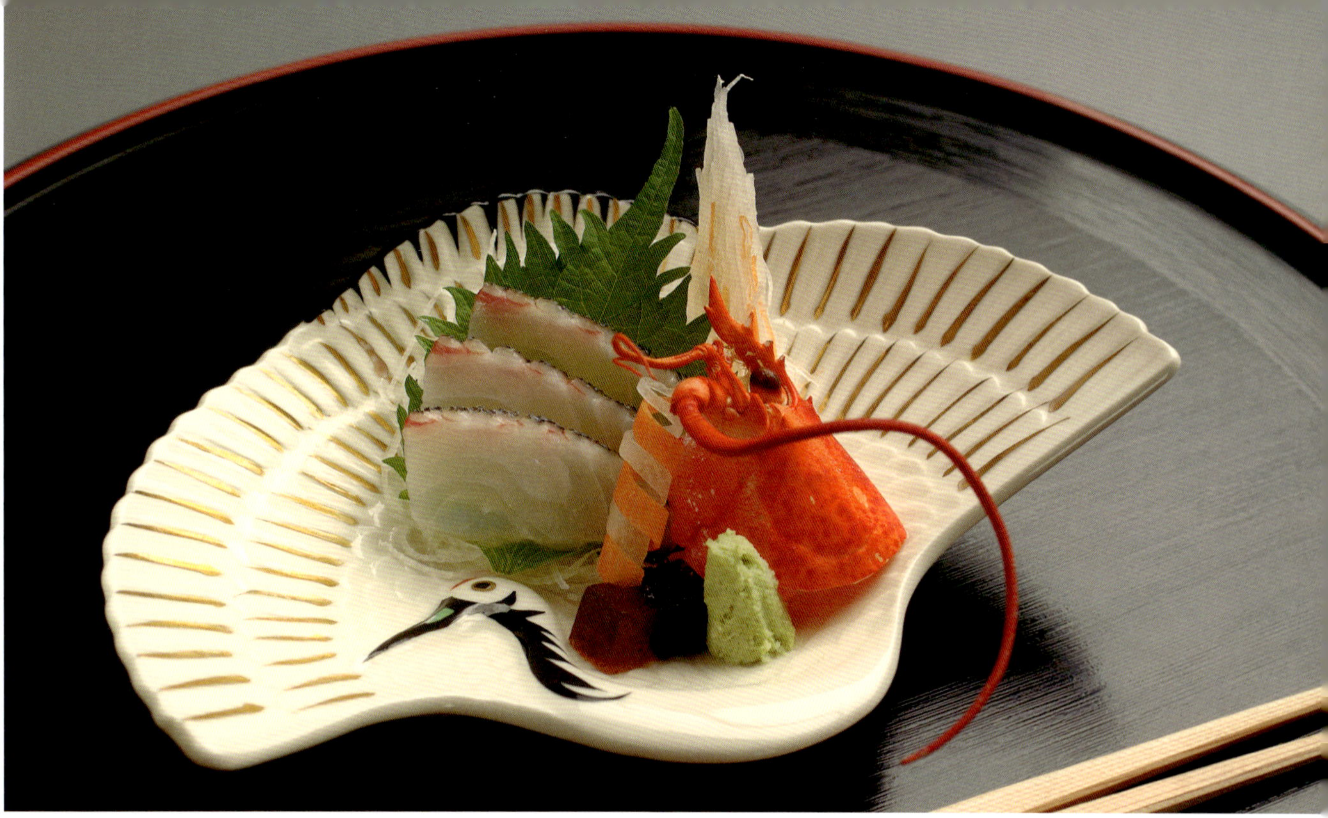

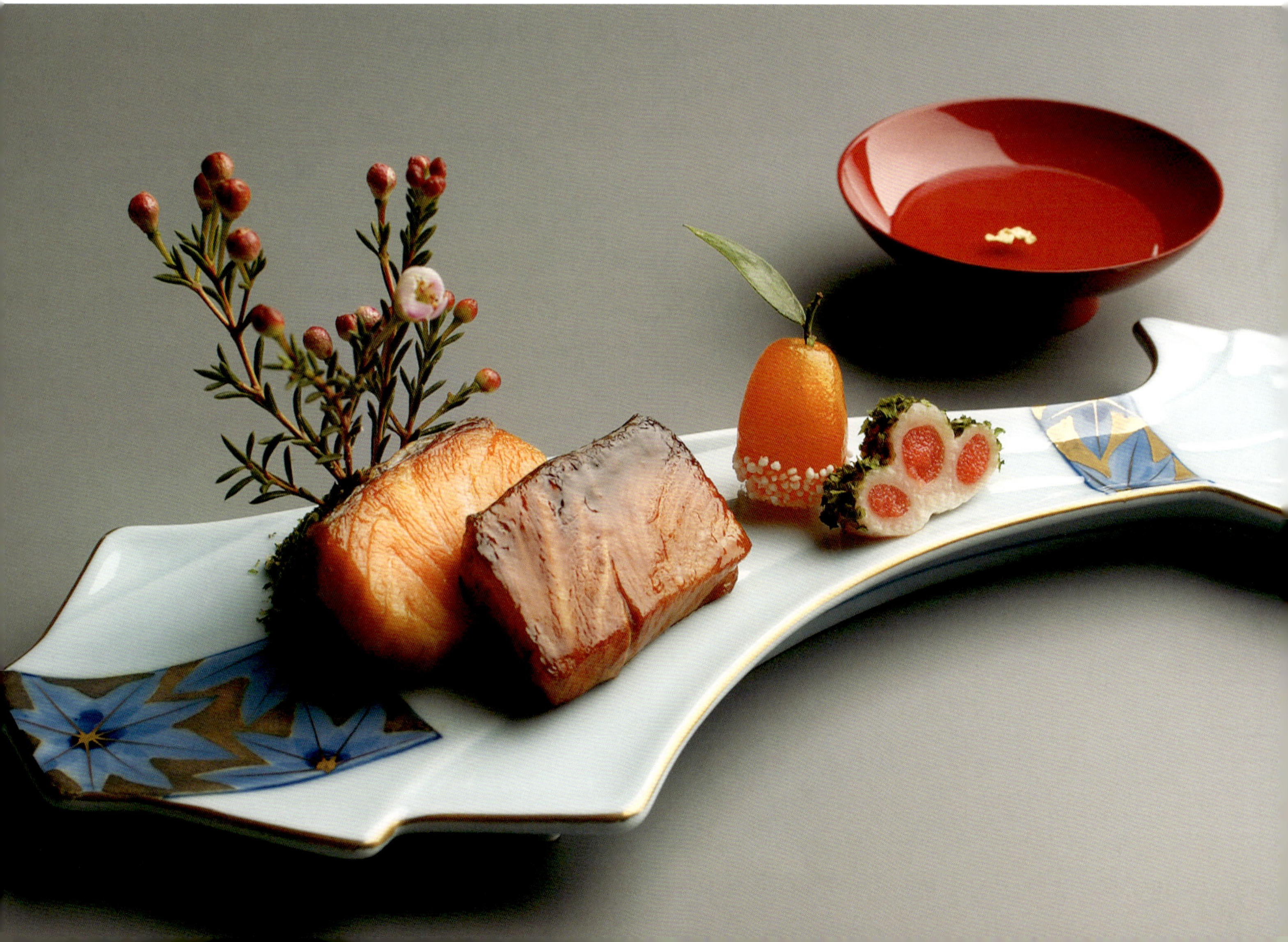

EARLY SPRING MENU **Hatsuharu**

NIMONO
Nishime

SIMMERED COURSE
Slowly simmered rolls of kelp around eel, with taro and lotus root, bamboo shoot and sugar snaps

SUNOMONO
Hirame ryūhimaki

SALAD COURSE
Vinegary brill rolled up with kelp and 'flowers' of turnip and cucumber

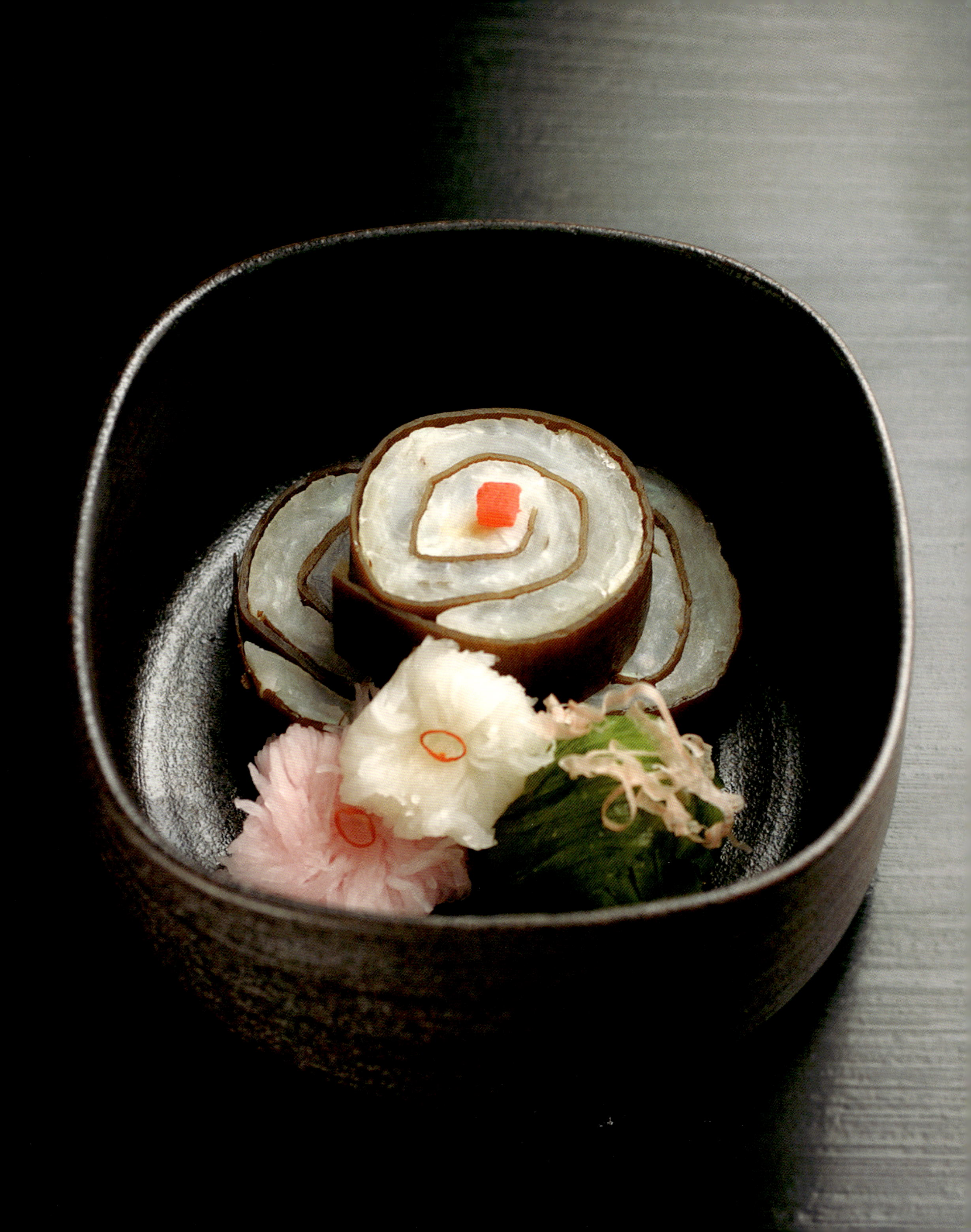

EARLY SPRING MENU
Hatsuharu

SHOKUJI
Wakakusa gohan
Kōnomono

THE MEAL
Rice with water horsbane
Chinese cabbage and gourd pickled in *sake* lees with dried and salted *konbu*

KASHI
Kuri zenzai

DESSERT
Sweet soup of red *azuki* beans and chestnuts

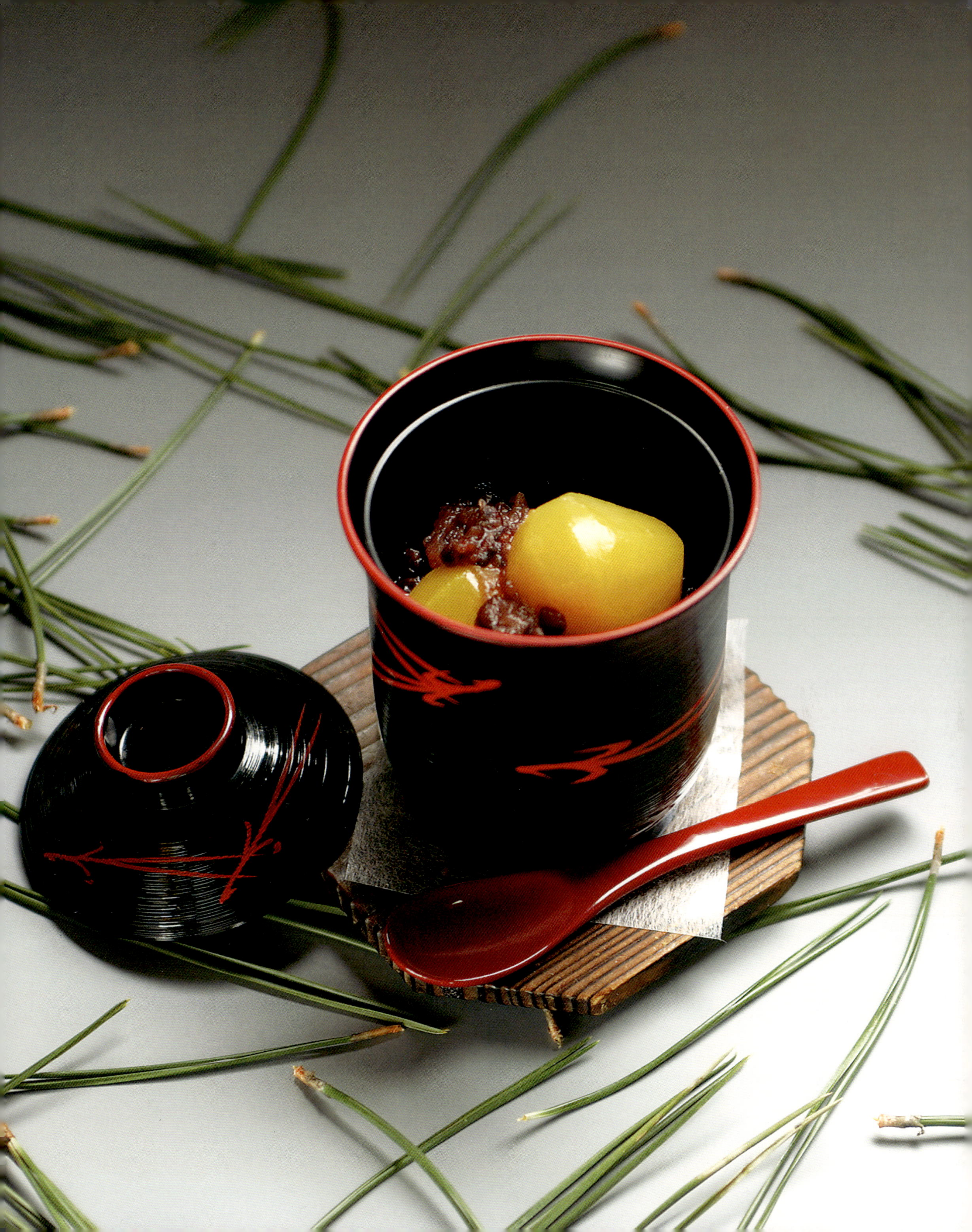

'In the menus I try to communicate aspects of Japanese culture, so I include prawns, which represent evil, and sardines, which are said to be disliked by impious forces, in the Winter Kaiseki Menu. Some of these references may not be entirely clear to Dutch guests, but Dutch and Japanese winters are both cold, so it also makes sense here to drink a warming soup of salmon and sake lees. Also in Holland the nabe stew makes a perfect winter dish, for which the rich harvest of the North Sea is very suitable.'

— Oshima —

冬
Fuyu
Winter

New Year is so prominent that it overshadows other winter feasts, but elements of these other festivals are found in the winter menus of *kaiseki ryōri*. One of those festivals is *Setsubun*, which is nowadays celebrated on the third or fourth of February. The festival involves purification rituals to drive demons out of the house – especially the two hairy ogres Akaoni and Aooni – by throwing roasted soya beans from every external door and window of the house. Good spirits are invited in by throwing beans into the house as well, with the accompanying spell: *'Oni wa soto, fuku wa uchi'* – 'demons out, luck come in'. Children eat the beans that fall on the floor, and try to consume one for each year of their lives.

In the *Kaiseki* Winter Menu, references are also made to *Kamakura Matsuri*, the Snow Hut Festival of the northern Akita prefecture. Families build igloos of snow in their garden, called *kamakura*, in which a little niche contains an image of the water god. This festival serves to ensure fresh drinking water for the rest of the year. Children spend an evening in these huts, drink hot soup of *sake* lees and eat rice cakes.

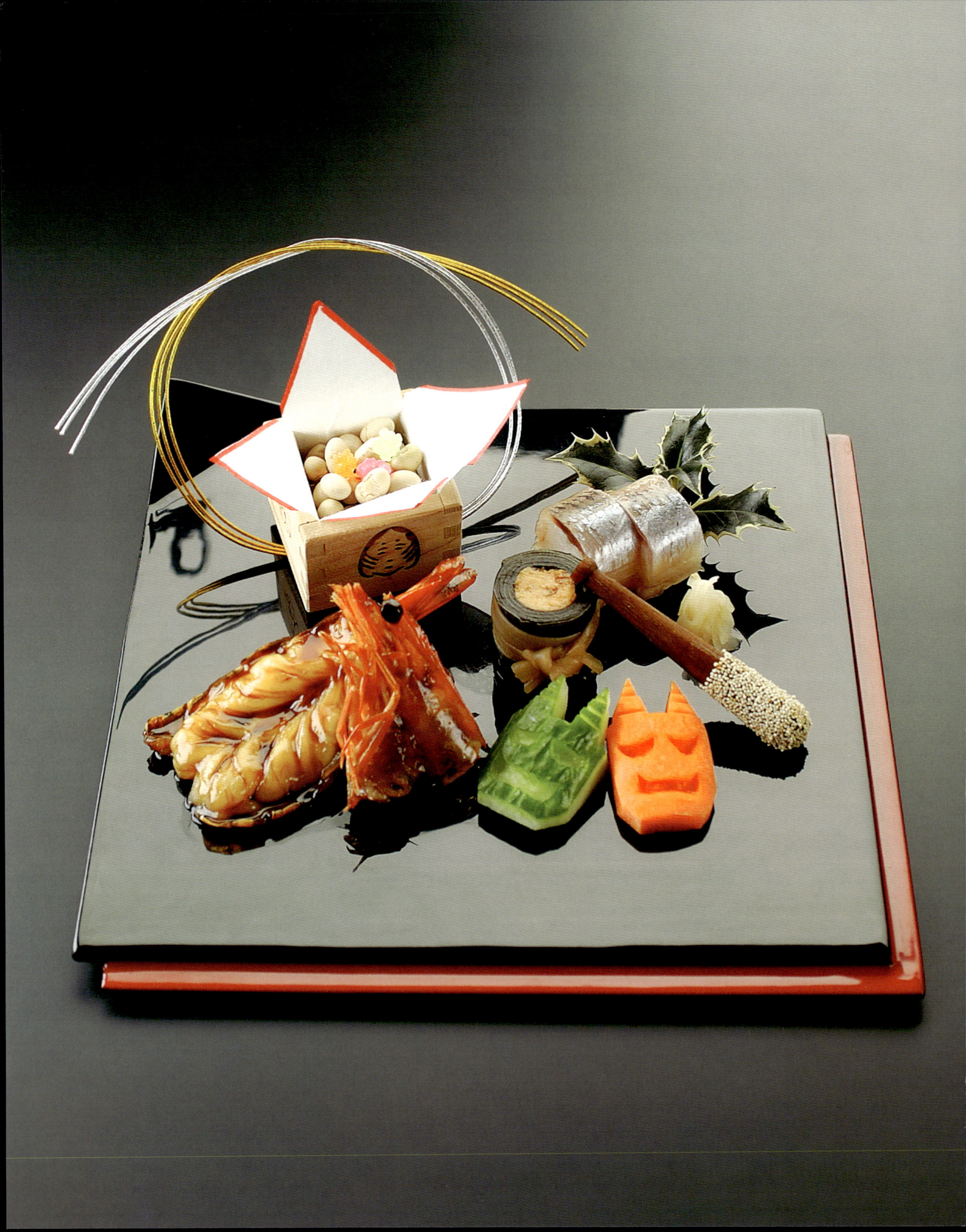

Setsubun

Winter menu

節分

ZENSAI — **APPETISERS**

Fukumasu — Roasted soya beans in a traditional measuring cup

Akaoni, aooni, konbō — A red ogre made from carrot and a green one from cucumber with a 'bludgeon' of burdock

Iwashi bōzushi — *Sushi* of sardine

Kuruma ebi onigarayaki — Grilled prawn in its 'demonic' shell

Tainoko kobumaki — Drum of kelp filled with the roe of sea bream

OWAN — **SOUP**

Sake kasujiru — Soup of sake lees with salmon, *daikon, shiitake*, burdock, watercress, a firm *konnyaku* jelly and dried red pepper

Winter menu # Setsubun

TSUKURI
Kamakuramori

RAW FISH COURSE
Sashimi of blue-fin tuna, 'camellia flower' of brill with salmon caviar, and pink shrimp in an igloo of snow

YAKIMONO
Amadai negimaki

GRILLED COURSE
Red mullet grilled with sweet *miso* rolled around a Japanese leek with green pepper and *hajikami* ginger pickle

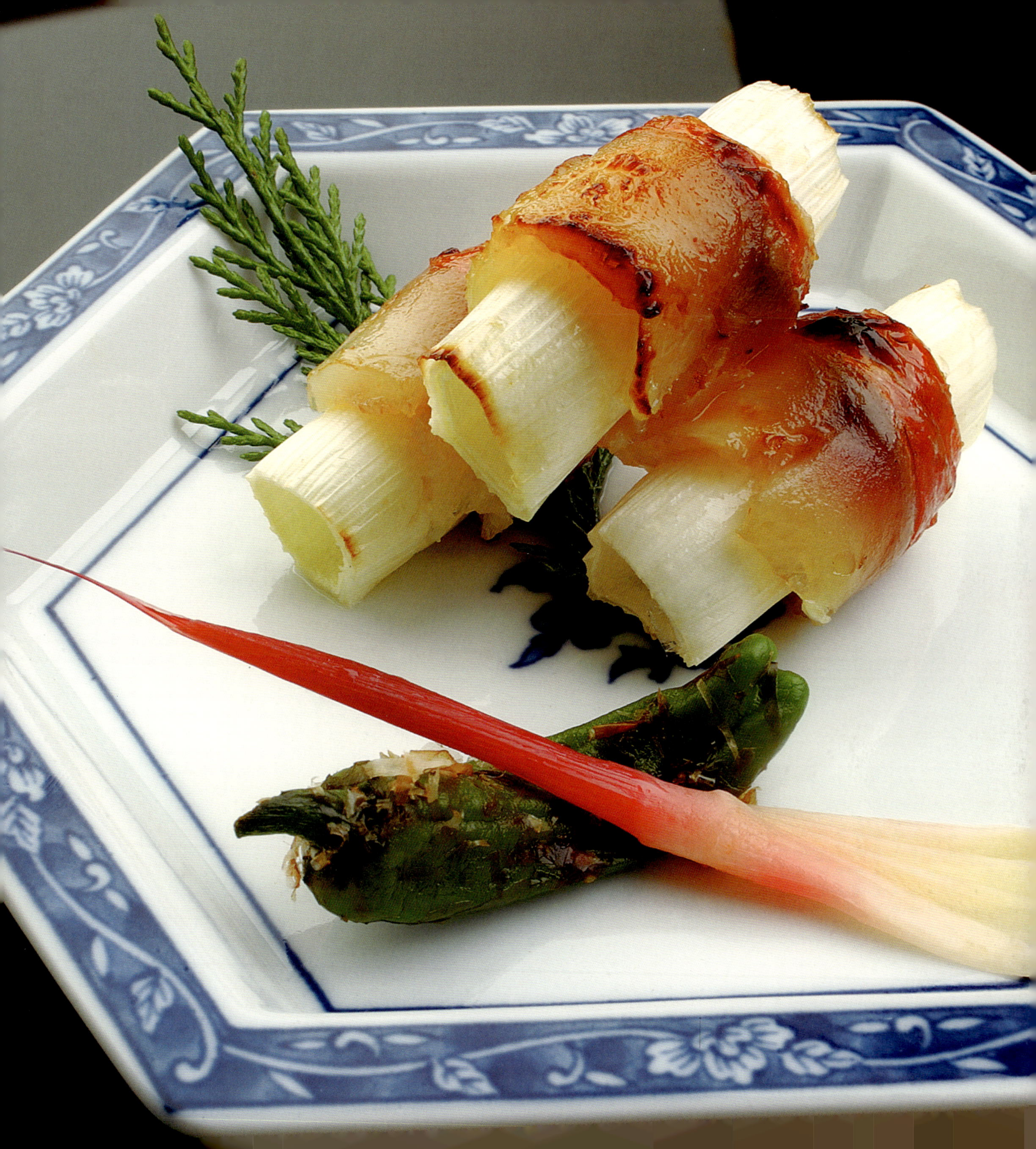

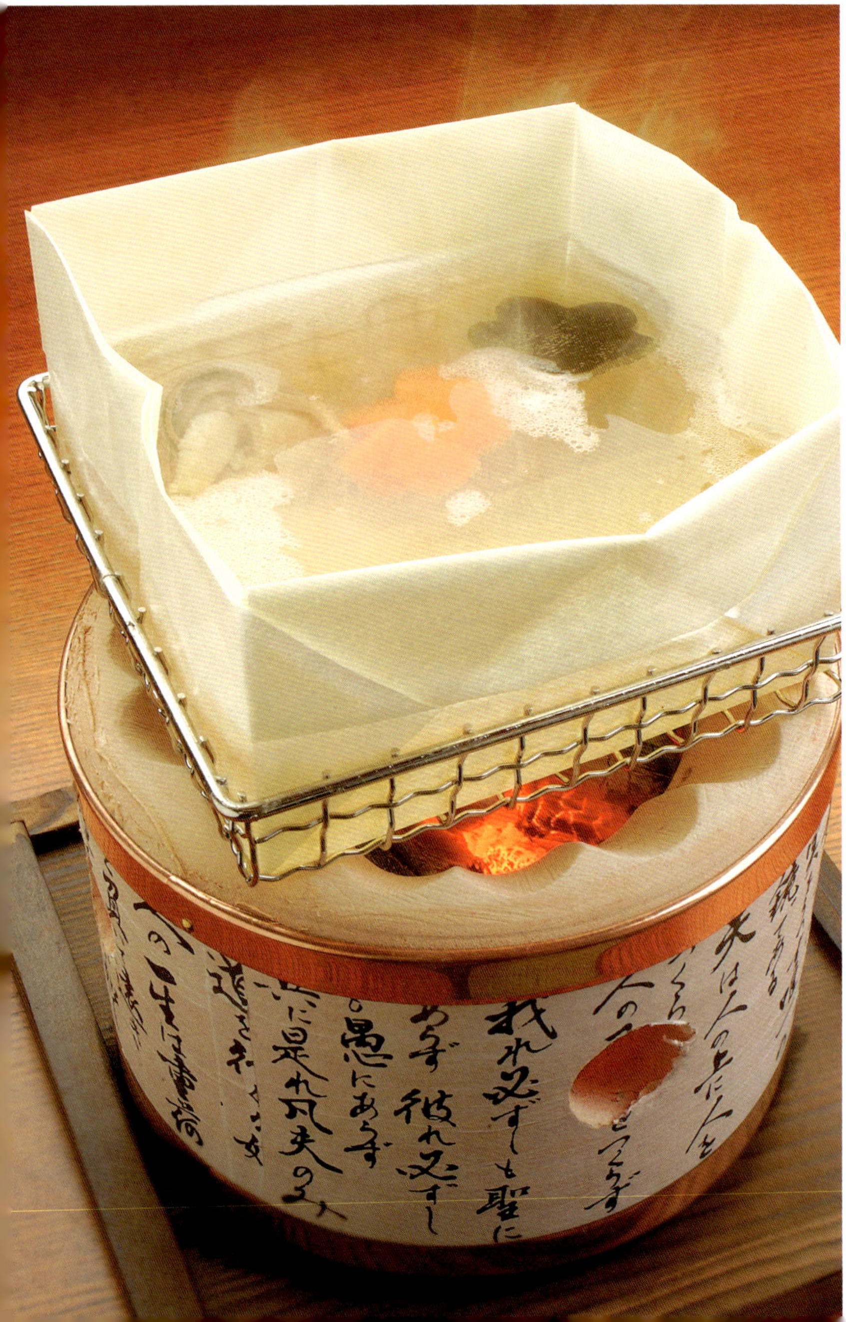

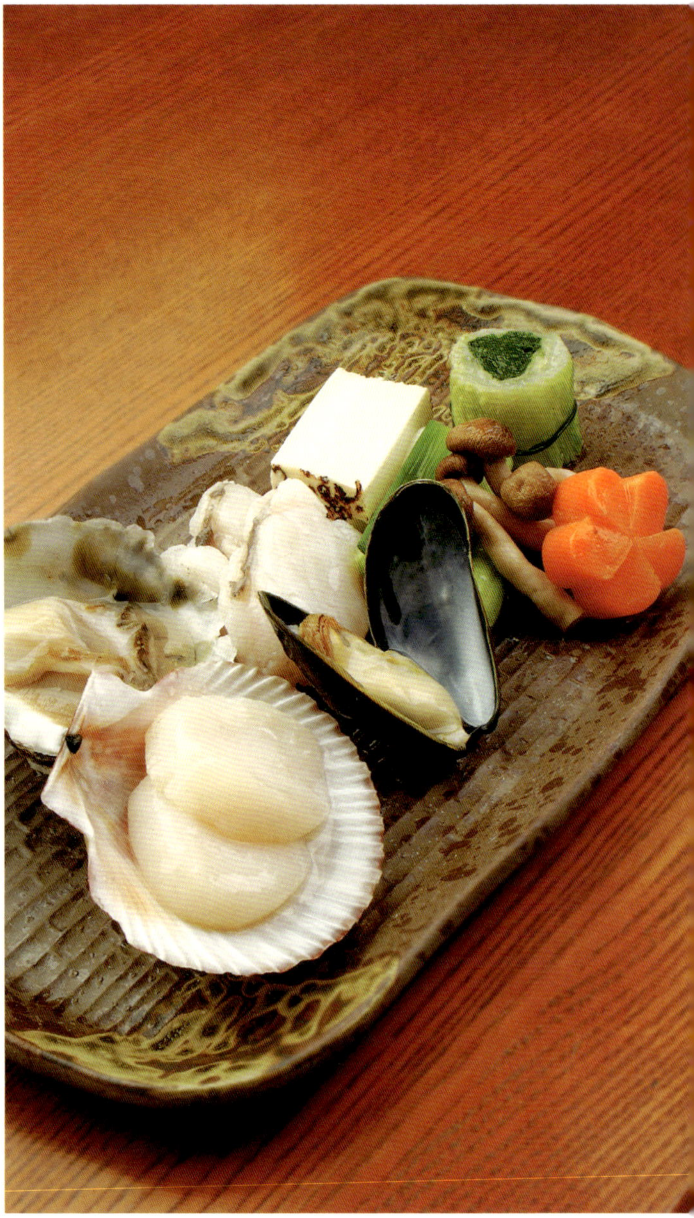

Setsubun

WINTER MENU

KAMINABE
Hokkai no sachi kaminabe

PAPER POT
Individual paper pot on a small *hida* stove, with delicacies of the North Sea

SUNOMONO
Kani kaburamaki

SALAD COURSE
King crab rolled in sheets of turnip, topped with egg yolk and vinegar with sturgeon caviar, beside checkered green and yellow pepper and dressed cucumber

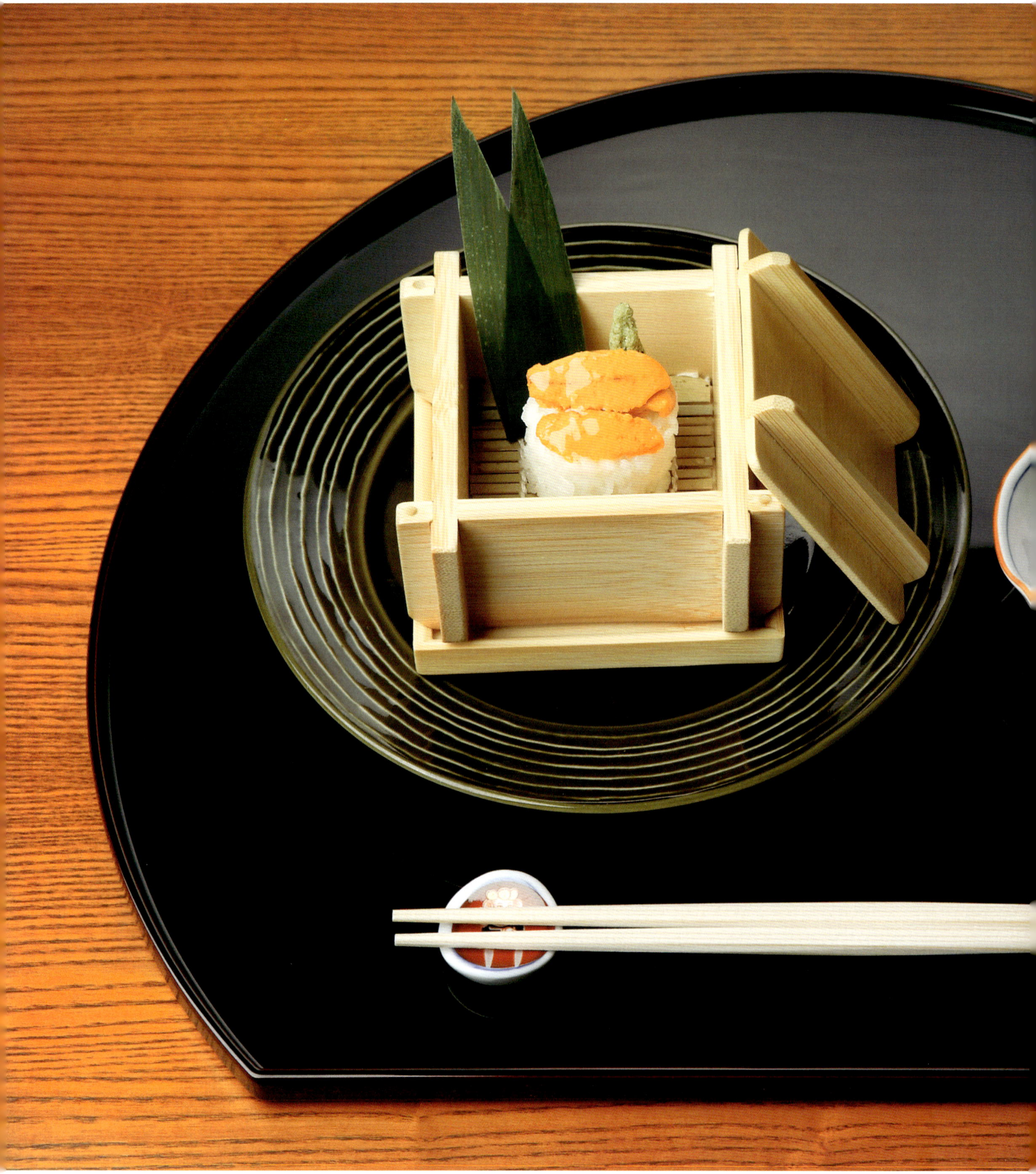

Setsubun   Winter menu

SHOKUJI
Uni iimushi
Kōnomono

KASHI
Umeshu zeriiyose

THE MEAL
Steamed rice with *wasabi* and sea urchin
Pickles of cucumber, *mibuna* cabbage
and red turnip rolled in white turnip

DESSERT
Jelly of red *ume* apricot liqueur

'Feminine qualities predominate in the menus of spring. In this season that sees the blooming of many trees, we scatter peach-flower petals over sake, as they are supposed to be beneficial to the health and bring some colour to the cheeks. Our meals should be as delicate and becoming as the most gracious girl.'

— Oshima —

The festival for girls is called *Hina no Sekku* or *Hina Matsuri*, which both mean Dolls' Festival. It can also be refered to as *Momo no Sekku*, meaning Peach Festival. When the lunar calendar was in use, the third month saw the blooming of peach blossoms – hence the latter name. Because March comes a month earlier than the original 'third month', peach trees are not yet in bloom. Plum and cherry blossoms are nowadays associated with the festival. The cherry tree (*sakura*) blooms in March or April and this is a feast in its own right. During *hanami* (flower viewing) scores of people collect under the trees day and night to have picnics, drink *sake* and admire the blossom. In medieval times the cherry blossom became an icon of the poetic sensitivity of the aristocracy, but in the Edo period it started to represent the whole of Japanese culture.

On Dolls' Festival, dolls representing the emperor, the empress, courtiers and court musicians are usually set up in a conspicuous spot in the house and admired for several days. Diamond-shaped rice cakes *hishimochi* (representing a pattern used by suppliers of the imperial family) are placed as offerings, and a special kind of sweet 'white *sake*' *shirozake*, made with rice malt, is drunk. In front of the altar, girls play games such as *kaiawase*, with clams or other shells. The two halves are separated and have to be matched by the contestants. Sometimes one half of the shell is decorated with the drawing of a plant and the other with its flower, or with other combinations that need to be matched.

In 1948 the Boys' Festival on May 5th was designated a national holiday and named Children's Day (*Kodomo no Hi*). However, May 5th is still observed in most families as a festival for boys, while the Dolls' Festival is celebrated as a day for girls.

春
Haru
Spring

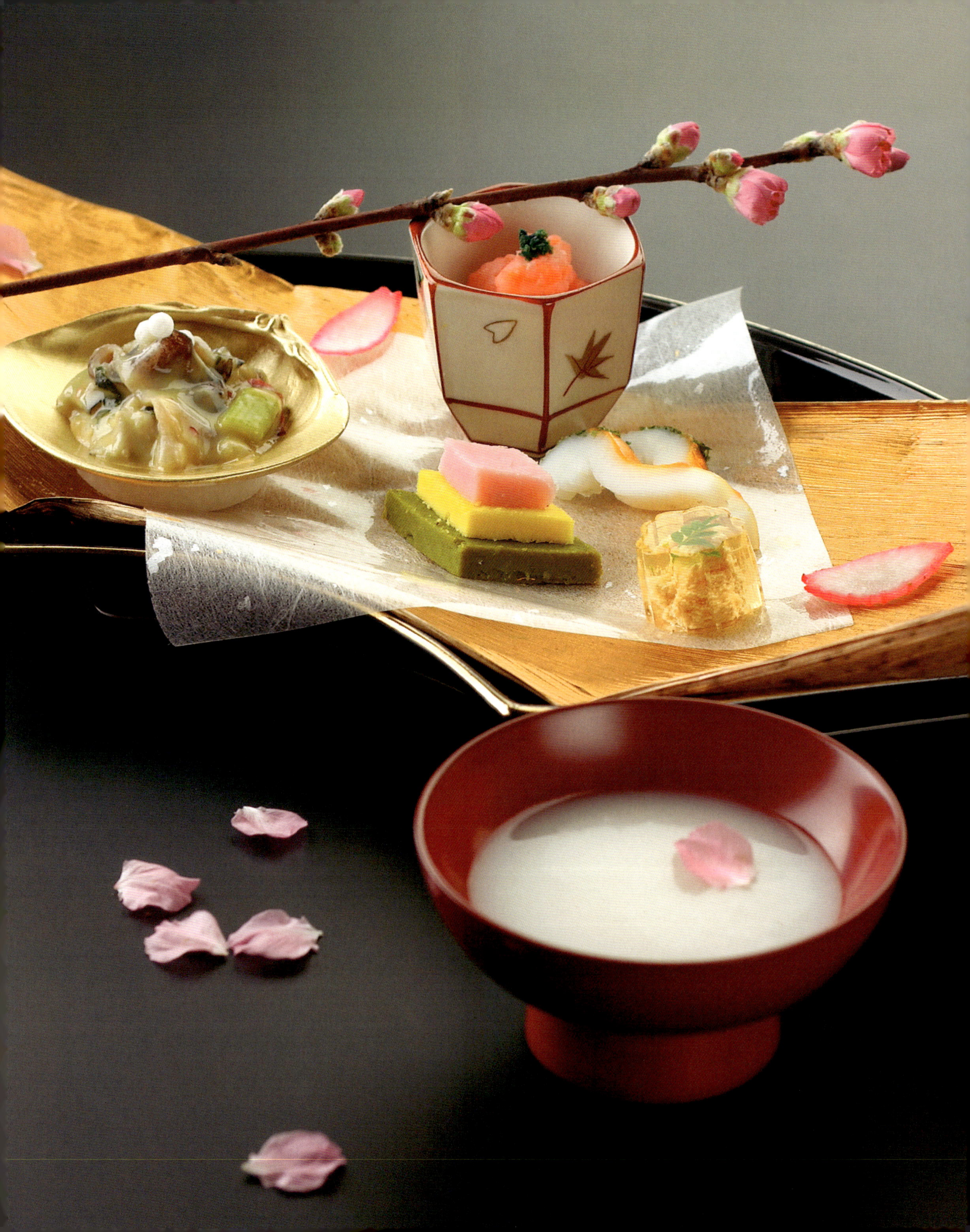

Hina Matsuri

DOLLS' FESTIVAL MENU

雛祭り

IKKON — APERITIF
Shirozake — White milky *sake* for Girls' Day, with peach blossom

ZENSAI — APPETISERS
Hishimochi — Diamond-shaped rice cakes coloured pink with *ume* apricot, green with peas, and yellow with egg
Hokkigai sumisoae — Clam salad with vinegary mustard sauce
Amaebi baikōae — Pink shrimp with dressing of *umeboshi* and *sake* lees
Warabi ika — Grilled cuttlefish shaped like fern shoot with laver and sea urchin
Tainoko nikogori — Roe of sea bream and ginger in jelly

OWAN — SOUP
Hamaguri shinjō — Soup with clam fishcake, carrot, salted cherry blossom and *kinome*

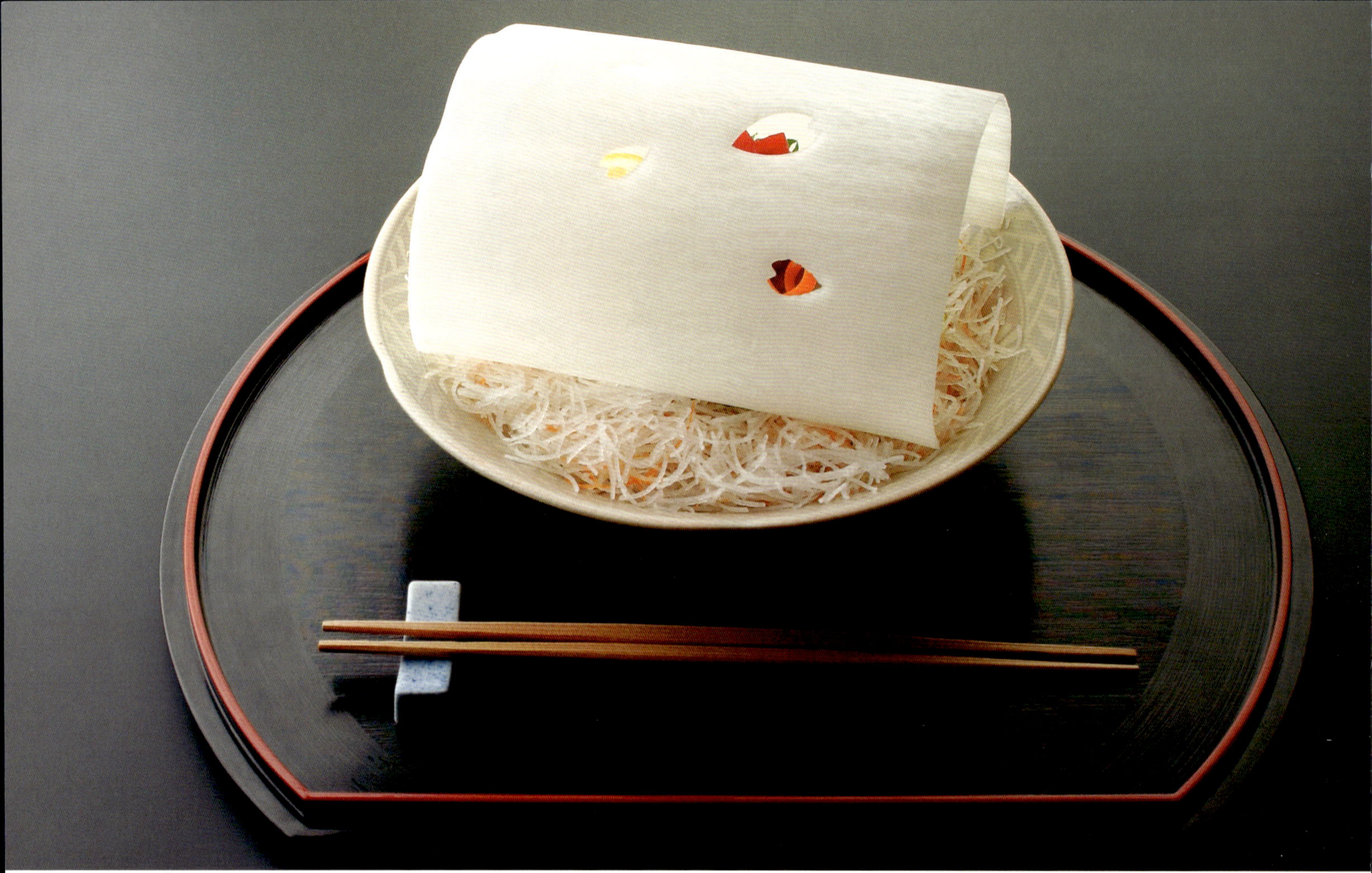

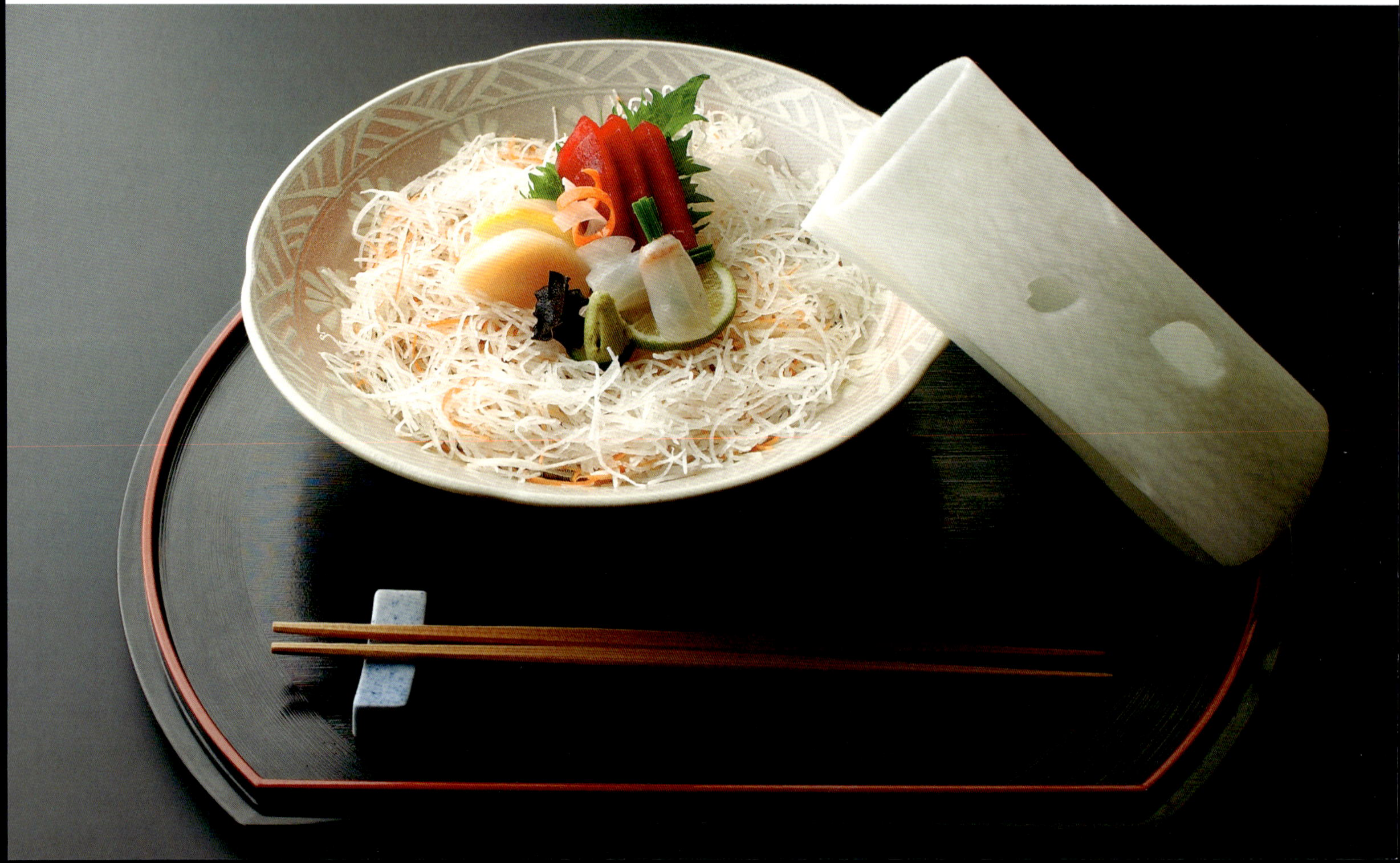

DOLLS' FESTIVAL MENU

Hina Matsuri

NIMONO
Ume daikon fukiyose

SIMMERED DISH
'Flower' of poached *daikon* with king crab, *temari* gluten ball, carrot, grated *yuzu* zest and a broad bean ahead of season.

SUNOMONO
Kaimori

SALAD COURSE
Three shellfish in vinegar dressing: abalone, red Venus clam and cockle with *wakame* seaweed and ginger jelly.

Dolls' Festival menu

SHOKUJI
Temarizushi

THE MEAL
Sushi balls (since girls play games with balls) of transparent sea bream over a twig of *kinome*, salmon, prawn and omelette, beside slices of sweet-and-sour ginger

KASHI
Sakura mochi

Sakura aisu

DESSERT
Cake of pounded rice with red *azuki* bean paste *(an)* wrapped in a salted cherry leaf

Ice-cream of cherry blossom with puffed and sugared rice

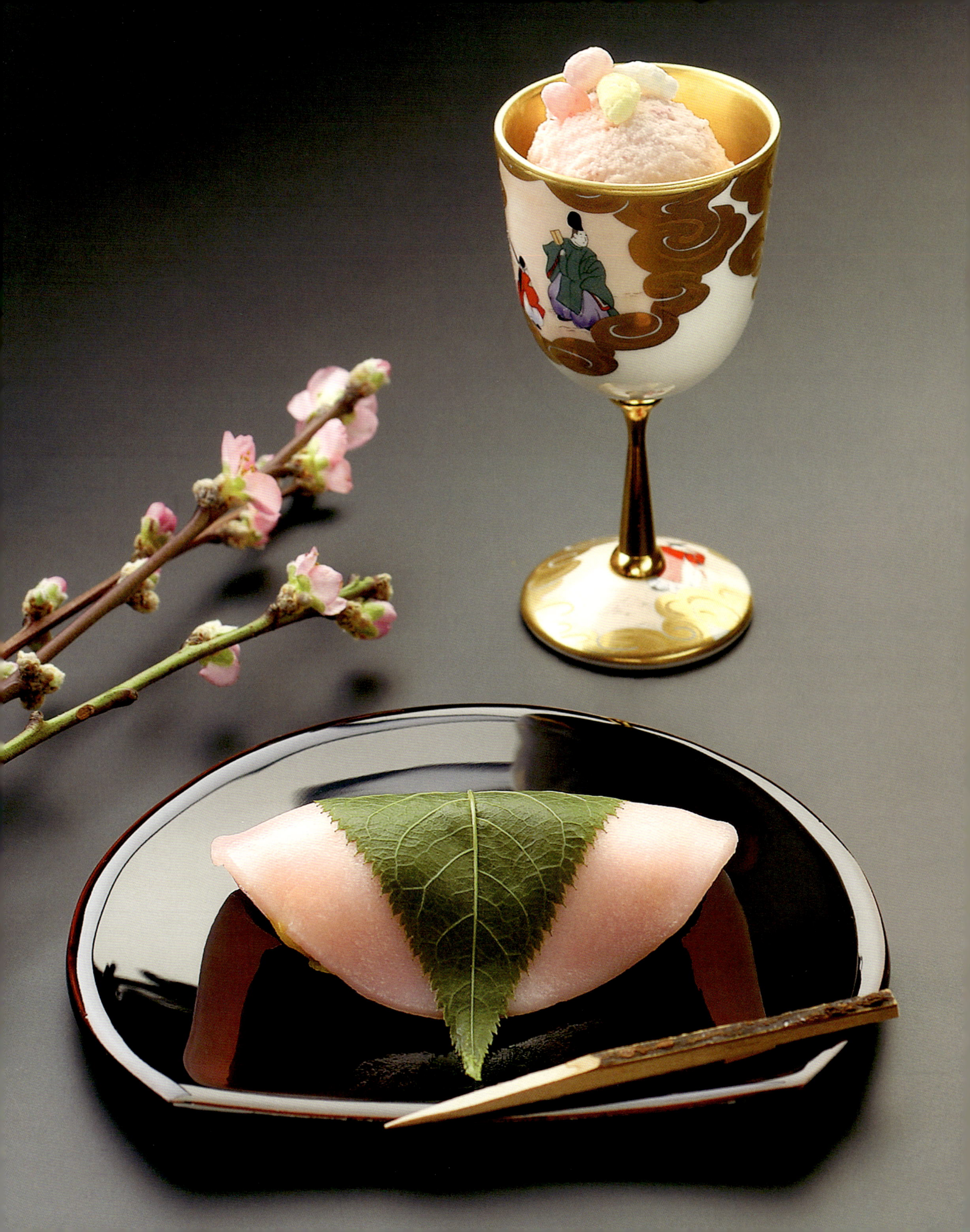

'Besides fresh vegetables, traditional Japanese cuisine includes fish, but vegetarianism is on the increase everywhere. Spring brings many young shoots and tender new vegetables, which are especially delectable for vegetarians.
We are grateful for the many Japanese vegetables now grown in the Netherlands, such as daikon, kaiware, shiitake *and* shiso, *but also for Dutch ones like asparagus, peas, tomatoes, carrots and lettuce, which have a wonderful quality of their own, thanks to a special salinity of the Dutch soil.*'

— Oshima —

精進
Shōjin
Vegetarian

Vegetarianism is deeply rooted in Japan because of Zen-Buddhist doctrines, but secular vegetarianism is quite rare. It is rather difficult to find completely vegetarian meals outside temples and monasteries. Normally *kaiseki* restaurants in Japan do not offer whole vegetarian menus. The fact that the Yamazato Restaurant in Amsterdam always has a vegetarian menu may be regarded as a nod towards local tastes.

Buddhist vegetarianism came to Japan from China. In the 13th to 14th century the Japanese vegetarian cuisine, *shōjin ryōri*, developed and with it vegetarian products like *tōfu*, *yuba*, soy sauce, *miso* paste, and a wheat gluten called *fu*. *Shōjin ryōri*, which helped to spread the use of the vegetarian products over Japan has greatly influenced *kaiseki ryōri*.

Unlike vegetarian cuisines in China, in *shōjin ryōri* no attempts are made to imitate meat dishes – like duck, chicken and pork made of gluten.

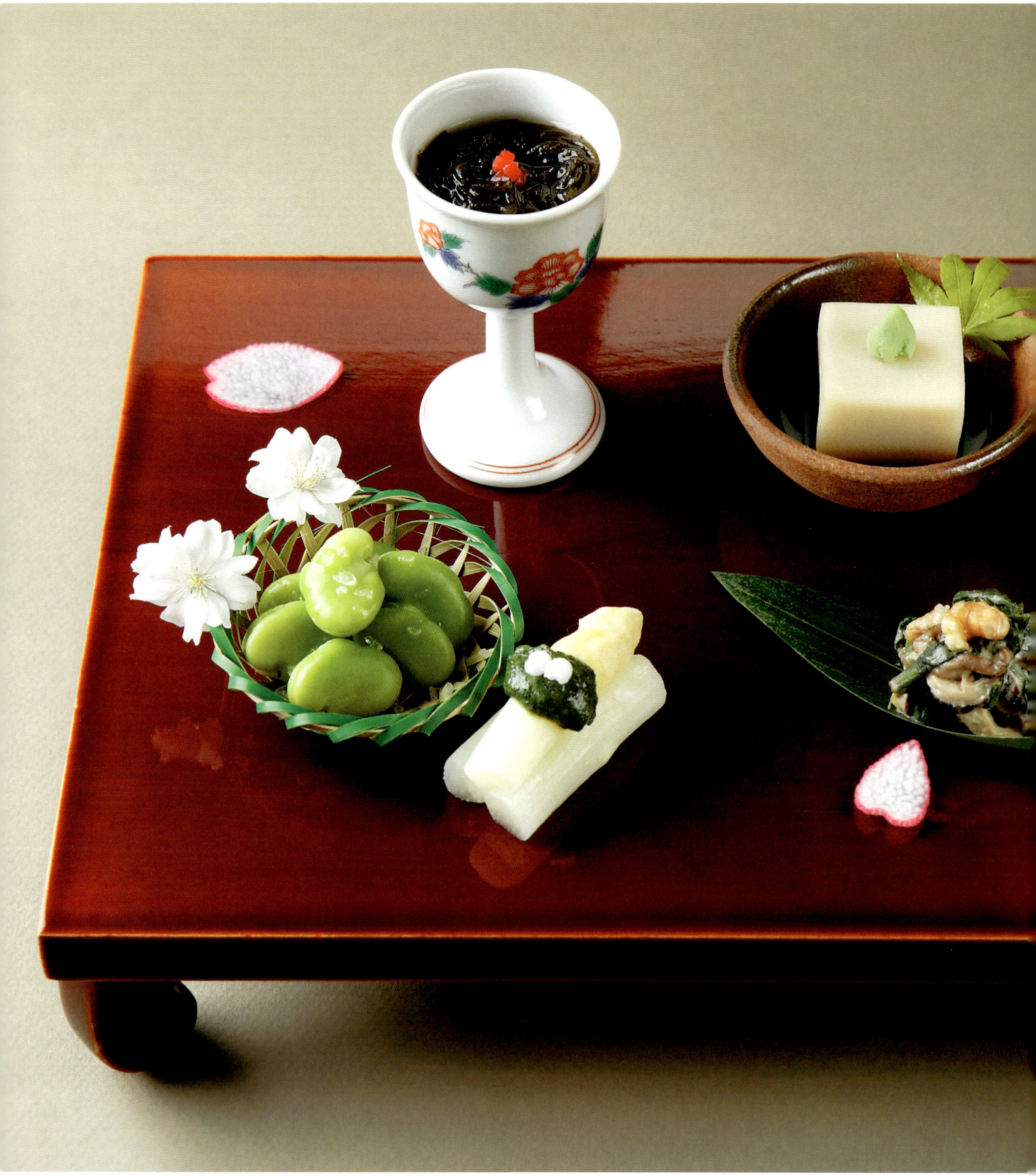

ZENSAI
 Yuzu mozuku

 Gomadōfu
 Hōrensō kurumiae
 Asuparagasu
 Soramame

OWAN
 Endō surinagashi

Wakana

YOUNG SHOOTS MENU

APPETISERS

Long filaments of *mozuku* seaweed in dressing
with *yuzu* peel, topped with red ginger
Firm jelly of white sesame paste topped with *wasabi*
Spinach, grilled *shiitake* in a walnut dressing
New white asparagus with *kinome miso* sauce
Boiled broad beans with salt, dented with a thumbnail

SOUP

Japanese pea soup with truffle and gold leaf

若菜

113

YOUNG SHOOTS MENU

Wakana

TSUKURI
Shōjin sashimi

VEGETARIAN SASHIMI COURSE
Fresh bamboo shoots, avocado, yam wrapped in laver, *iwatake* mushrooms

YAKIMONO
Takenoko sanshōyaki

GRILLED COURSE
Grilled bamboo shoots in *teriyaki* sauce, sprinkled with chopped *kinome*

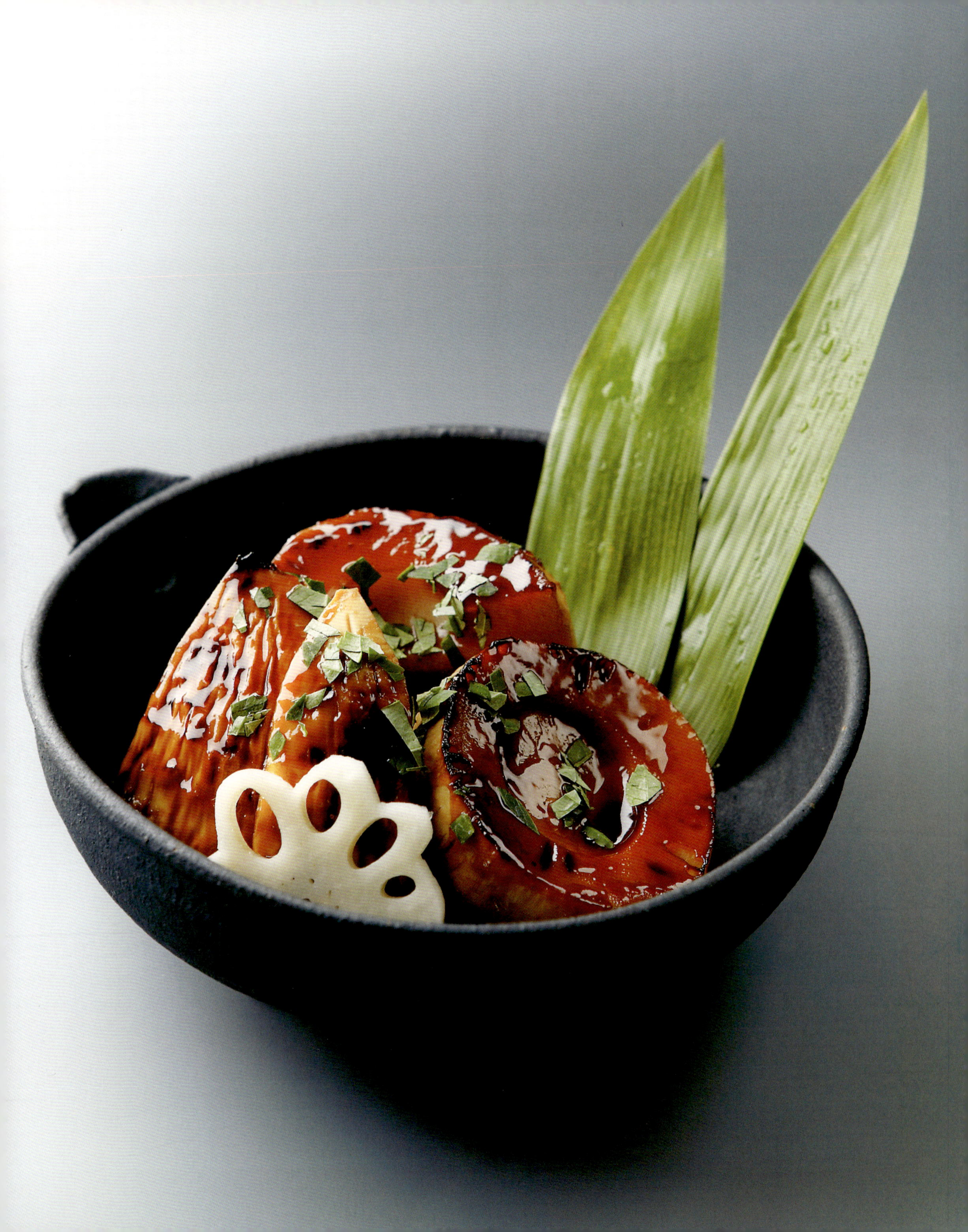

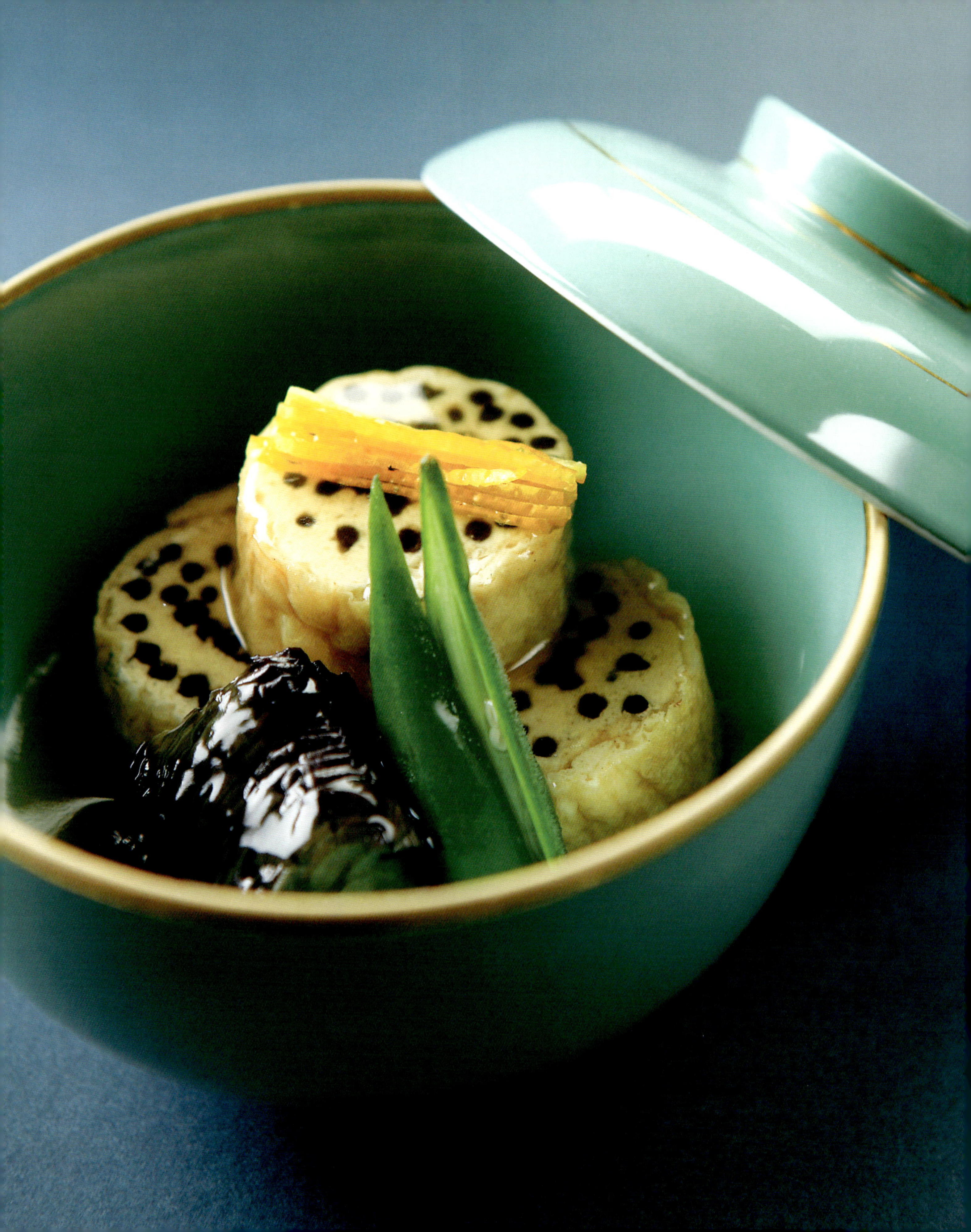

Wakana

YOUNG SHOOTS MENU

NIMONO
Nagahijiki shinodamaki

SIMMERED COURSE
Rolls of *tōfu* and *hijiki* seaweed, with Japanese aubergines, okra and *yuzu* zest.

AGEMONO
Yasai tempura

DEEP-FRIED COURSE
Deep-fried vegetables; spring onions, *shiso* leaf, aubergine, *shiitake*, lotus root, red pepper, green asparagus, *myōga* ginger and green pepper

SUNOMONO
Mitsuba moyashiae

SALAD COURSE
Salad of *mitsuba*, bean sprouts, red pepper and *suizenji* laver with *tosazu* dressing

YOUNG SHOOTS MENU # Wakana

SHOKUJI
Sakura gohan
Kōnomono

THE MEAL
Steamed rice with salted cherry blossom and *kinome*
Pickles of *takuan* radish, *nozawana*, and aubergine with *shiso*

KASHI
Hanami dango

DESSERT
Five sweet rice balls, one pure, the rest coloured and flavoured with *ume*, green tea, egg yolk and red *azuki* beans

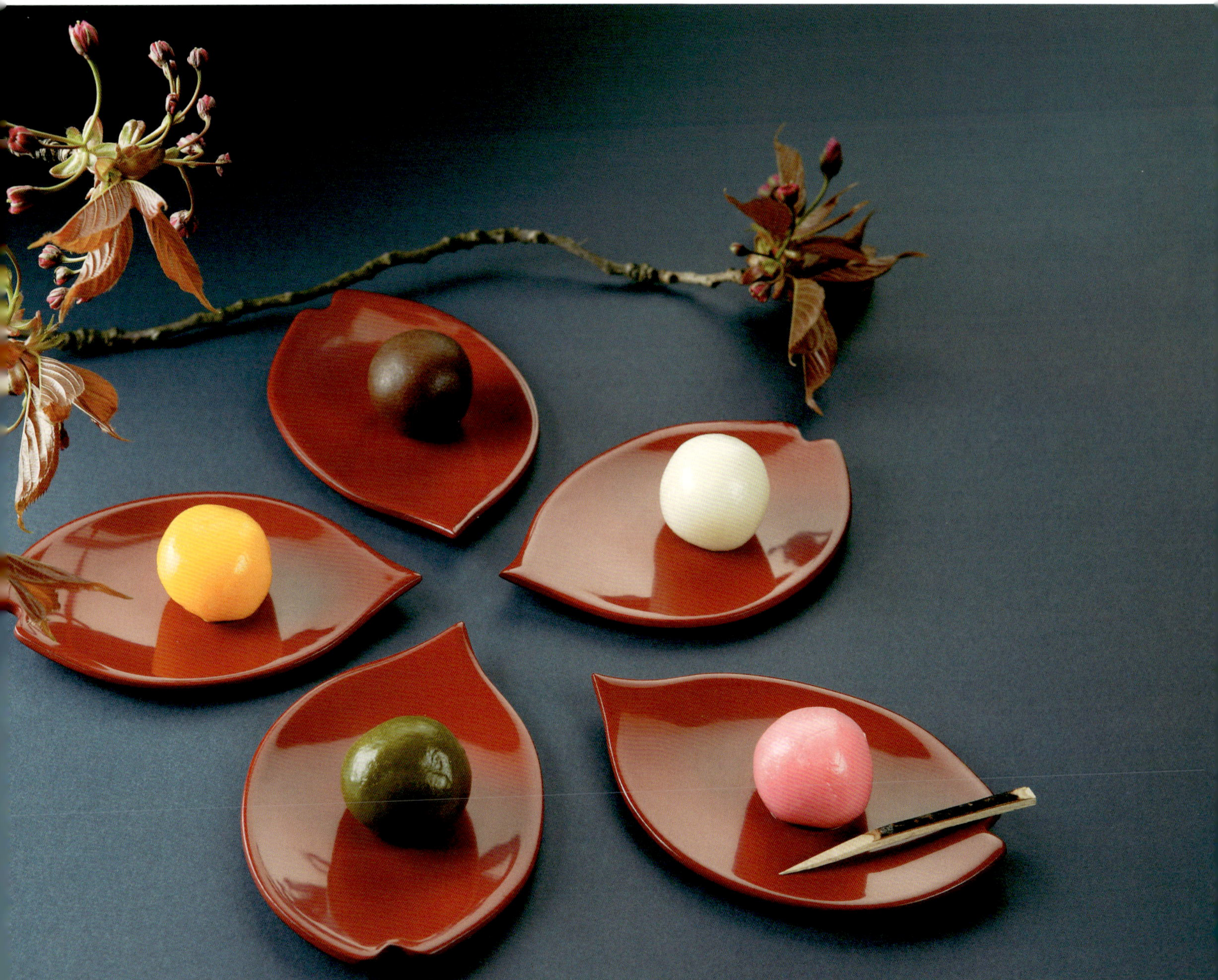

'When I started at the Japanese Traditional Restaurant Tsuruya some four decades ago, we might have served chimaki as a starter and kashiwa mochi as a dessert on Tango no Sekku, but nowadays it has become fashionable to include many more references to festivals in the courses of kaiseki menus. The traditions of the Boys' and Girls' Festivals include many seasonal aspects that go beyond the pleasures aimed at children and we endeavour to present a wide range of Japanese traditions in our dishes.'

— Oshima —

Shoka
Early summer

Officially called Children's Day, *Kodomo no Hi*, this feast is also known as *Tango no Sekku* (Boys' Festival). Children's Day remains a male affair. On that day, warrior dolls with miniature weapons and ritual offerings are displayed, and invariably a flying carp (*koi nobori*) is hoisted outside. For every boy born into the family, the parents attach a paper or cloth carp at the end of a long pole in the garden or to the roof of the house. As the wind fills it out, it swims in the air like a real fish. The carp has traditionally been attributed with high courage and fearlessness. *Samurai* connections are clearly recognisable in the appetizers of the Boys' Day *kaiseki* menu.

The carp is not only a brave fish that swims against the stream, but an old myth has it that the carp turns into a dragon when it comes to the top of the stream. Eastern dragons are water spirits and in China the festival on the fifth day of the fifth month is celebrated as the Dragon Boat Festival, in which the river, dragons, rice and bamboo feature.

The Boys' Festival is also called *Shōbu no Sekku* (Iris Festival). Irises grow along river banks, and the blue variety is much associated with the fifth of the fifth. It is a very straight and strong flower, which was used (along with bamboo) to repel evil spirits. Children still fence with the leaves of the blue iris. The Japanese word for this kind of iris is *shōbu*, which (spelled with different characters) also means 'martial valour'.

Photo: Hisanori Saito

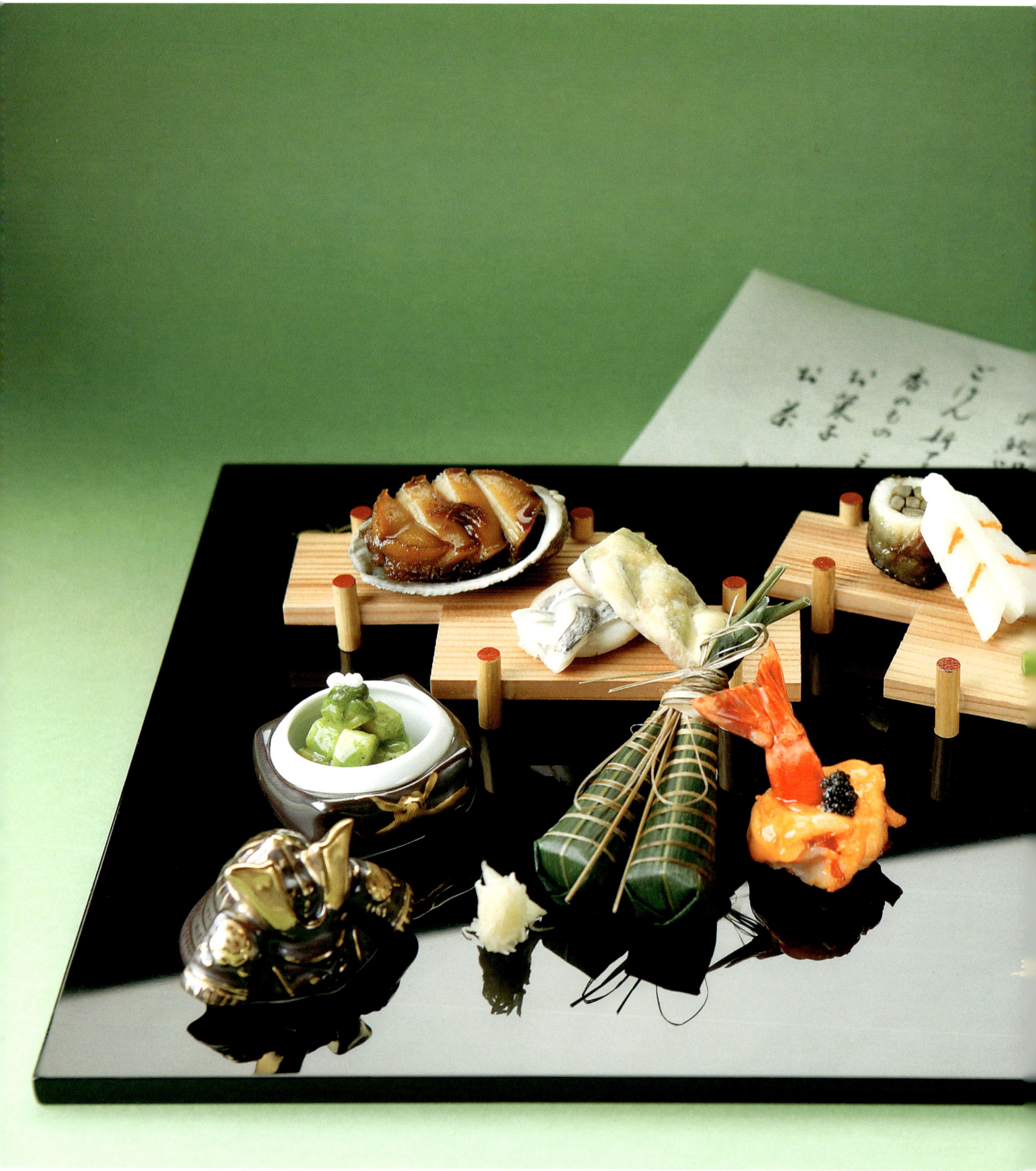

Tango no Sekku

Boys' Festival menu

端午の節句

ZENSAI

Chimakizushi

Takenoko kinomeae
Tokobushi mannenni
Tazunayaki
Unagi yawatamaki

Asupara saikyōzuke
Kabuto ebi

APPETISERS

Brill and crab *sushi* wrapped in bamboo leaf beside sweet ginger
Bamboo shoots with *kinome* sauce
Abalone simmered with ginger
'Braided horse reins' of salt grilled hairtail.
'Bull's eye' of grilled eel around burdock with 'arrow' of yam
Green asparagus marinated in white *miso*
'*Samurai*'s helmet' of prawn in sea-urchin paste with caviar

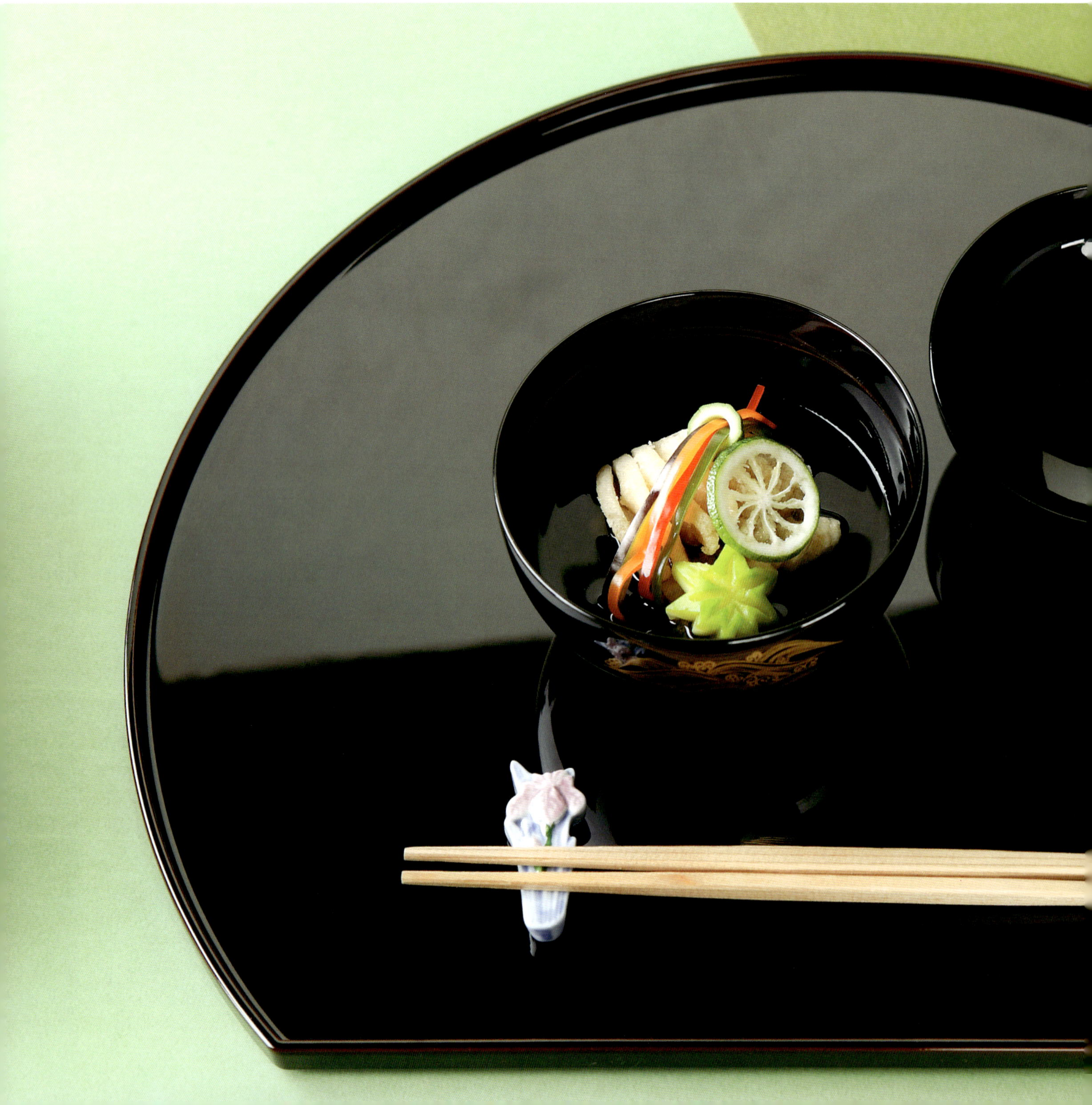

Boys' Festival menu

Tango no Sekku

OWAN | **SOUP**
Koi karaage usukuzujitate | Soup of deep-fried carp with streamer in five colours, maple leaf of courgette and *yuzu* wheel

Boys' Festival menu
Tango no Sekku

TSUKURI   RAW FISH COURSE
Hon maguro, ika, suzuki   Sashimi of blue-fin tuna, rolls of squid with laver and cucumber and sea bass wrapped around chives

YAKIMONO   GRILLED COURSE
Tai sanshōyaki   Grilled sea bream with *sanshō* pepper and 'lance' of *hajikami* ginger

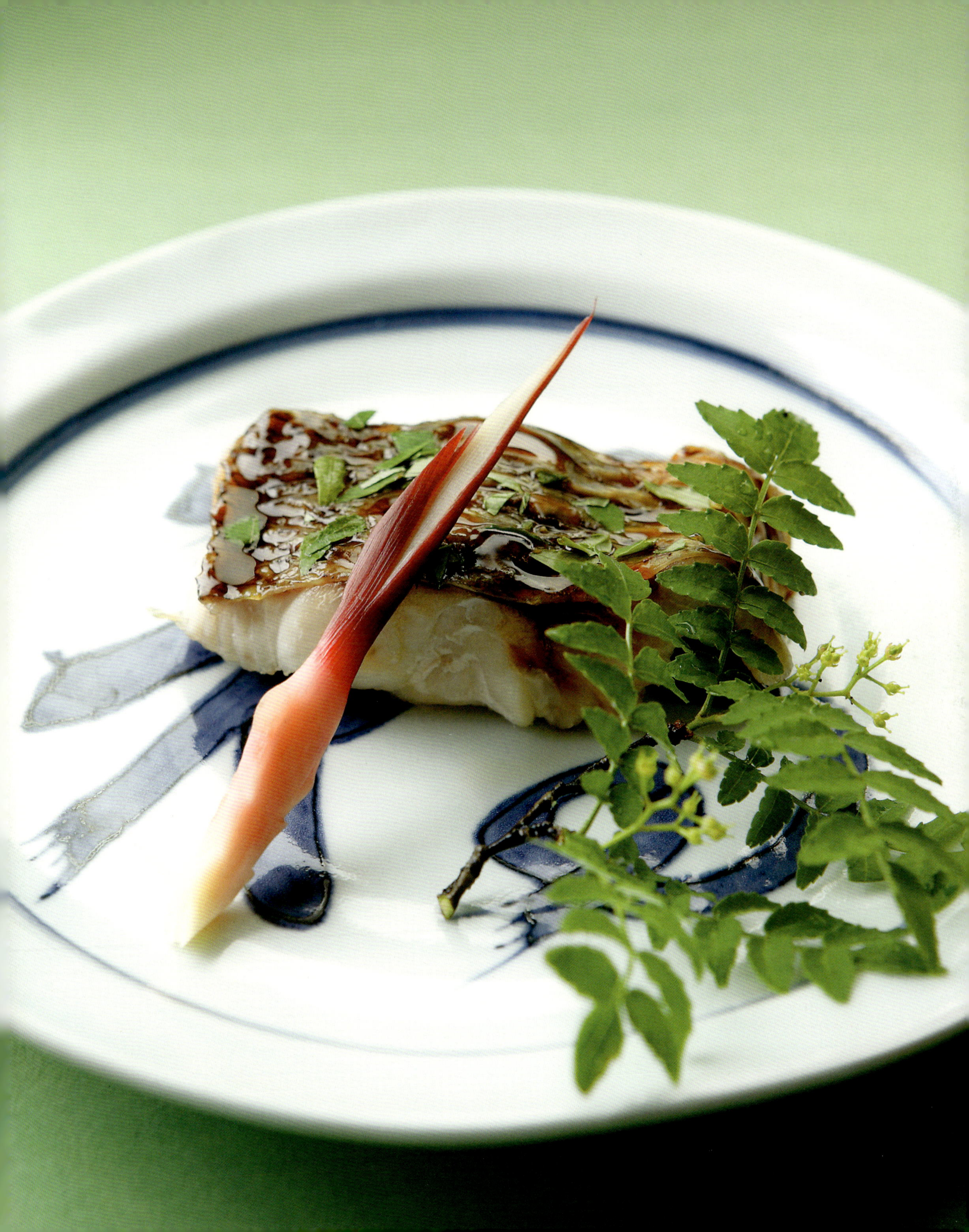

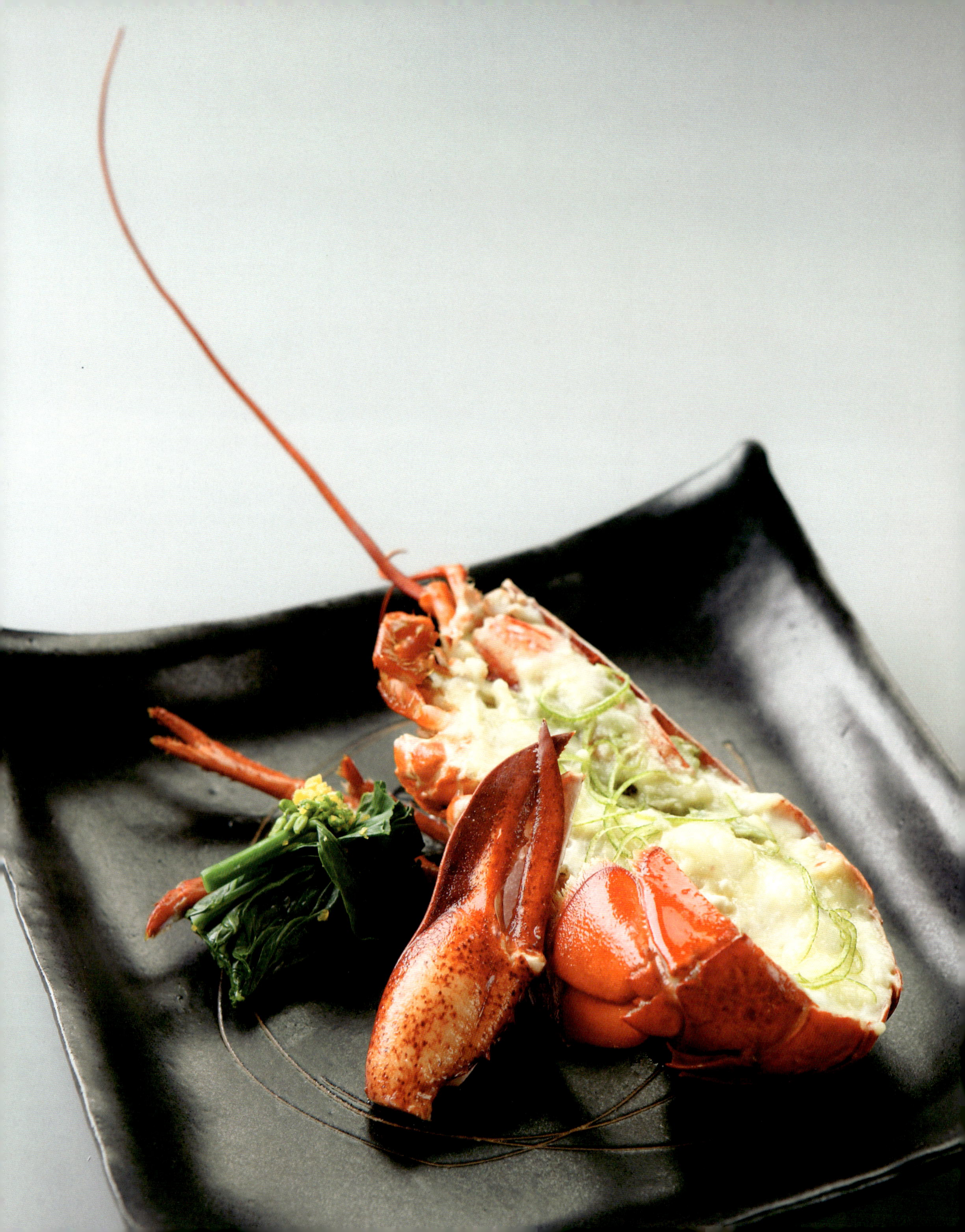

BOYS' FESTIVAL MENU

NIMONO
Saikyō gusokuni

SIMMERED COURSE
Lobster poached in white *miso* sauce, served with rape and egg yolk

SUNOMONO
Katsuo tatakiae

SALAD COURSE
Salad of seared bonito with onion and *ponzu* dressing

BOYS' FESTIVAL MENU
Tango no Sekku

SHOKUJI THE MEAL
Shin asuparagasu gohan Rice with white asparagus.
Kōnomono Salt pickled Cos lettuce with kelp, aubergine and *daikon*

KASHI DESSERT
Kashiwa mochi Rice cake with *azuki* bean paste wrapped in oak leaf

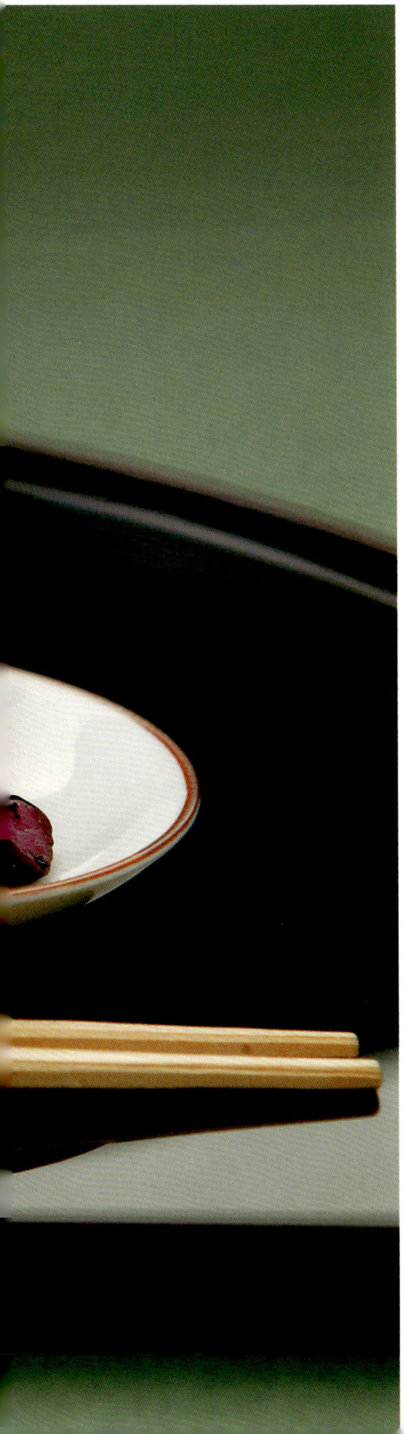
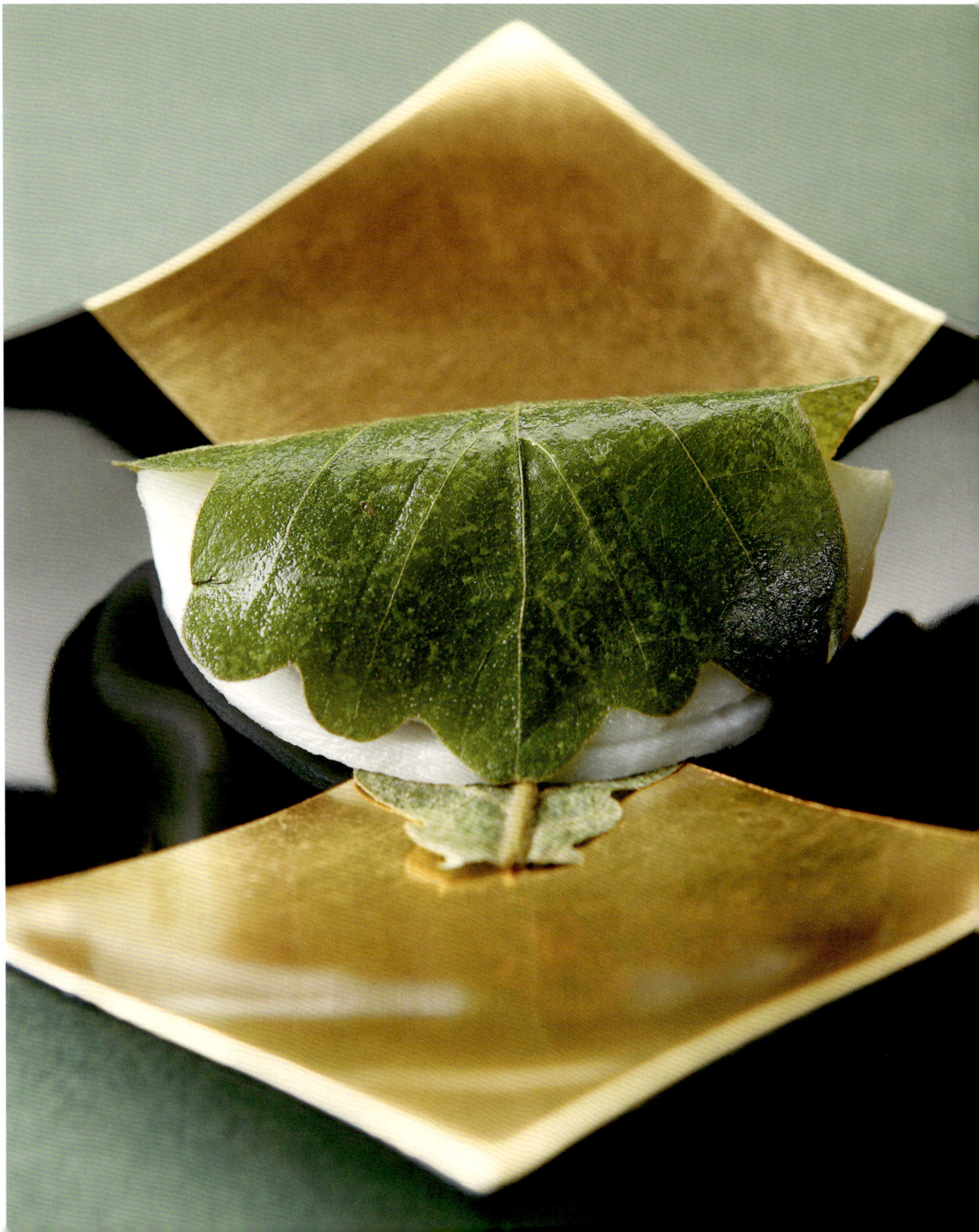

'In many parts of Japan, summer is excruciatingly hot and before modern air-conditioning was invented people were gasping for coolness. Kaiseki dishes are therefore light and refreshing. The presentation of the food and the tableware also reflects relief from the heat. Plates are not heated, but tableware is chilled and has water sprinkled over it. Bamboo is soaked to make it look more refreshing. In the Summer Kaiseki Menu sashimi are presented in a dome of clear ice, which is very different to the warmly insulated igloo of snow we make in winter.'

— Oshima —

Photo: The Tourist Society of Joyo City, Fuk

Natsu
Summer

In the summer *Tanabata* is celebrated – a romantic affair in which some old-fashioned ladies and gentlemen still sit in lines opposite each other and exchange poems that they write on the spot. There are many local customs connected to *Tanabata*, but very few hold throughout the whole country. *Origami* birds often feature, as do colourful ribbons. Children hang these cheerful decorations on a bamboo stick outside the house, together with poems and wishes. After *Tanabata* everything is thrown into the river.

The official festival is based on an old myth about Orihime who wove beautiful cloth for her father the emperor god to wear (in Chinese mythology she is a spinster). She was very successful in her work, but wanted to marry. Her father chose Hikoboshi as a husband for her, a shepherd, who might not seem the ideal party for such a lady, but the simple man would at least not interfere with her work. Daddy's plan did not work, however, since the couple fell very much in love and the shepherd did interfere with her work – all manner of coarse cloth was the result. The chief god was furious and cast the two to opposite sides of the Milky Way, where they still stand as stars. Once a year however, on the seventh night of the seventh month the lovers are joined by a temporary bridge of magpies. The name *Tanabata* means 'loom in storage,' obviously referring to the fact that the girl is not at work. Since the adoption of the Gregorian calendar *Tanabata* is celebrated on July 7th, but previously it was closely linked to the *Obon* festival, which is nowadays usually celebrated in mid August.

Obon is the Japanese version of All Souls, on which the spirits of the ancestors return to Earth. Many people return home for the occasion and tend the graves of their dead relatives, which are decorated with flowers, lanterns and the favourite foods of the dead. Sometimes packets of cigarettes are placed on graves. During the period that the ghosts are on Earth, dances are held (*Bon odori*). These can be traditional or modern. On the departure of the spirits, paper boats containing candles are placed in the river to flow downstream and accompany the spirits back home. Now summer has ended.

Departure of the spirits

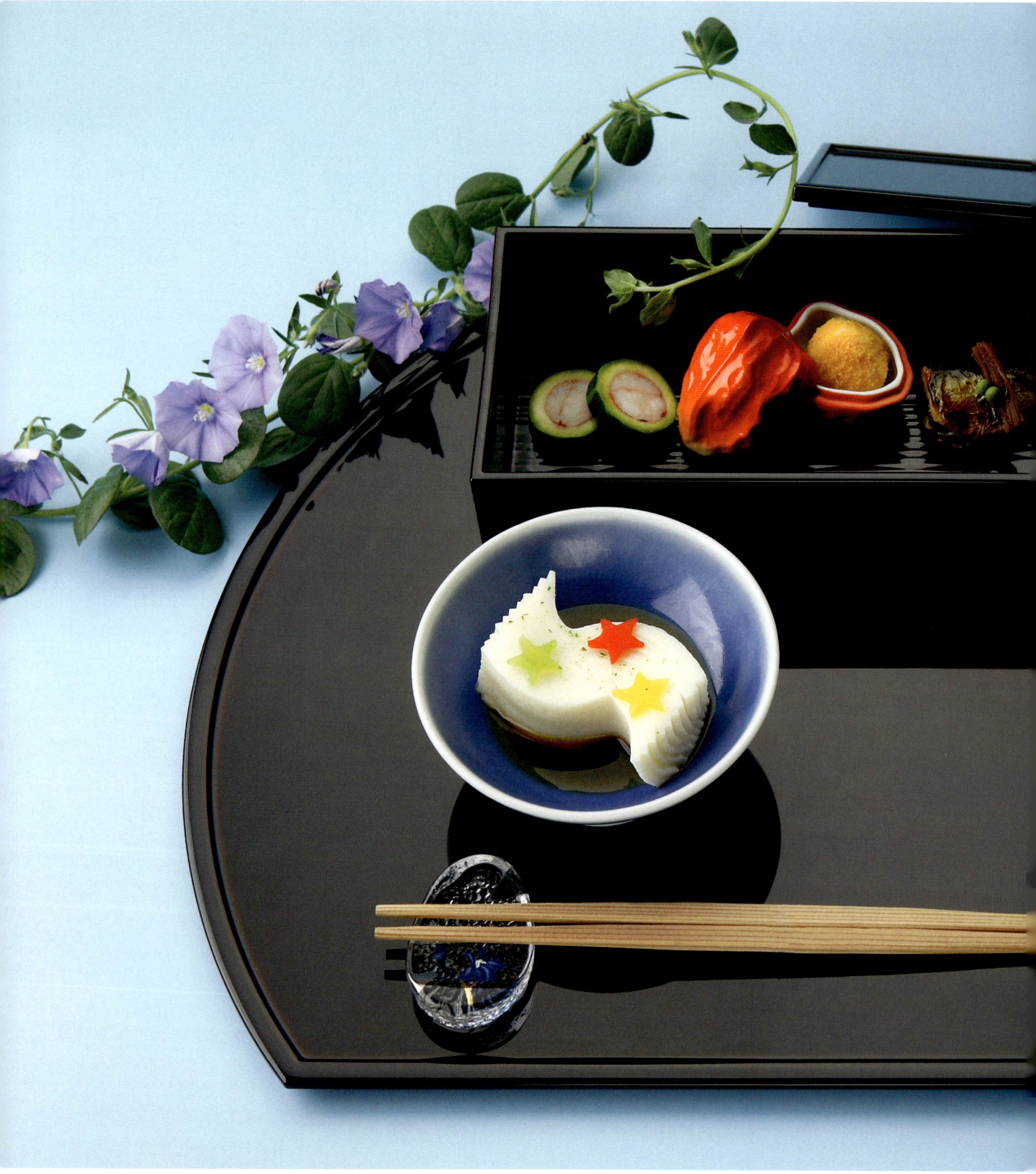

Tanabata

Kaiseki summer menu

ZENSAI
Shirouri kobujime

Hōzuki

Iwashi mannenni
Unagi bōzushi
Takigawadōfu

OWAN
Himeji kuzuuchi

APPETISERS

White *uri* melon marinated between layers of kelp and filled with crab
'Lantern fruit' of minced shrimp sprinkled with dried roe of grey mullet
Sardines simmered with ginger
Sushi of grilled eel with *myōga* ginger
Milky Way of *tōfu* with 'stars' of pepper in *dashi*

SOUP

Soup with red mullet, wax gourd, burdock and *umeboshi* paste

七夕

Kaiseki summer menu
Tanabata

TSUKURI
Himuromori

RAW FISH COURSE
Dome of ice containing *sashimi* of lobster, tuna that has been briefly cooked by pouring over hot water and squid

YAKIMONO
Fukko sugiitayaki

GRILLED COURSE
Grilled sea bass, *shiitake* and green pepper wrapped in sheet of cedar wood with *hajikami* ginger and sweet potato, ahead of season

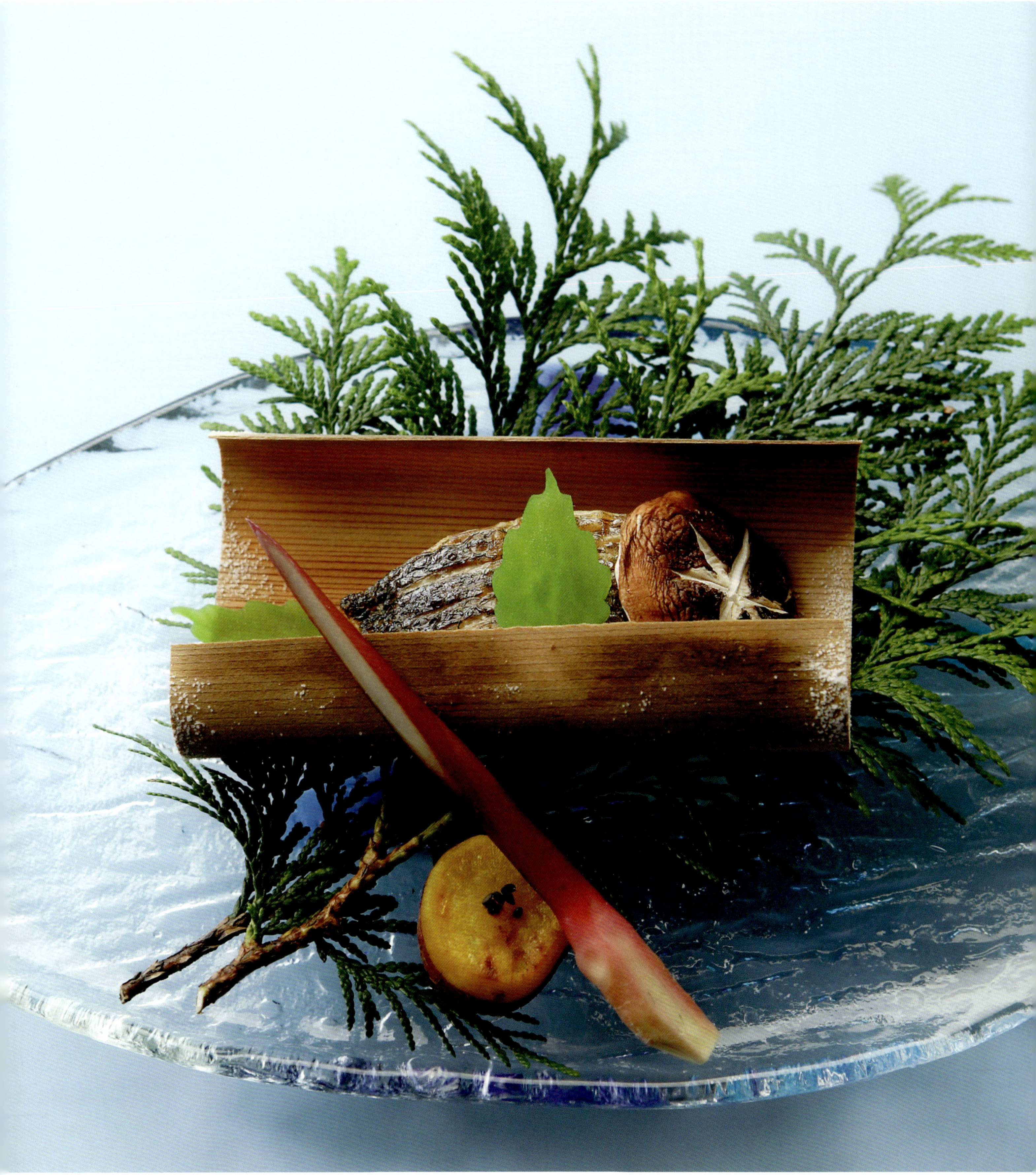

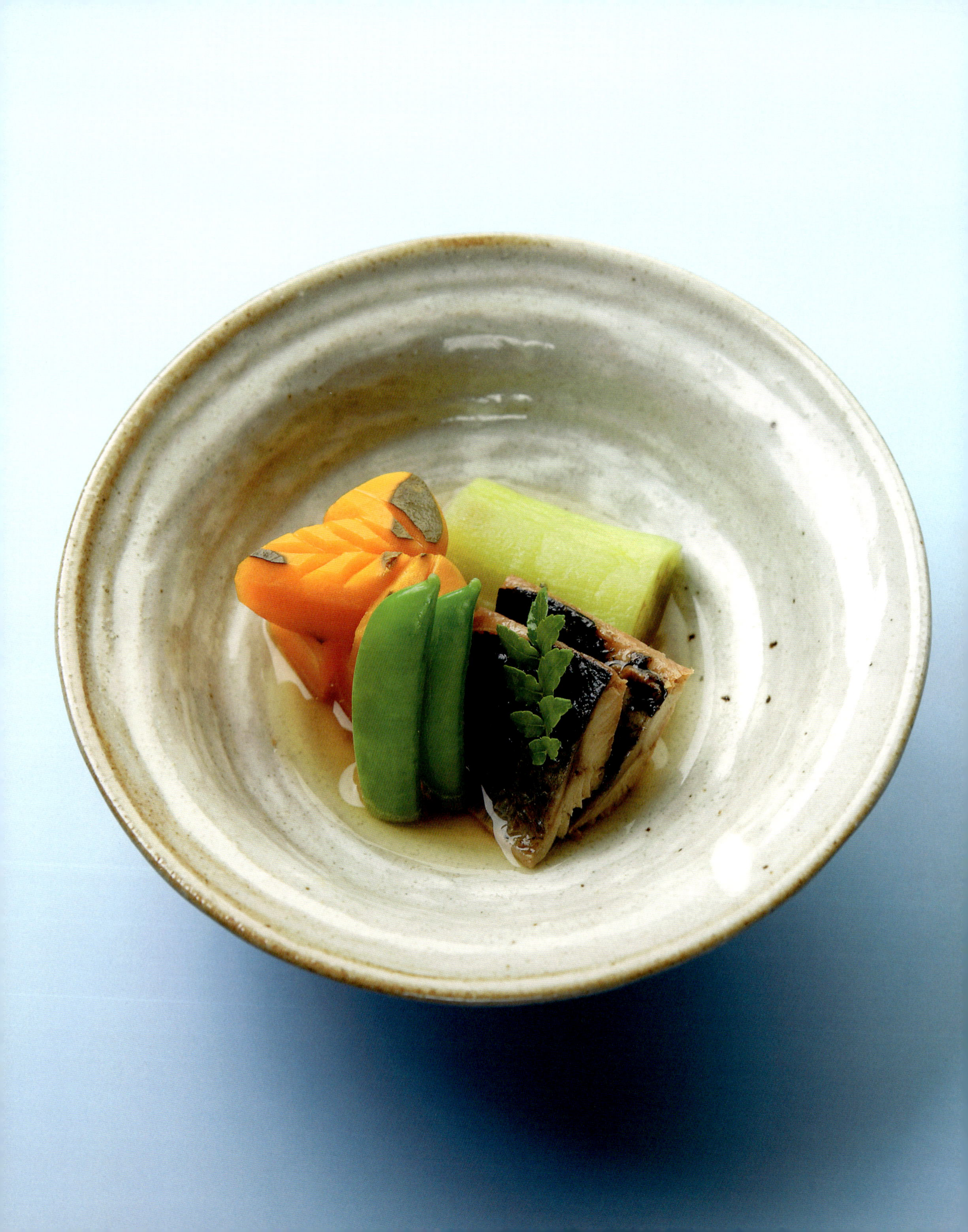

KAISEKI SUMMER MENU

Tanabata

NIMONO
Takiawase

SUNOMONO
Aji kinutamaki

SIMMERED COURSE
Jade-coloured aubergine, roasted and peeled, dried herring, pumpkin, sugar snaps and *kinome*

SALAD COURSE
Rolls of *daikon* and seaweed filled with red pepper, omelette with *kimizu* dressing (of egg yolk and vinegar), salted cucumber, radish and a sprinkling of bonito flakes

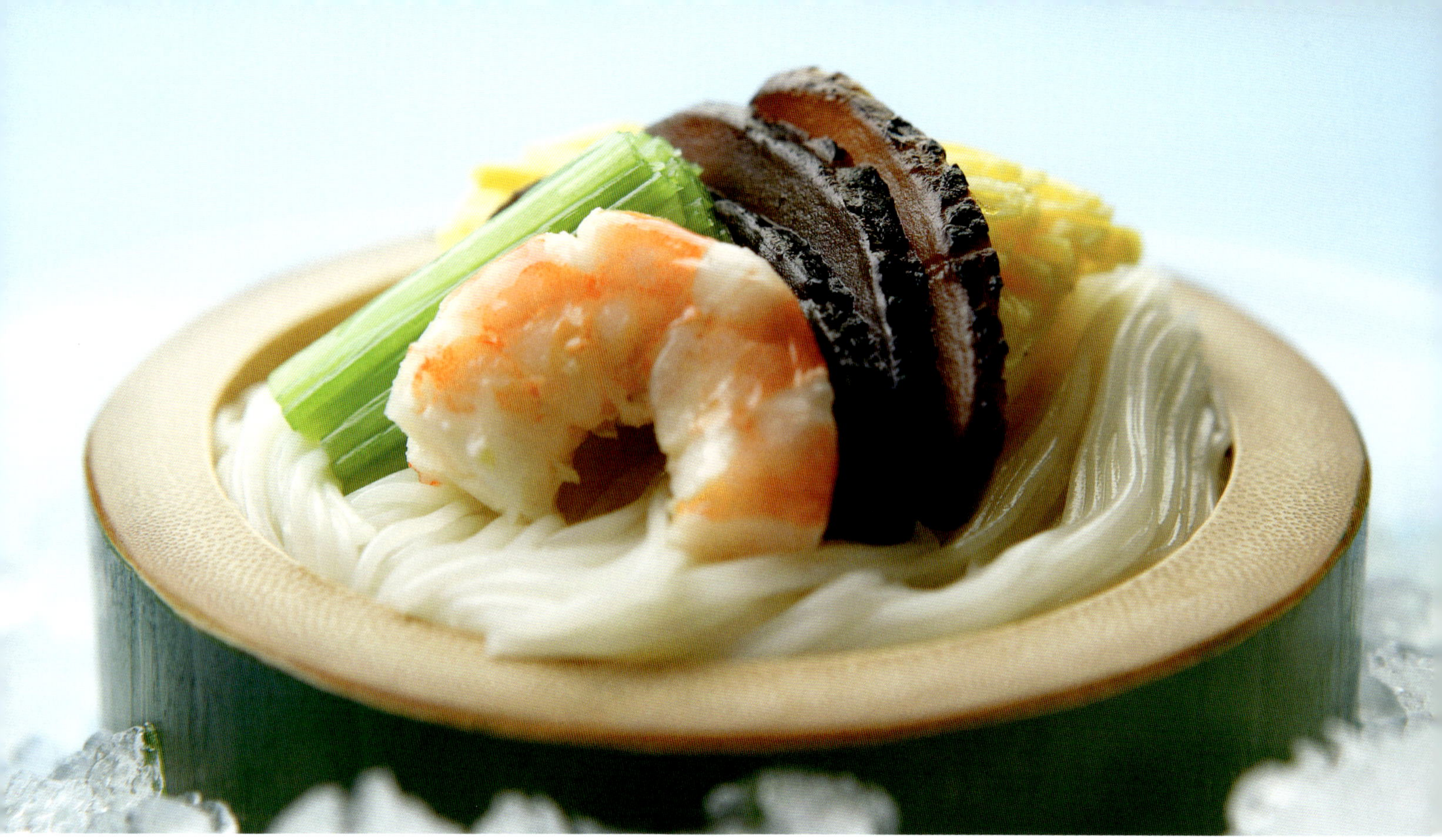

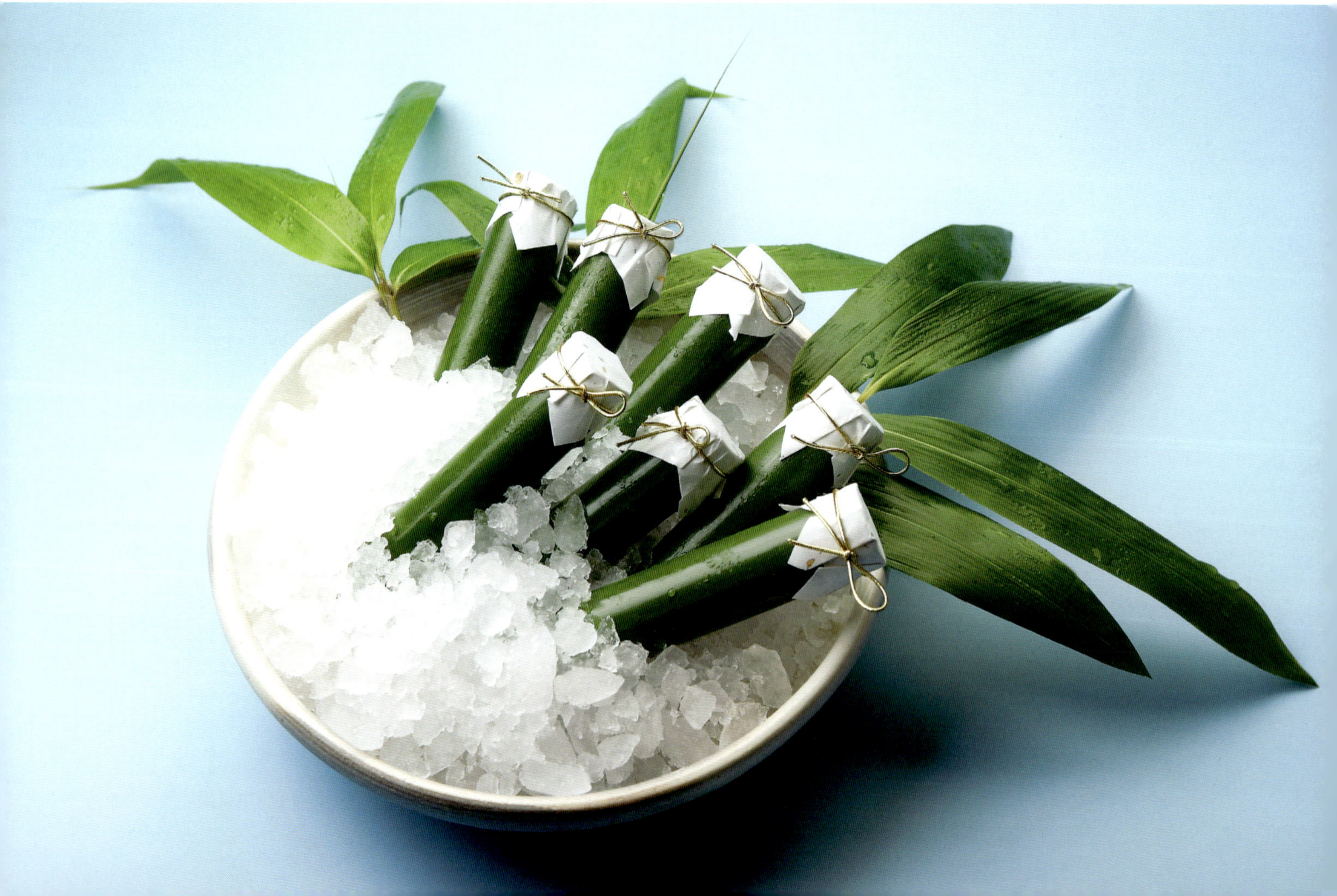

SHOKUJI
Aodake sōmen

KASHI
Mizu yōkan

Tanabata
KAISEKI SUMMER MENU

THE MEAL
Chilled *sōmen* noodles served in bamboo on ice, with pink shrimp, dried and sweetened *shiitake*, *mitsuba* stems, brocade of omelette and grated ginger

DESSERT
Bamboo with light watery jelly of *azuki* bean paste *(an)*

'Fall is marked by the brilliant colours of the autumn leaves. Especially the red, yellow and golden colours of the maple are much appreciated. Autumn brings many nuts like chestnuts and fruits, such as the popular kaki, *as well as many types of mushrooms, among which is the* matsutake, *an unchallenged delicacy. Because many foods are at their best in this season – such as mackerel, salmon, brill, tuna, turnip, pumpkin and aubergine – autumn is also known as* mikaku no aki: *the season of the memorable taste.'*

— Oshima —

Aki
Autumn

The official *sekku* on the ninth day of the ninth month is *Kiku no Sekku*, the Chrysanthemum Festival, also known as *Chōyō no Sekku*. It is hardly celebrated anymore, but used to include an elegant ritual: on the previous night blooming chrysanthemum flowers were covered with silk fluff, which was removed the next morning when the morning dew – subtly scented by the touch of the flower – had been drawn into the silk. Washing oneself with this dew would procure a long life. Nowadays horticultural events, in which the chrysanthemum plays a central role, are still held around this period.

More important in autumn is the feast of moon viewing, *tsukimi*, on the fifteenth night of the eighth month in the moon calendar, nowadays celebrated somewhere in the beginning of September. Even though *tsukimi* (moon viewing) is not as popular as the *hanami* (cherry blossom viewing) in spring, many people still gather under the clear autumn sky to drink *sake*, make music (especially on the bamboo flute) and stare at the mesmerising beauty of the moon. As opposed to the Europeans, who recognize a face in the patterns of the moon, East-Asians see a rabbit and the Japanese note that this rabbit holds a large pestle in his paws, such as the Japanese use for pounding steamed rice into sticky *mochi* dough. Thus the Japanese see 'a rabbit making *mochi*' in the moon.

Poets claim that the magnificence of the moon is so great that it can best be observed when a little cloud passes in front, or from behind a bush of pampas grass and bush clover (both closely connected to the feast), so as to avoid exposure to a splendour that would be too overwhelming.

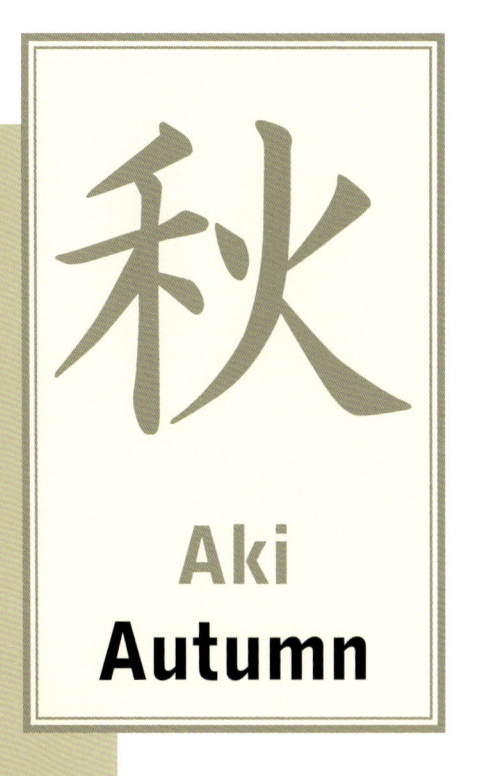

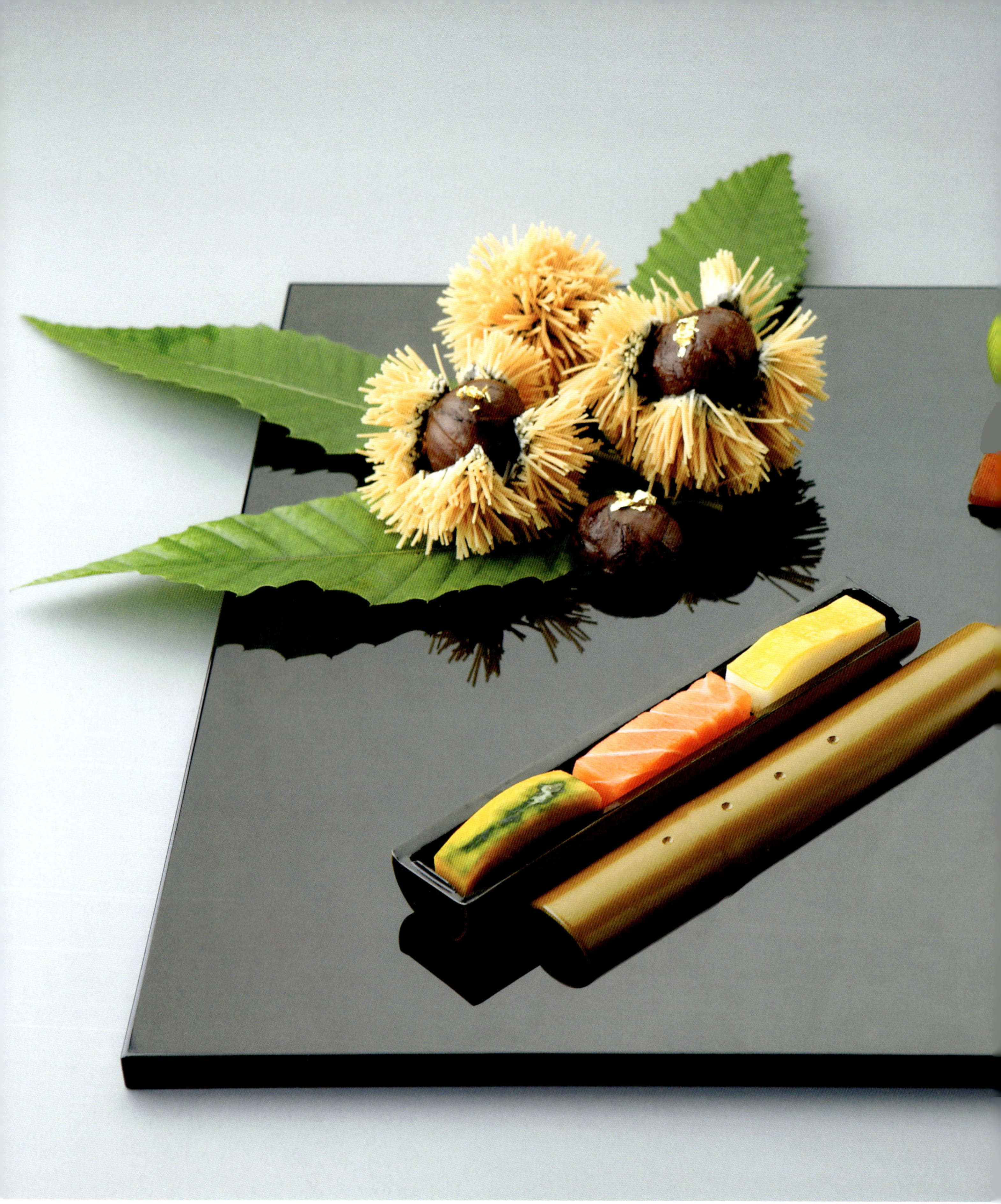

Momijitsuki

TINGED AUTUMN LEAVES MENU

紅葉月

ZENSAI
Igakuri shibukawani

Shimeji shiraae

Karasumi daikon
Hirame kikukazushi
Yokobue sanshokumori

APPETISERS
Sweet brown chestnuts in shell of shrimp paste and *somen* noodles
Garland of chrysanthemum leafs with *shimeji* mushroom in dressing of *tōfu* and white sesame
Cured roe of grey mullet with *daikon*
'White chrysanthemum' *sushi* of brill
Grilled squid with egg yolk, salmon pressed between kelp, and *ebisu kabocha* in bamboo flute

TINGED AUTUMN LEAVES MENU
Momijitsuki

OWAN　　　　　　　　　　　　SOUP
Dobin mushi　　　　　　　　　Clear soup of shrimp, *matsutake* mushrooms, ginkgo nuts and *yuzu* served in a small teapot

TSUKURI　　　　　　　　　　RAW FISH COURSE
Suzuki, toro, hamachi　　　　Thinly sliced sea bass, fatty tuna and yellowtail

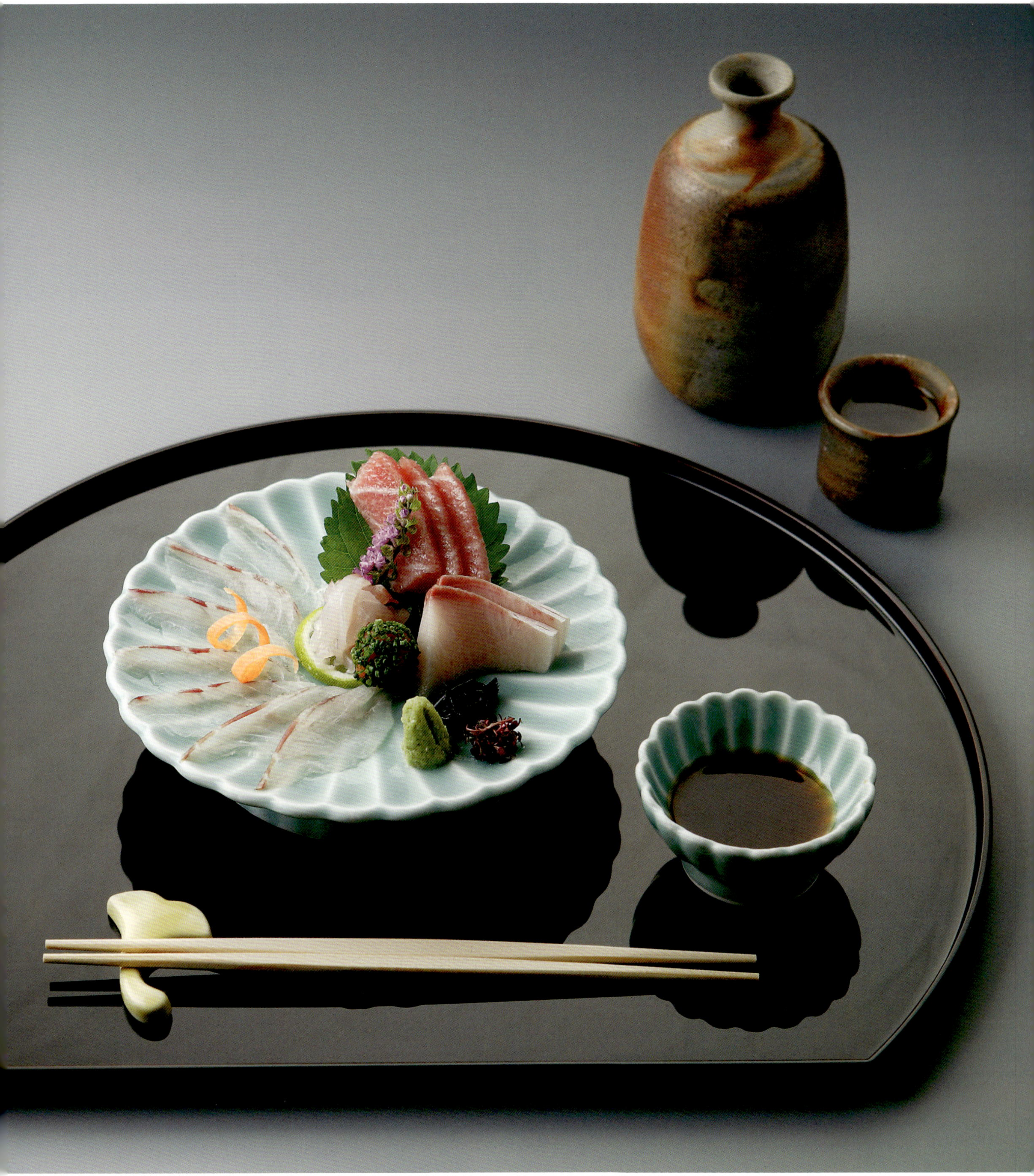

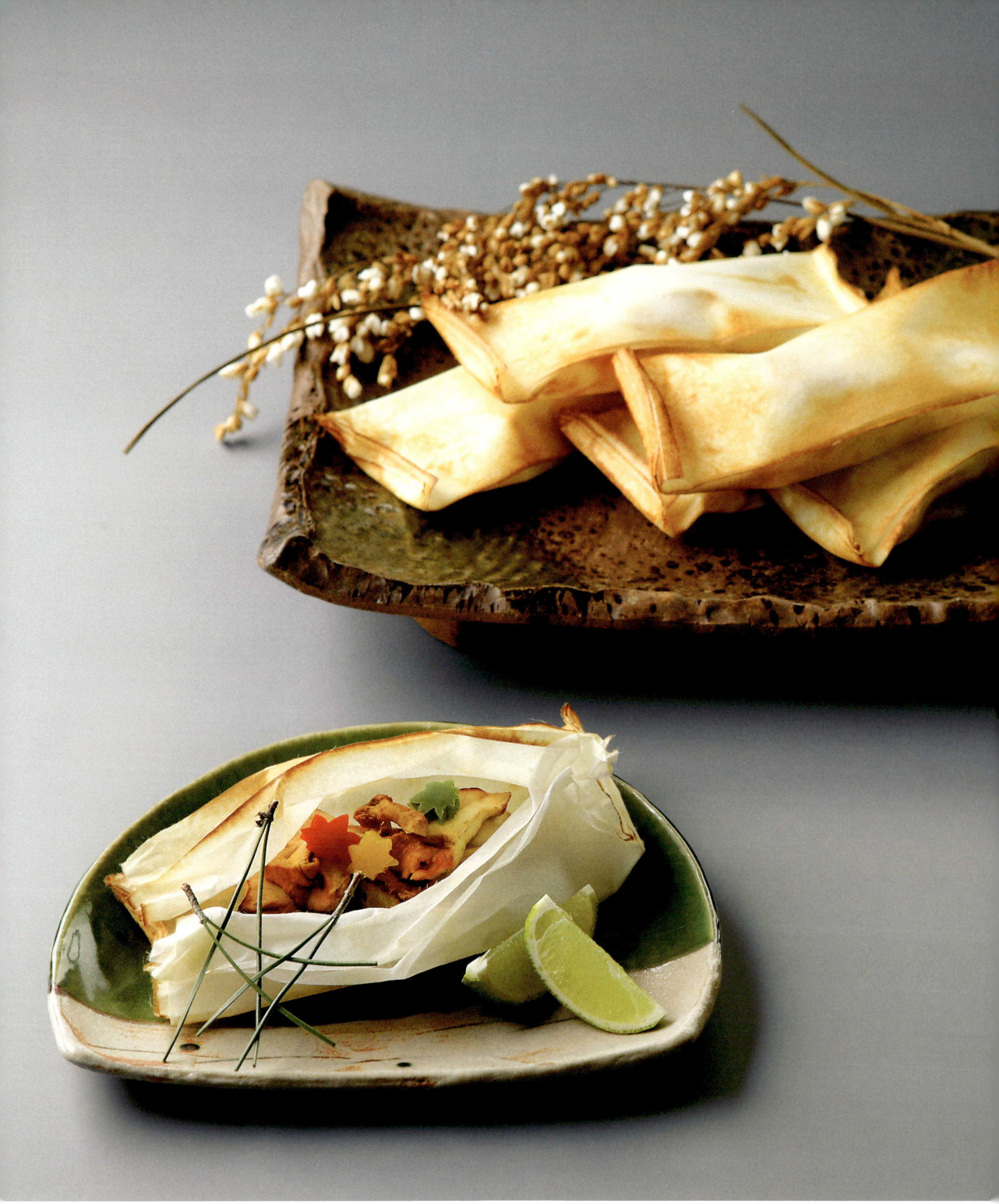

Momijitsuki

TINGED AUTUMN LEAVES MENU

YAKIMONO
Sawara hōshoyaki

NIMONO
Kikuka kabu

GRILLED COURSE
Spanish mackerel, chanterelles, red and green pepper wrapped and roasted in Japanese handmade paper

SIMMERED COURSE
Steamed 'chrysanthemum' cut from turnip, stuffed with lobster and served with a thick sauce of yellow chrysanthemum flower petals

TINGED AUTUMN LEAVES MENU
Momijitsuki

SUNOMONO
Kaki namasu

SALAD COURSE
Julienne of carrot, *daikon* and *kaki*

SHIIZAKANA
Kamonasu ishiyaki

CHEF'S SPECIAL
Hida brazier with grilled aubergine stuffed with duck, quail, *shishitō* pepper, *shiitake*, topped with *miso* sauce

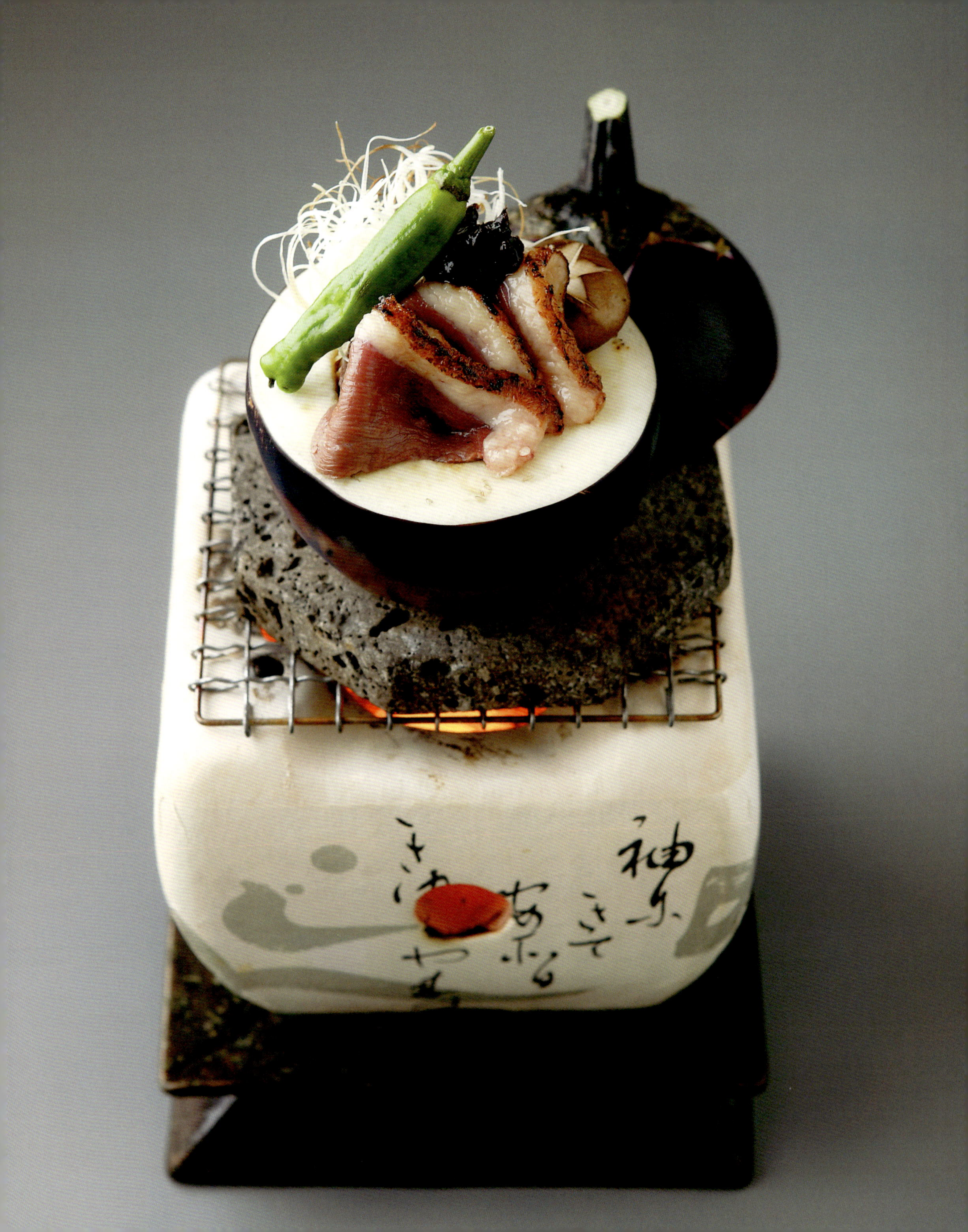

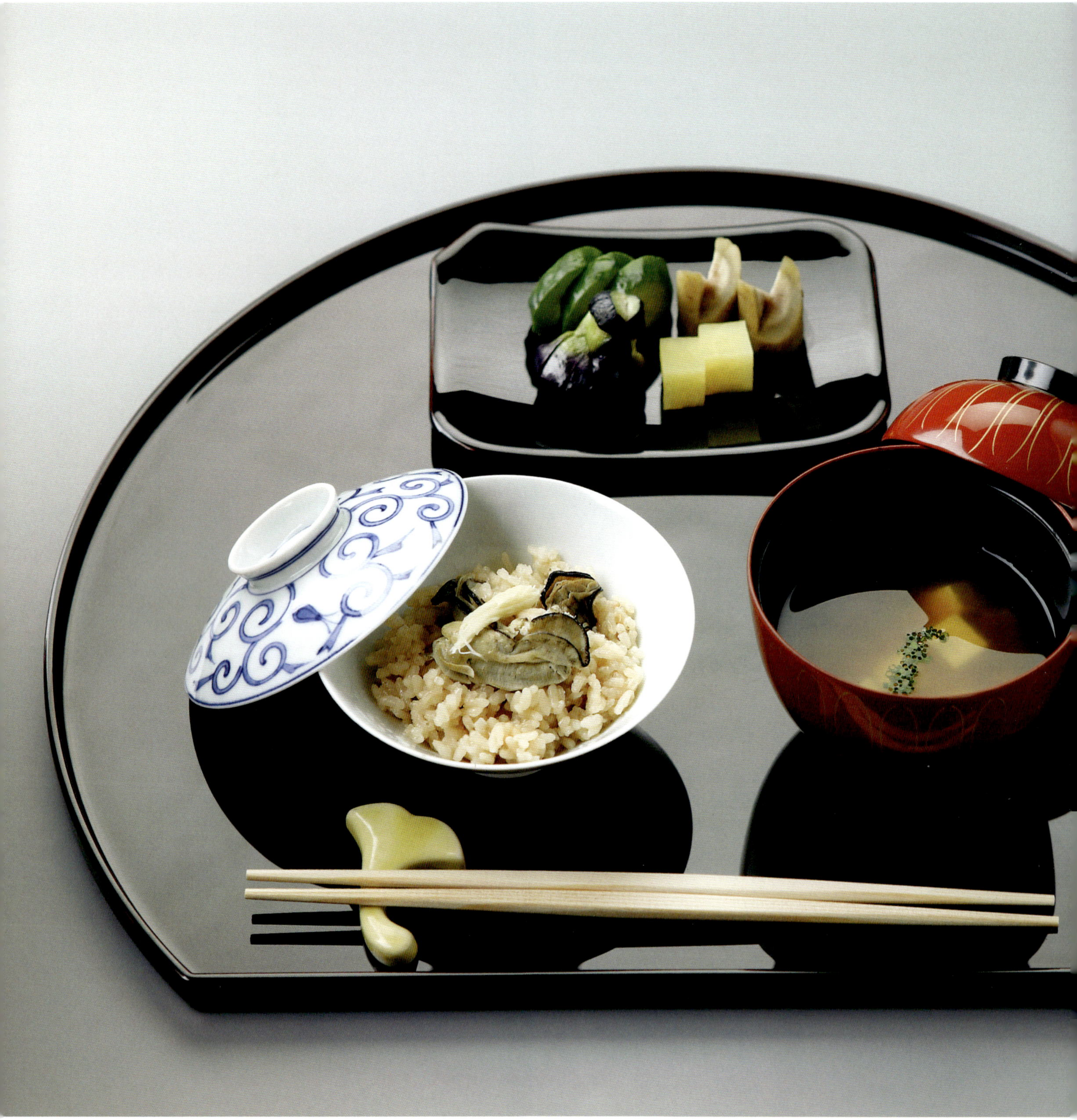

Momijitsuki
TINGED AUTUMN LEAVES MENU

TOMEWAN — END SOUP
Misojitate — Miso soup with slippery *nameko* mushrooms and *tōfu*

SHOKUJI — THE MEAL
Kaki gohan — Rice with Zeeland oysters flavoured with soy sauce, *sake* and ginger
Kōnomono — Pickles of aubergine, burdock, cucumber and *takuan*

KASHI — DESSERT
Tamago sōmen — Strands of egg yolk cooked in syrup

寿司

Sushi

Sushi are among the most popular Japanese foods, both in and outside Japan. *Sushi* consist of rice that has been flavoured with sugar, salt and vinegar. Some *sushi* are made of rice and other ingredients wrapped in a cone of *nori* seaweed; others are shaped into rolls of seaweed and cut in slices.

Nigirizushi consist of little loaves of pressed rice, topped with a delicacy such as raw tuna, mackerel, shrimp, sea urchins, grilled eel, omelette. A little *wasabi* is spread on each piece.

Originating in casual street stalls, *sushi* can be eaten by hand. They are merely dipped in a sauce comprising soy sauce with *wasabi*. In restaurants, however, and generally when one wants to keep the fingers clean, chopsticks are used.

The eating of *nigirizushi* requires some skill. Care is taken to dip the topping in the sauce and not the rice, which might fall apart in the liquid. The hand is turned with the palm upward and thus the *sushi* is taken between thumb and index finger. The *sushi* are turned upside down, while the fingers keep the topping from falling off, and thus the fish can be dipped in the sauce. With chopsticks this procedure of turning the *sushi* can be more of a challenge, unless the topping is tied to the rice with a ribbon of *nori*, which is often done for convenience.

Sushi

There are many local variations of *sushi* and new ones are being invented constantly. The California roll, containing crab, cucumber, mayonnaise and avocado, originated in the USA, as the name indicates, but is popular also in Japan.

All types of *sushi* have in common that they are made of vinegary rice, and raw fish is the most common topping, but this is not how *sushi* originated. The rice used to be sour because it was fermented, and the fish was not always fresh either. Originally it too was fermented. *Narezushi*, a forerunner of modern *sushi*, was made (beginning in about the 8th century) by keeping freshwater fish weighted down in boiled rice and salt water for several months. The rice turned brown and was discarded, but it preserved the fish and gave it a sour flavour and a strong cheesy smell.

As time passed fermentation was modified. By the 15th century *nama nare* appeared; 'raw' *narezushi*. The rice was no longer discarded, but fermented for 'only' three to ten days, which still gave it a sour flavour. By the 18th century rice was no longer fermented at all, but vinegar was added to make it sour. These were called 'quick sushi', *hayazushi*.

Sushi

In the 19th century many types of *sushi* appeared that we still know today. *Sushi* rolled in *nori* seaweed, *norimakizushi*, were first made in this period, as were *inarizushi*, parcels of deep fried *tōfu* stuffed with sour rice. These *sushi* are called after the household and rice god Inari, who used foxes as his messengers. Foxes are reputedly fond of deep fried *tōfu*. *Nigirizushi*, mentioned earlier, are from the early 19th century.

In the course of the last 200 years *sushi* have become ever more popular, initially within Japan and in the last few decades also abroad. As refrigeration techniques improved and transport became faster, the fish no longer had to be preserved in soy sauce and could be sold raw and fresh at any location. *Sushi* became the national dish of Japan. Speed is essential with *sushi*. They are nearly always made on the spot, at the customer's request, though nowadays they sometimes also appear in fast-food restaurants on high-tech conveyor belts.

鉄板焼

Teppanyaki

The word *teppanyaki* means 'grilled on a griddle.' Meat, shellfish and vegetables are fried on a hot metal plate directly before the customers' eyes. The origins of *teppanyaki* go back to the time of the American occupation (1945-1952). The invention of this new dining style is officially claimed by Mr Fujioka, owner of Misono restaurant in Kobe. His little restaurant made *okonomiyaki* – wheat pancakes with shredded cabbage and diced seafood fried on a griddle.

Okonomiyaki derive from *monjayaki*, a 19th century play-food for children. They would write Japanese characters with a batter of water and wheat flour on a hot griddle, then eat the snack. After the Tokyo earthquake of 1923, restaurants serving *okonomiyaki* pancakes were thriving. At these times of severe food shortages, *okonomiyaki*, which means 'fry it as you please', implied rather 'fry whatever is available'. The restaurants were also called *issen yōshoku*, 'Western food for a penny,' because European ingredients like cabbage were included, and because bottles of Worcestershire sauce stood on the tables.

Despite the supposedly Western overtones, the American soldiers who frequented the restaurant were not very impressed by the absence of meat, so Fujioka bought beef on the black market and fried it on his griddle. At first the meat was thinly sliced, as for *sukiyaki*, but later, upon customers' request, he also tossed thicker chunks onto the hot plate. His business did well. Fujioka improved his style and aimed more at a Japanese public. In 1960 he opened a fashionable *teppanyaki* restaurant in the centre of Tokyo, which became a

TEPPANYAKI

Teppanyaki

big hype with television stars and other celebrities. All kinds of food, including live shrimps, were baked on a griddle before the guests. Soon even grand international hotels, like the Okura, also began to offer *teppanyaki* griddles for their foreign guests. The Yamazato restaurant at the Amsterdam Okura already had such tables in the mid 1970s, before it opened the specialized *teppanyaki* restaurant Sazanka in 1978.

The popularization of *teppanyaki* outside Japan, however, would probably not have taken place in such a swift tempo without the American *teppanyaki* restaurant chain, Benihana of Tokyo. The first restaurant opened in West Side Manhattan in New York City, in 1964. Within two decades, the formula had been imitated all over the world, including in Japan. The style of serving is a long way from *kaiseki ryōri*, with all its restraint. Vegetables, fish, shell fish, chicken and meat were chopped, sliced and tossed with amazing dexterity, but flashy knife-swinging and pepper-mill-juggling chefs mostly provided entertainment. However, the same attention is paid to the quality of the ingredients and to not over cooking them as in Japanese *haute cuisine*. With its typically Japanese concern for quality, *teppanyaki* has surprised many. An American, Italian and a Frenchman may all have very different ideas of how the perfect beef steak should be, but when they try the succulent cubes that come from the *teppanyaki* table, they all agree it comes pretty close to an international standard of perfection. As Oshima himself puts it: '*Teppanyaki* is a first introduction to Japanese cuisine.'

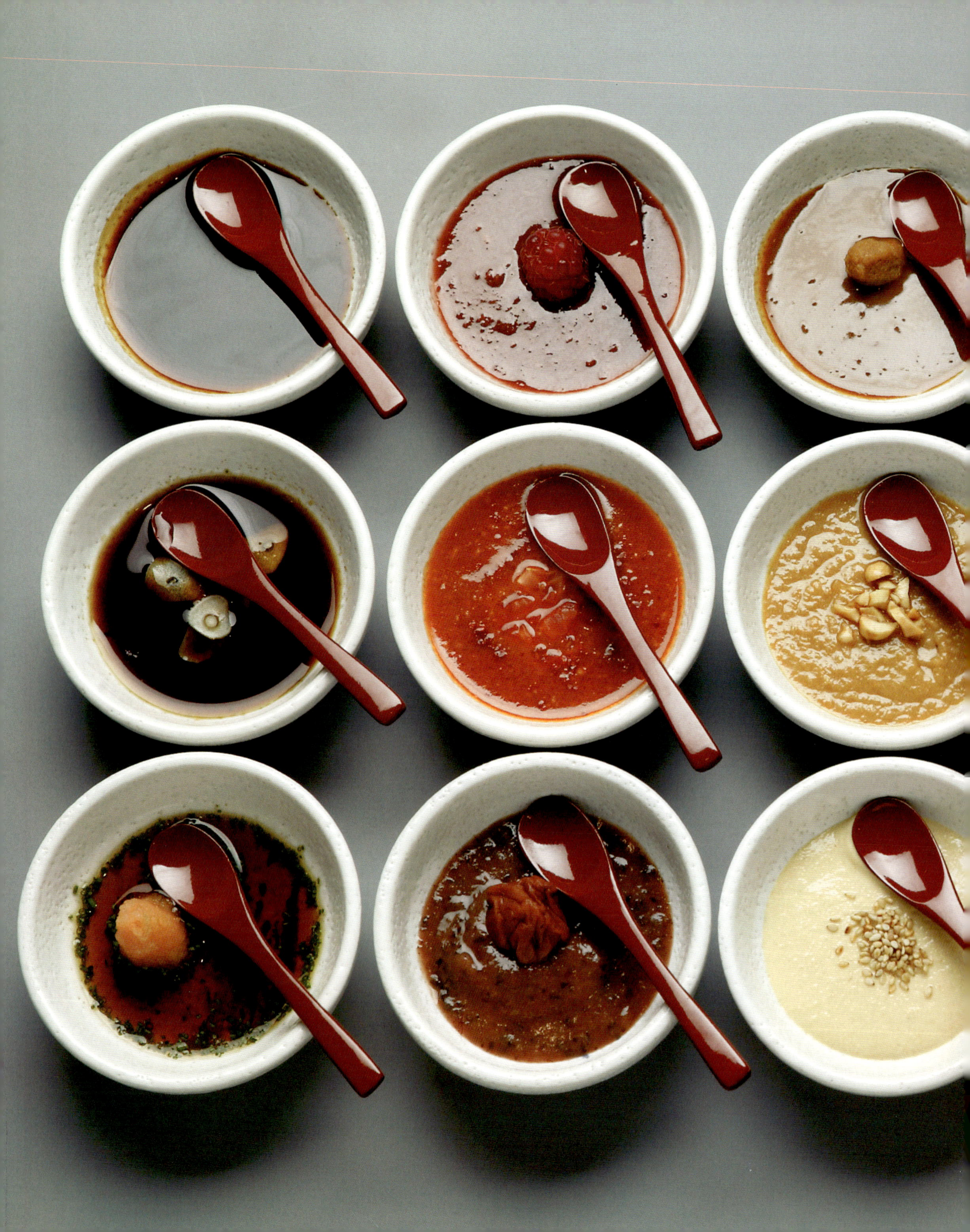

Sauces for *teppanyaki* form left to right:

Teriyaki sauce

Raspberry sauce

Red *miso* sauce

Mustard-remoulade sauce

Wasabi-remoulade sauce

Garlic sauce

Chilli-tomato sauce

Peanut sauce

Pickles remoulade sauce

Green pepper sauce

Soya vinaigrette

Umeboshi sauce

White sesame sauce

Lemon butter sauce

Ravigotte sauce

鰻

Unagi

Eel

Kabayaki is a Japanese favourite way of preparing eel that few people in Europe can prepare as well as Oshima. The name comes from *kaba*, which is the cigar shaped plume of rush, so often seen along the shores of Dutch lakes and ditches. In the olden days eels were skewered in the length, without filleting, and seemed to resemble these cigars after being grilled in a dark brown sauce. Nowadays there are two main ways of preparing eel *kabayaki*: Osaka style and Tokyo style. Oshima performs the latter. In both cases the eel is filleted alive, but in Osaka the fish is opened along the belly, as they do in Holland, and in Tokyo along the back, which leaves the fillets with the soft white belly in the middle. In Osaka eels are skewered on long metal rods, in Tokyo on short bamboo ones.

Then they are grilled 'white' (i.e. without sauce), *shirayaki*, on very hot *binchō* charcoal, which is made from oak wood, but smokeless. The eel is cooked and the fat comes out.

In Tokyo style the eels are now washed in cold water to make them more resilient and to rinse off excessive fat. Then the fish is steamed, which makes it softer and more succulent. This stage is skipped in Osaka.

In all cases the eel is then dipped in *kabayaki* sauce, which consist of *mirin*, reduced to half and then mixed with *tamari* soy sauce and some glucose syrup. Roasted eel bones and an eel head are also added. The sauce is ones again brought to the boil and strained. The sauce can be kept for a long time. The one in the Hotel Okura Amsterdam dates back to 1971. Reduced *mirin* and soy sauce are regularly added and a few times per year the sauce is sterilised by setting it on fire with burning *sake* and bringing it briefly to the boil.

Now the eel is grilled again, but this time the heat of the fire is reduced by removing some of the charcoal, to avoid burning the sauce. When the eel is cooked and glazed the

Eel *Unagi*

skewers are removed and the eel is served. This may seem a simple recipe, but Oshima assures us that it takes nine years to learn how to fillet an eel and three years before one is able to skewer them properly. Acquiring the perfect roasting technique takes a life time.

Eel dishes

Yawatamaki [1]	*Teriyaki* rolls of eel and burdock
Shirayaki [2]	'White' grill of eel with soy sauce and *wasabi*
Unajū [3]	*Kabayaki* of eel in *unajū* (eel box) *Kimo sui* (liver soup) with green *mitsuba*, gluten ball and liver of eel, next to tin with *sanshō* pepper to be scattered over the eel

Unagi EEL

[1]

[2]

[3]

Eel *Unagi*

Kabayaki [1] Grilled eel in *kabayaki* sauce

Mushizushi [2] Warm steamed *sushi* rice with *kinshi tamago* (brocade of egg), *kabayaki* eel and *kinome* on top

Yanagawa [3] Willow river. This little stew of eel used to be made of *dojō (misgurnus anguillicaudatus)*, a little fish that dwells between the roots of willows – hence the name. Burdock root has been cut in the shape of willow leafs

Uzaku [4] Cucumber rings and *wakame* seaweed
Eel *kabayaki* with *wakame* seaweed and cucumber

Unagi bōzushi [5] Sushi of *kabayaki* eel and flower of *myōga* ginger pickled in vinegar

[1]

[2]

[3]

[4]

[5]

169

味
Aji
Condiments

SAKE

The Japanese use the word *sake* for all alcoholic drinks, including gin and whisky. The Japanese 'rice wine' is called *nihonshu*, which means 'Japan' and 'alcoholic drink.' Although it is not made of grapes like European wine, it has a similar cultural significance and also has great religious importance. There are countless *shintō* rituals in which *sake* plays a role.

Different types of *sake* vary in quality and price, but the distinction is based on the reputation of the producer and the ingredients used (the rice and especially the water), rather than the year in which it is made. *Sake* does not have vintage years, since it is consumed shortly after bottling.

Dry as well as sweet *sake* is produced. In Europe the sweetness of wine is connected to the tradition of a particular château, while in Japan fashion dictates the sugar level. In the course of the 19th and 20th centuries different periods can be distinguished in which all *sake* becomes sweeter and then again dryer. The temperature at which *sake* is drunk does not depend on the colour, as with grape wine, but on the season. In the heat of summer *sake* is drunk cold, but at other times it is warmed until it is just above body temperature. It is not polite to pour out one's own sake. The waitress will do it for you and otherwise table companions serve each other.

Sake is made with the help of the *kōji* mould (*kōjikin; aspergillus oryzae*). First the rice is pearled by removing 30 to 70 per cent of the outer skin – the larger the reduction the better the *sake*. Then it is washed, soaked and steamed. One quarter of the rice is mixed with the *kōji* mould and kept moist and warm (30 °C) for 35 hours, after which it is mixed again with the other three quarters of the rice and cooled to 5 °C. The need for cooling was the reason that *sake* production was restricted to winter in the days before refrigeration. *Kōji*, rice and water are added three times until, after about three months, the mould turns the rice into sugars and the sugars into alcohol. The lees are pressed to release a murky white *sake*, which will become clear by letting it stand or by filtration. It is then sterilized at 60 °C and allowed to mature for several months in wooden barrels, then it is bottled sold and drunk.

Mirin is an almost syrupy liquid, made by adding distilled *shōchū* (of rice, buckwheat, or barley) containing up to 45 per cent alcohol to fermenting rice, from which *mirin* can be drawn after 40 to 60 days. *Mirin* is used frequently in cooking. In most cases the sweet flavours in Japanese dishes derive from (often reduced) *mirin*.

WASABI

There are two types of *wasabi:* real *wasabi* and fake *wasabi*.

Real *wasabi (wasabia japonica)* is a plant that grows along river banks. Its green root is grated and eaten on *nigirizushi*, or mixed into the sauce eaten with *sushi* and *sashimi*. Fake *wasabi* is made with grated horseradish and green dye. Horseradish *(armoracia rustica)* is called *wasabi daikon* in Japan, which adds to the confusion. Depending on the quality, tubes of *wasabi* may contain a percentage of real *wasabi*, but pure *wasabi* is not exported. Only occasionally does Oshima manage to get real *wasabi* for the Yamazato restaurant.

SHŌYU

Soy sauce *(shōyu)* is so very crucial to Japanese cuisine that it is part of nearly every dish. It gives flavour to nearly every sauce. Its use is very comparable to the ancient Roman *garum*, made of fermented fish and related to the present-day fish sauces of South East Asia such as *nam pla* from Thailand and *nuoc nam* from Vietnam. Fish sauce was used in ancient Japan as well, and leftover from this product called *shottsuru*, is still made in northern prefecture af Akita.

Before the 17th century soy sauce was a luxury. It did not overtake *miso* as the most used condiment until the early 20th century.

Soy sauce is made of steamed soya beans and crushed wheat, which has been lightly roasted. The mixture is exposed to the *kōji* mould for three days and soaked in salt water. This mash, called *moromi*, is left to ferment for two summers, after which it is strained and pressed. Soy sauce is released, as is soya oil. The sauce is pasteurized and bottled.

Before this method developed throughout the 17th century, soy sauce used to be acquired by draining the liquid that separates during the process of *miso* fermentation. In fact, until the end of the 19th century, soy sauce remained a luxury for the farmers who formed the majority of the population. However, it became the prevalent flavouring in the urban areas already from the 18th century onwards.

The most ubiquitous soy sauce is *koikuchi shōyu*, a dark sauce made with equal portions of wheat and soya beans. *Usukuchi shōyu* is lighter and saltier. It has been fermented for a shorter period. White soy sauce, *shiroshōyu*, is made with a large quantity of pearled wheat, fewer soya beans and less salt, is slightly sweeter

CONDIMENTS

and useful in dishes that should keep their colour, but it does not keep well. *Tamari* is made of soya beans alone, and is predominantly used for pickling vegetables and for *sashimi*.

MISO

Until the 20th century *miso* was the most used condiment of the Japanese people. Nowadays it is predominantly added to *dashi* to make *miso* soup *(misoshiru)*, the soup eaten at every meal including breakfast. In addition, *miso* is used to pickle vegetables and fish. Grilled dishes are coated with *miso* and it goes into simmered dishes also.

Miso is a thick fermented paste, made from soya beans and rice *(komemiso)*, or rice and barley and rye *(mugimiso)*, or of soya beans alone *(mamemiso)*. Other types of *miso* have additional ingredients like vegetables, fish or herbs and can be eaten as dishes in their own right.

A common ancestor of *miso* and *shōyu* is *hishio*. It came to Japan from China around the 7th century and became one of the standard flavourings, along with salt, vinegar and *sake*.

Hishio consisted of cereals fermented with vegetables or fish, similar to a mixture of pickles and *miso*, but in the 13th century *miso* was developed as a separate product.

To produce *miso*, first rice (and/or barley) is steamed and mixed with the *kōji* mould at body temperature and left for several days. Then the soya beans are washed, boiled, mashed and mixed with the cereal. Depending on the salt content (5 % to 15 %) and the length of maturation (six months to several years), white *miso* *(shiromiso)* is the result, or red *miso* *(akamiso)*.

DASHI

The basic stock in Japanese cuisine is *dashi*, from which most soups and many sauces are made. *Dashi* consists of water in which kelp and *katsuobushi* have been soaked. Kelp is a seaweed that grows many meters long. It is carefully wiped instead of being washed after harvesting, since the flavour is contained in the outer skin. This is also why there is little point in simmering kelp for more than twenty minutes to make a stock. For a vegetarian stock, kelp is sufficient on its own, even though *shiitake* mushrooms are often added for a richer flavour. To all other stocks the shavings of *katsuobushi*, which resemble wood shavings, are added. *Katsuobushi* indeed looks like driftwood, but is made of *katsuo* (bonito, *katsuonus palamis*), which is closely related to the tuna. First the fillets are removed from this fish and simmered for twenty minutes to set the protein. They are smoked for several hours a day over a period of one or two weeks, a process which partially dries them. After this the fish is further dried in a careful fermentation process. For several months the fillets are matured in the dark and exposed to the *kōji* mould, but to avoid too fierce a fermentation they are removed from the dark every so often and exposed to sunlight, which kills the *kōji* mould. When the fish is dry and as hard as wood, it can be preserved for a very long time.

The best stock is made with freshly shaved *katsuobushi*. The flakes are merely submerged in a hot (not boiling) broth of kelp and filtered out after only a few minutes to create a 'first stock' *ichiban dashi*. The best *nimono* is simmered in this stock and it is the basis of clear soups. A second infusion *(niban dashi)* can be made by boiling the strained *katsuobushi* again in new kelp water. This second stock is most suitable for making *miso* soup and many sauces.

In some cases *dashi* is made of little dried anchovies *(niboshi)* from which the heads and guts have been removed.

Condiments
AJI

Index

Aemono — Cooked salad with thick dressing — p. 22, 41
Agemono — Deep-fried dish, also a kaiseki course — p. 117
Aji — (Trachurus Japonicus) jack, horse mackerel — p. 139, 170
Amadai — (Branchiostegus japonicus) kind of sea bream — p. 94
Amaebi — (Pandalus borealis) pink shrimp — p. 103
An — Sweet paste of azuki beans — p. 108, 141
Awabi — (Hliotis asinina) abalone — p. 9
Azuki — (Vgna angularis) a little red bean — p. 88, 108, 118, 130, 141
Benihana of Tokyo — Teppanyaki restaurant chain — p. 161
Binchō — Smoke free oak charcoal — p. 35, 165
(O)Bon — Buddhist observance honouring the spirit of ancestors — p. 26, 71, 133
Buri — (Seriola quinqueradiata) fully grown yellowtail horse mackerel — p. 81
Chakaiseki ryōri — Tea kaiseki cuisine — p. 21, 22, 23, 68
Chawan mushi — Steamed, savoury custard — p. 46
Chimaki — Flavoured rice wrapped in bamboo leaf — p. 123
Chūtoro — Low-fatty belly of tuna — p. 8
Daidai — (Citrus aurantium) a kind of mandarin — p. 84
Daikon — (Raphanus sativus) giant white radish — p. 10, 26, 47, 78, 83, 84, 93, 107, 110, 130
Daimyō — Feudal lord — p. 18
Dashi — Stock (usually made of katsuobushi and konbu) — p. 26, 41, 47, 52, 74, 135, 172
Dashijiru — See dashi — p. 172
Ebi — (Penaeidae spp.) prawn — p. 78, 81, 93, 123
Ebisu kabocha — (Cucurbita moschata) winter squash — p. 145
Edo — Previous name of Tokyo — p. 18
Edo period — 1600–1867 — p. 71
Enkaiseki ryōri — Banqueting kaiseki cuisine — p. 22, 25
Fu — Wheat gluten, made by kneading dough under water — p. 111
Fugu — (Fugu rubripes en f. namerafugu) blowfish — p. 7
Furai — Meat or seafood deep-fried in a coating of flower, egg and breadcrumbs — p. 47
Gobō — (Arctium lappa) burdock (root) — p. 77, 81
Gohan — Cooked rice, can also mean 'a meal' — p. 88, 118, 130, 153
Gyō — Loose style in food presentation — p. 63, 64
Hajikami — Shoot of ginger (zingiber off.) — p. 94, 126
Hamachi — (Seriola quinqueradiata) young yellowtail horsemackerel — p. 146

Hanami — (Cherry) blossom-viewing picnic — p. 101, 118, 143
Hashiri — Food product ahead of season — p. 25
Hassun — A chakaiseki course — p. 22
Hida — Little portable stove of plaster and paper — p. 97, 150
Hijiki — (Hizikia fusiforme) a black seaweed — p. 117
Himeji — (Mullus surmuletus) mul — p. 135
Hina Matsuri — See Hina no Sekku — p. 101
Hina no Sekku — Dolls' Festival/Day — p. 71, 101
Hirame — (Paralichthys olivaceus) brill — p. 78, 86, 145
Hishimochi — Diamond-shaped rice cakes — p. 101, 103
Hishio — Fermented vegetables, legumes, cerials and/or seafood — p. 17, 172
Hokkigai — (Spisula sachalinensis) surf clam or sand gaper — p. 103
Honzen ryōri — A formal banqueting style — p. 17, 18, 20, 22
Ichijū sansai — 'One soup and three side dishes' – the basis of a Japanese meal — p. 25
Ika — (Various dibranchiate cephalopods) squid and cuttlefish — p. 103, 126
Ikebana — Art of flower arrangement — p. 62
Ikizukuri (or ikezukuri) — Sashimi of living fish — p. 26
Ikura — Salmon roe — p. 77
Iwatake — (Umbilicaria asculenta) lichen that grows on cliffs — p. 114
(O)jūbako — lacquer boxes for food — p. 72, 74
Kabayaki — A way of grilling eel — p. 35, 165, 166, 168
Kadomatsu — 'Gate pine', New Year's decoration — p. 73, 83
Kagamimochi — New Year's rice cake decoration — p. 73
Kaki — 1. (diospyros kaki) Japanese persimmon, 2. (crassostrea gigas) oyster — p. 150, 153
Kakushibōchō — Hidden cuts — p. 69
Kamakura Matsuri — Snow Hut Festival — p. 91
Kaminabe — Stewing pot of paper — p. 97
Kanten — Agar-agar, jelly drawn from tengusa — p. 69
Karaage — Chicken or seafood dusted with seasoned flour and deep fried — p. 47, 125
Karasumi — Botargo, dried and salted roe of grey mullet — p. 77
Kashi — Confection and sweets — p. 43, 88, 99, 108, 118, 130, 141, 153
Kashiwa mochi — Rice cake wrapped in oak leaf — p. 120, 130
Katsuo — (Katsuwonus pelamis) bonito — p. 129, 172
Katsuobushi — Dried, smoked and cured bonito — p. 52, 172
Kazunoko — Salted or dried and cured herring roe — p. 9, 74, 77, 83

Ki — A formal name for receptacles for serving food — p. 57, 58
Kihada maguro — (Thunnus albacares) yellowfin tuna — p. 8
Kiku no Sekku — The Chrysanthemum Festival — p. 71, 143
Kimizu — Dressing of egg yolk and vinegar — p. 139
Kinome — Young leaves of sanshō — p. 103, 108, 113, 114, 118, 123, 139, 168,
Kobumaki — Poached rolls of kelp — p. 74, 81, 93
Kodomo no Hi — Children's Day — p. 101, 121
Koi nobori — Streamer looking like flying carp — p. 121
Konbu (or kobu) — (Laminaria spp.) kelp — p. 52, 74, 88
Konnyaku — Gelatinous paste made of the root of elephant foot (amorphophallus rivieri) — p. 81, 93
Kõnomono — See tsukemono — p. 43, 99, 118, 130, 153
Kuromaguro — (Thunnus thunnus) bluefin tuna — p. 8
Kuromame — Sweetened black soya beans — p. 74, 78, 83
Ma — Empty space — p. 64
Matsuri — Local festival — p. 71
Matsutake — (Tricholoma matsutake) pine mushroom — p. 142, 146
Mebachi maguro — Big-eye tuna — p. 8
Mibuna — (Brassica japonica) Japanese cabbage — p. 99
Mirin — Sweet liquid flavouring made of glutinous rice — p. 47, 74, 165, 170
Miso — A fermented paste of soya beans, salt and barley or rice — p. 10, 17, 41, 43, 67, 94, 111, 113, 123, 129, 150, 153, 163, 172, 171
Misoshiru — Miso soup — p. 172
Mitsuba — (Cryptotaenia japonica) trefoil (wild chervil) — p. 46, 83, 117, 141, 166
Mochi — Paste of steamed and pounded rice — p. 74, 84, 108, 130
Momo no Sekku — See Hina no Sekku — p. 101
Monjayaki — Griddle-fried batter — p. 159
Moritsuke — Art of food arrangement — p. 62
Mozuku — (Nemacystis deciens) a dark brown seaweed — p. 113
Mukōzuke — A chakaiseki course — p. 21
Mushimono — Steamed dish, also a kaiseki course — p. 46
Myōga — (Zingiber mioga) mioga ginger (shoot) — p. 117, 135, 168
Nabemono — One-pot stew — p. 52
Nagaimo — (Dioscorea opposita) Chinese yam — p. 77
Namasu — Vinegary dish of strips of raw meat, fish, or vegetables — p. 25, 78, 83, 150
Nameko — (Pholiota nameko) a Japanese mushroom — p. 153

Nanakusa no Sekku — Seven Herb Festival — p. 71, 73
Narezushi — Ancient form of sushi — p. 156
Nattō — Sticky soya beans fermented with the bacillus natto — p. 67
Nenchū gyōji (or Nenjū gyōji) — A sequence of seasonal festivals observed all over Japan — p. 71
Nigirizushi — Hand-pressed sushi — p. 155, 157
Nimono — Simmered dish, a kaiseki course — p. 25, 41, 86, 107, 117, 129, 139, 149, 172
Noren — Hangings in the restaurant door — p. 60
Nori — (Porphyra spp.) laver — p. 10, 155, 157
Nouvelle cuisine — p. 15, 69
Nozowana — (Brassica Campestris var. Hakabura) the foliage and stem of turnip — p. 118
'O' — Used as an honorific prefix, which can often be omitted Okonomiyaki — Griddle fried pancake with vegetables and diced seafood — p. 159
Origami — Art of folding paper into figures and ornamental objects — p. 133
Ōtoro — Fatty belly of tuna — p. 8
Ponzu — Sauce made of soy sauce and juice of citrus — p. 129
Renkon — (Nelumbo nucifera) rhizome of the lotus — p. 84
Sakana — Drinking snack (written with a different character can also simply mean 'fish') — p. 52
Sake — 1. Alcoholic drink from rice, 2. (Oncorhyncus keta.) salmon — p. 10, 17, 20, 21, 22, 23, 43, 46, 52, 68, 74, 91, 93, 100, 101, 103, 153, 170
Sakizuke — Amuse — p. 46
Sakura — Cherry tree — p. 101, 108, 118
Samurai — (Man of) the warrior class — p. 17, 18, 57, 71, 121, 123
Sashimi — Dish of raw fish — p. 8, 10, 15, 25, 26, 58, 62, 84, 94, 105, 126, 136, 171
Sanshō — (Zanthoxylum piperitum) pepper of the ground seeds of the Japanese prickly ash — p. 35, 126, 166
Sawara — (Scomberomus niphonius) Spanish mackerel — p. 149
Sazanka restaurant — Teppanyaki restaurant in the Hotel Okura Amsterdam — p. 10, 161
Sekku — See nenchū gyōji — p. 71, 143
Setsubun — A winter festival — p. 91
Shiitake — (Lentinus edodes) mushroom that grows on shii (castanopsis cuspidata) — p. 10, 26, 67, 81, 84, 93, 110, 113, 117, 136, 141, 150, 172
Shiizakana — A kaiseki course: chef's special dish — p. 52, 150
Shikibōchō — Cutting of fish as high art — p. 26
Shimeji — (Lyophyllum spp.) clustered straw coloured mushrooms — p. 145
Shin — Formal style in food presentation — p. 63, 64, 130

Shinnen — See (O)Shōgatsu — p. 73
Shintō — Indigenous religion of Japan — p. 71, 170
Shioyaki — Salt grilling — p. 35
Shirayaki — White grilling (without sauce) — p. 165, 166
Shirozake — Sweet, white sake for Dolls' Festival — p. 101, 103
Shishitō — (Capsicum annuum) green pepper — p. 150
Shiso — (Perilla frutescens) perilla — p. 63, 110, 117, 118
Shōbu no Sekku — See Tango no Sekku — p. 121
(O)Shōgatsu — New Year's Festival — p. 71, 72, 74
Shōgun — Head of the warrior class, ruler of Japan between the 12th and 19th century — p. 17
Shōjin ryōri — Vegetarian cuisine — p. 111
Shokuji — 'The meal', also a kaiseki course containing rice, miso soup and pickles — p. 88, 99, 108, 118, 130, 141, 153
Shun — In season — p. 25
Sō — Wild style in food presentation — p. 63, 64
Sōmen — Thin wheat noodles usually served chilled — p. 141, 145
(O)suimono — Clear soup — p. 26
Suizenji nori — (Aphanothece sacra) a fresh water alga — p. 83
Sukiyaki — Beef and vegetable stew — p. 159
Sunomono — Salad dressed with seasoned vinegar — p. 22, 41, 86, 97, 107, 117, 129, 139
Sushi — Vinegary rice with a topping or filling — p. 10, 15, 93, 108, 123, 145, 154, 155, 156, 157, 171
Suzuki — (Lateolabrax) sea bass — p. 126, 146
Tai — (Fam. Sparidae) sea bream — p. 77
Takenoko — (Phyllostachys heterocycla) bamboo shoot — p. 81, 114, 123
Takii — Japanese seed distributor — p. 10
Takuan(zuke) — Pickled daikon radish — p. 118, 153
Tanabata — A summer festival — p. 71, 133, 135
Tango no Sekku — Boys' Festival/Day — p. 71, 120, 121, 123
Tatsukuri — Tiny dried and simmered sardines — p. 77, 83
Tempura (or tenpura) — Deep frying in batter — p. 10, 18, 47, 117
Tengusa — (Gelidium amansii) Ceylon Moss of which kanten is made — p. 69
Tentsuyu — Dipping sauce for tempura of dashi, soy sauce and mirin — p. 47
Teppanyaki — Grilling on an iron plate — p. 10, 15, 158, 159, 161, 163
Teriyaki — Lustre grilling — p. 35, 81, 84, 114, 163, 166
Tōfu — Bean curd — p. 41, 111, 117, 135, 145, 153, 157

Toro — Medium fatty belly of tuna — p. 8, 146
(O)Toso — New Year's sake — p. 74
Tsukemono (or kōnomono) — Pickles — p. 43
Tsukimi — Moon viewing (picnic) — p. 143
(O)tsukuri — Restaurant term for sashimi — p. 26, 84, 94, 105, 114, 126, 136, 146
Umami — The fifth flavour, savoury — p. 67
Ume — (Prunus mume) Japanese apricot — p. 81, 99, 107, 118
Umeboshi — Dried and salt pickled ume apricot, often coloured with perilla — p. 22, 103, 135
Unagi — (Anguilla) eel — p. 81, 123, 135, 164, 166, 168
Uni — (Echinoidea) sea urchin — p. 99
Uri — (Cucumis melo) cucumbers and pumpkins — p. 135
Urushi — Lacquer ware — p. 59
Wabi — An aesthetic and moral principle — p. 20, 21, 57
Wagashi — Japanese confectionary — p. 43
Wagyū — Breed of Japanese beef cattle — p. 54
Wakakusa — (Oenanthe phellandrium) Water dropwort — p. 88
Wakame — (Undaria pinnitifida) green seaweed — p. 107, 168
(O)wan — Soup, a kaiseki course — p. 26, 84, 93, 103, 113, 125, 135, 146
Wasabi — (Wasabia japonica) plant related to horseradish — p. 26, 67, 99, 113, 155, 163, 166, 171
Yakimono — Grilled dish, course of kaiseki — p. 21, 25, 35, 84, 94, 105, 114, 126, 136, 149
Yakitori — Chicken satay — p. 35
Yamazato restaurant — Traditional Japanese restaurant in the Hotel Okura Amsterdam — p. 43, 69, 71, 111
Yōgashi — Western sweets — p. 43
Yōkan — A kind of wagashi made of an and kanten — p. 141
Yosenabe — A kind of nabemono — p. 52
Yuba — The skin on soya milk, consumed fresh or dried — p. 111
Yuzu — (Citrus junos.) Japanese citron — p. 26, 107, 113, 125, 146
Zen Buddhism — One of the Buddhist sects introduced in Japan in the 12th century — p. 15, 111
Zensai — Appetizers — p. 25, 26, 83, 103, 113, 123, 135, 145
(O)Zōni — New Year's Soup — p. 74, 84

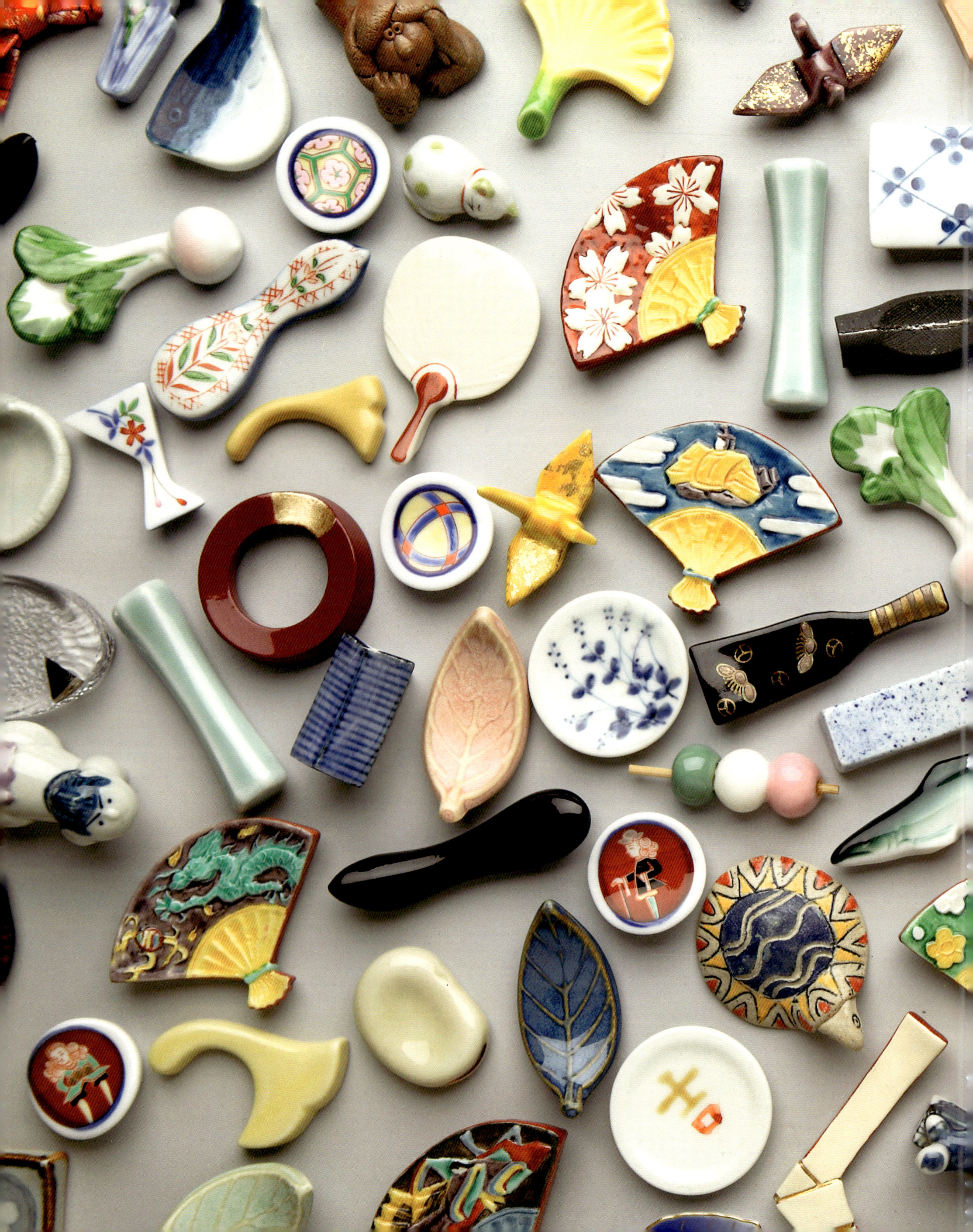